Cont

Macromedia®
Contribute™ 3

Ned Averill-Snell

in a
Snap

SAMS
**Teach
Yourself**

Sams Publishing, 800 East 96th Street, Indianapolis, Indiana 46240 USA

Macromedia Contribute 3 in a Snap

International Standard Book Number: 0-672-32516-0

Library of Congress Catalog Card Number: 2002116066

Printed in the United States of America

First Printing: July 2004

07   06   05   04   4   3   2   1

Trademarks

All terms mentioned in this book that are known to be trademarks or service marks have been appropriately capitalized. Sams Publishing cannot attest to the accuracy of this information. Use of a term in this book should not be regarded as affecting the validity of any trademark or service mark.

Macromedia is a registered trademark of Macromedia, Inc.

Contribute is a trademark of Macromedia, Inc.

Warning and Disclaimer

Every effort has been made to make this book as complete and as accurate as possible, but no warranty or fitness is implied. The information provided is on an "as is" basis. The author and the publisher shall have neither liability nor responsibility to any person or entity with respect to any loss or damages arising from the information contained in this book.

Bulk Sales

Sams Publishing offers excellent discounts on this book when ordered in quantity for bulk purchases or special sales. For more information, please contact

U.S. Corporate and Government Sales

1-800-382-3419

corpsales@pearsontechgroup.com

For sales outside of the U.S., please contact

International Sales

1-317-428-3341

international@pearsontechgroup.com

Acquisitions Editor
Betsy Brown

Development Editor
Jonathan Steever

Managing Editor
Charlotte Clapp

Senior Project Editor
Matthew Purcell

Production Editor
Seth Kerney

Indexer
Ginny Bess

Proofreader
Tonya Fenimore

Technical Editor
Robyn Ness

Publishing Coordinator
Vanessa Evans

Designer
Gary Adair

Page Layout
Michelle Mitchell

About the Author

Ned Averill-Snell has been making technology make sense since 1986, when he began writing beginner's documentation for one of the world's largest software companies. After writing manuals and training materials for several major technology companies, Ned switched sides and became a computer journalist, serving as a writer and editor for two national magazines, *Edge* and *Art & Design News*.

A freelance writer since 1991, Ned has written more than two dozen computer books and hundreds of articles. Between books, Ned works as a professional actor in regional theater, commercials, and industrial films.

Dedication

For my family.

Acknowledgments

This book—as many, many others—is the better for the imagination, experience, and hard work of Mark Taber, Betsy Brown, Jon Steever, Matt Purcell, Seth Kerney, and Alice Martina-Smith. Hats off, please.

We Want to Hear from You!

As the reader of this book, *you* are our most important critic and commentator. We value your opinion and want to know what we're doing right, what we could do better, what areas you'd like to see us publish in, and any other words of wisdom you're willing to pass our way.

You can email or write me directly to let me know what you did or didn't like about this book—as well as what we can do to make our books stronger.

Please note that I cannot help you with technical problems related to the topic of this book, and that due to the high volume of mail I receive, I might not be able to reply to every message.

When you write, please be sure to include this book's title and author as well as your name and phone number or email address. I will carefully review your comments and share them with the author and editors who worked on the book.

Email: consumer@samspublishing.com

Mail: Mark Taber
            Associate Publisher
            Sams Publishing
            800 East 96th Street
            Indianapolis, IN 46240 USA

Reader Services

For more information about this book or others from Sams Publishing, visit our website at www.samspublishing.com. Type the ISBN (excluding hyphens) or the title of the book in the Search box to find the book you're looking for.

PART I

Getting Started

1

✔ Start Here

As just about every company, large and small, has developed its own Web site in recent years, a problem has emerged. Contribute is a first-of-its-kind website maintenance program designed to address this problem.

So What's the Problem?

In many companies, the person who develops and maintains the website (the *webmaster*) is an IT staffer or an out-of-house website designer. In either case, it's a person who has the technical expertise to create and maintain websites, but who might not be sufficiently involved in the day-to-day operations of the company to independently update all the website content when it needs changing.

The people who do know what content needs to be changed—call them "content experts"—are often people who lack the technical knowledge to edit a website without inadvertently creating formatting problems or otherwise scrambling up the various kinds of code that make up the website files, principally *Hypertext Markup Language (HTML)* and *JavaScript*.

> **NOTE**
>
> Contribute isn't designed to be an all-purpose web authoring tool. In fact, the range of ways you can edit and format pages in Contribute is more limited than in some freeware. If you want to build web pages from scratch, look to another program. Contribute's job is to manage the maintenance of *existing* websites created with other programs.

Whether the content experts have website expertise or not, webmasters are traditionally leery of allowing just anyone in the company to dive in and edit the website files, for both aesthetic and security reasons.

Traditionally this leaves the company with two solutions, neither ideal for keeping its site up-to-date, running smoothly and looking good: A) The content experts must submit their changes to the Webmaster, who actually edits the files (and might have trouble keeping up with the changes), or B) The content experts must be permitted (and trained) to edit the files—a risky proposition.

By adding Contribute to its website development environment, a company can strike a compromise to solve this dilemma. Serving as the *Contribute administrator*, the webmaster or another technologically-savvy staffer uses Contribute to control which sites and pages, and which content in those pages, individual content experts can open and edit. The content experts make their changes from within Contribute, which prevents them from changing content they're not authorized to change, and also helps them avoid changing the design of the page while editing its content.

Editing Content Versus Administering Sites

By design, then, two distinct kinds of people use Contribute within any one organization:

- **Content experts**, perhaps better dubbed "contributors," who use Contribute to edit, add, or delete content, and to publish their changes on the Web or company intranet.

- **Contribute administrators**, who use Contribute to set up and maintain two things: *connections*, which enable the content experts to open and edit pages and publish their changes online, and *roles*, which further control what each content expert can—and can't—change.

Although both types of users do their thing from within the Contribute program, different users use different parts of the program.

Content experts spend most of their time editing web pages in the Contribute workspace.

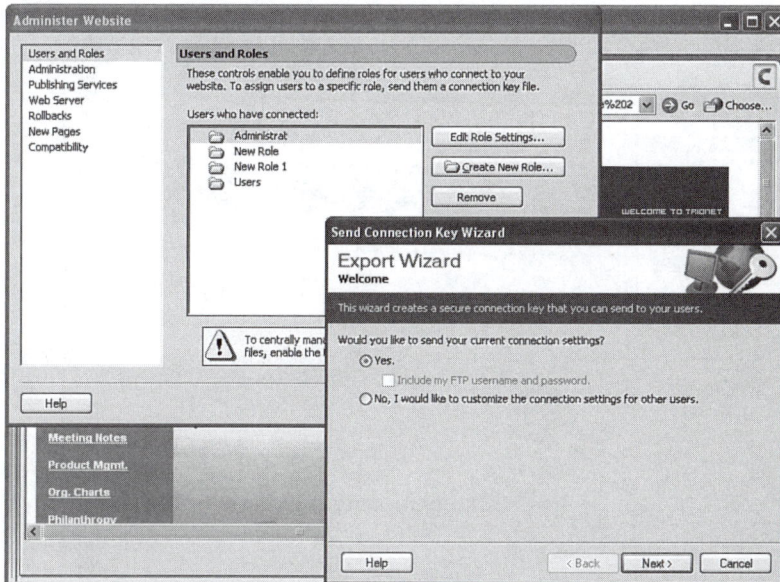

TIP

In many companies, the Contribute administrator may also be the webmaster, but that needn't be the case. The Contribute administrator can be anyone who has reasonable computer skills and is trusted to manage the activities of the content experts.

Administrators spend their Contribute time in dialog boxes in which they set up the connections and roles that control what each content expert can change.

Understanding the Contribute Interface

Both types of users will find using Contribute simple and straightforward, much like any latter-day Windows or Mac program, with most activities performed from the menu bar and toolbars. However, a few features of the Contribute interface are a little unusual, and although they're easy to use, they might cause a little confusion to some users upon their first Contribute encounter.

What follows is a quick tour of the Contribute interface, so you'll know how to get around.

Using the Sidebar

The Contribute interface features an optional *sidebar* on the left side of the screen. Exactly what appears in the sidebar at any given time depends somewhat upon what you're doing. The sidebar always appears automatically when you open Contribute.

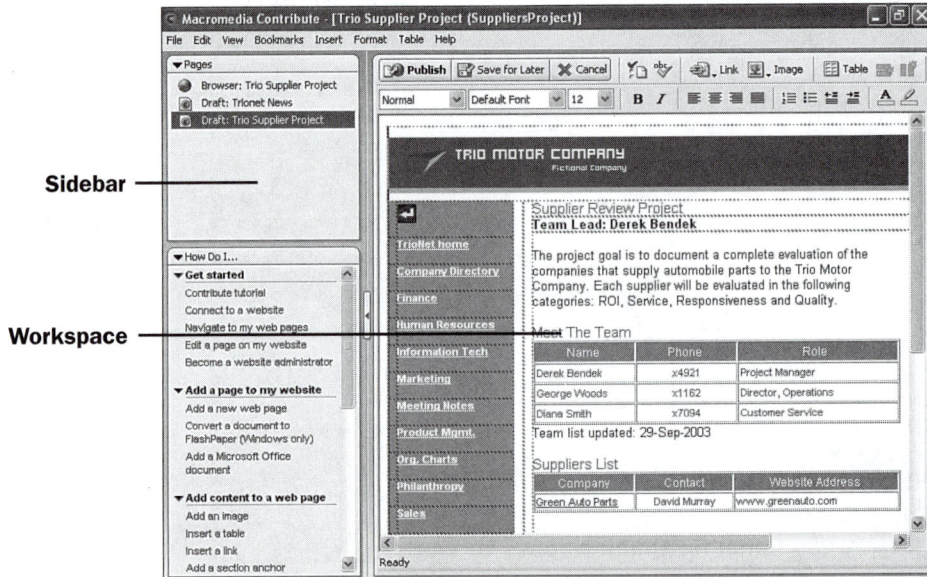

Contribute's optional sidebar offers information and links that relate to the activities you perform in the workspace.

However, when you're busy editing a web page and want to see the whole page filling the screen (as it would appear online), the sidebar is in the way. Therefore, it's good to know how to hide it, bring it back, and adjust its width to suit your needs.

- To hide the sidebar, choose **View, Sidebar**, or click the left-pointing arrow (or the triple vertical bar on the Mac) on the sidebar's right border.

- To redisplay the sidebar, choose **View, Sidebar**, or click the right-pointing arrow (or the triple vertical bar on the Mac) on the far left side of the screen.

- To adjust the width of the sidebar, point to the sidebar's right border to display the double arrow and then click and drag the border left or right until the width of the sidebar is what you want.

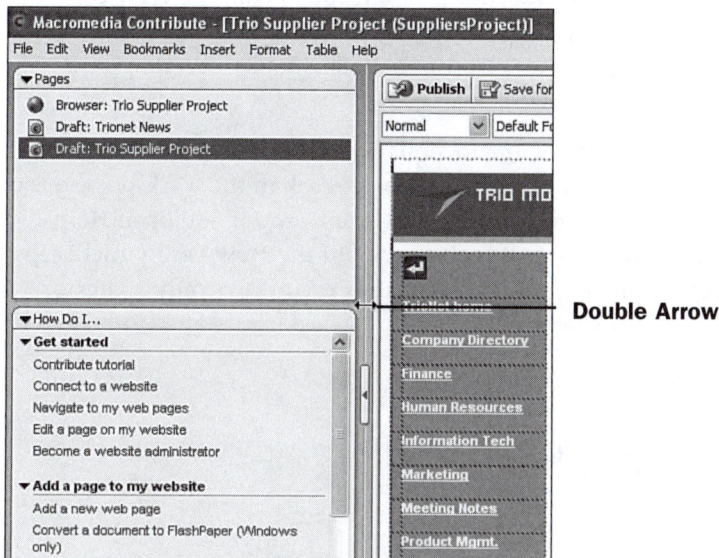

Drag the sidebar's right border to adjust its width.

Using the Pages Panel for Quick Access to Work in Progress

The top part of the sidebar is taken up by the **Pages** panel, which displays links to pages you've browsed or edited recently, but not yet published. Click on any page listed in the **Pages** panel to open it for editing.

Recently Edited Pages —

Pages Panel

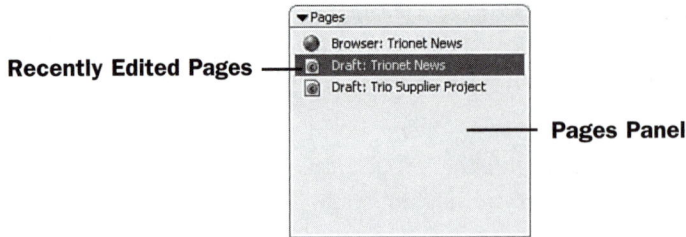

The sidebar's Pages panel offers one-click access to pages you've recently worked on.

Using the How Do I Panel for Step-by-Step Instructions

The bottom part of the sidebar is taken up by the **How Do I** panel, which displays links to step-by-step help text for common activities, such as editing a site. The topics listed vary depending upon what you're doing. When you're not yet connected to a site to edit, the **How Do I** panel offers links to help text explaining how to connect to a site. When you're editing a site, the **How Do I** panel offers topics covering basic editing tasks.

When you click a topic, the instructions appear in the **How Do I** panel, so you can refer to them as you perform the task in the workspace to the right. The instructions are the same text you'll read if you open **Help** (see "Getting Help," later in this chapter), but the **How Do I** panel keeps these instructions at your fingertips, so they are always only a click or two away when you need them.

Links to Instructions —

How Do I Panel

The sidebar's How Do I panel offers links to step-by-step help instructions for performing common tasks.

- To display the instructions for a topic, click that topic in the **How Do I** panel.

- To redisplay the list of main topics after reading instructions, click the **Topics** button in the **How Do I** panel.

- To go backward through help text you've already displayed, click the **Back** button in the **How Do I** panel.

Back Button   Topics Button

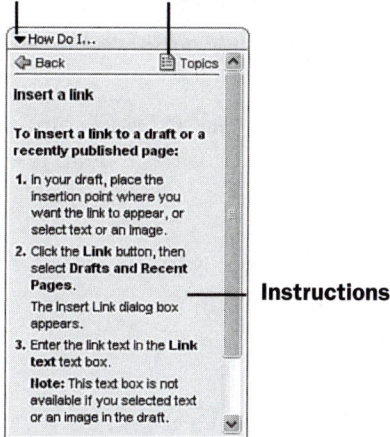

Instructions

After reading instructions in the How Do I panel, you can click Topics or Back to return to previous content.

Understanding Connections, Roles, Publishing, and Drafts

Four terms come up a lot in this book, and understanding exactly what they mean now will help you make sense of what you're doing when you dive in and start editing pages:

- **Connections:** To edit a page, you must "connect" to the copy of it that's currently online. Connecting copies the current online version of that page to your computer so that you can edit it into a *draft*. To connect, you use a special link, a *key*, given to you by your Contribute administrator (**see ❶ About Connections**). Contributors can edit only those pages for which they have a connection key.

🔖 **TIP**

It's easy to remember: If you've changed it, but still haven't published it, it's a draft. Drafts are labeled "Draft" in the Pages panel.

• **Roles:** The Contribute administrator assigns each user to a *role*. For each role, the administrator can choose from a list of options that control what users in that role can do. For example, the administrator may choose to grant or deny that role permission to change fonts in a site, or to add or delete pages in that site. Contributors can make only the kinds of changes their role allows.

• **Publishing:** You *publish* a page by sending your edited draft back to the Web (or your company's intranet), copying over the previous version. After you do that, the page is online, accessible to all, and is no longer a draft. You'll learn how to publish in Chapter 11, "Publishing Pages."

• **Drafts:** After a page has been copied from the Web (or your company intranet) to your computer for editing, it becomes a *draft*, or a working copy.

🔖 **TIP**

The **File, Save** menu item is grayed out—unavailable—until you've made at least one change to a draft. However, the **File, Save for Later** option (or **Save for Later** button), which saves the draft in temporary form so you can work on other things and come back to it later, is available as soon as you open a draft.

When you save a draft you're editing by choosing **File, Save**, you haven't published it—you've simply saved the draft with your changes on your computer.

Browse Mode Versus Edit Mode

You use the Contribute interface in either of two modes: Edit mode or Browse mode. Switching between the two is a snap:

• When in Edit mode, choose View, Browser to switch to the browser.

• When in Browse mode, click the Edit Page button to view and edit the same page in Edit mode.

🔖 **TIP**

When in Browse mode, you might see a **Create Connection** button instead of an **Edit Page** button. That means you have no connection to the site you're viewing, and cannot edit it. If it's a page you should be able to edit, you should contact your administrator to get a connection key.

In Edit mode, you actually make changes to Web pages. In this mode, the open page appears generally in WYSIWYG ("What You See Is What You Get") format, looking much as it would if published online and viewed through a browser. However, there are a few important deviations from WYSIWYG in Edit mode that are designed to help you edit. These include the following:

• Table borders designed to be invisible online appear as dashed lines, so you can work with the dimensions and designs of tables.

- Hyperlinks don't function.

- Some kinds of content don't perform exactly as they would online; for example, animations don't move, but instead appear as static pictures.

TIP

Often, the layout of a whole Web page is set by putting the page contents in a big table that fills the whole screen. You'll know this is the case when you see dashed lines around all of the content in Edit mode.

You edit pages in Edit mode, and Contribute alters the page's appearance in ways that help you work.

In Browse mode, you view pages you're working on to evaluate their appearance. Although you haven't left Contribute, the page appears largely as it would when viewed through a browser.

In fact, while in Browse mode, you can use the workspace as a Web browser. This capability gives you an easy way to navigate to a page you want to edit. After you've displayed the page you want to edit, you can click the **Edit Page** button to edit it.

To use Contribute as a browser, simply type a Web URL in the **Address** box above the workspace. (You don't have to type the "**http://**" part.)

NOTE

Browse mode shows you the online, published version of your page, not the version from any unpublished draft you might have been working on in Edit mode.

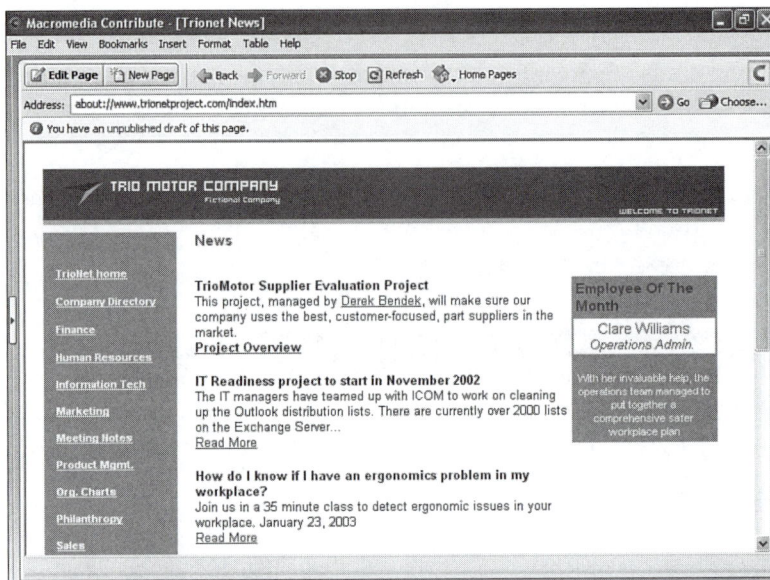

When in Browse mode, you can enter a URL in the Address box to use Contribute as a web browser.

The Browser Toolbar

When in Browse mode, the Contribute toolbar shows the same buttons you'd see on any browser—Back, Forward, Stop, and Refresh. They work just the way you would expect them to.

The Edit Toolbar

When in Edit mode, the Contribute toolbar shows the buttons and drop-down lists you'll use for editing and publishing Web pages. You'll learn how to use all of these buttons in Parts II and III of this book, when performing the tasks where they come into play. However, many of them might already be obvious to you because they match buttons that do the same things in other document-editing programs, particularly word processors.

When in Edit mode, the toolbar shows the buttons and lists you need to edit, create, and format content.

💡 **TIP**

The Edit mode toolbar has a **Save for Later** button. Clicking it saves your draft (just as if you had chosen **File, Save**) and then closes the draft so you can move on to another page or project.

For example, the **Table** button inserts a new table (**see 52 Create a New Table**).

Reviewing Pages with the Draft Console

Besides the Pages panel, Contribute offers another handy facility for not only opening your drafts, but also for managing those you've sent for review and those awaiting your review.

Open the Draft Console by clicking the **Draft Console** link on the Pages panel or by choosing **View, Draft Console**. The Draft Console reports three important matters concerning unpublished drafts:

- **Drafts I'm Editing**—Any unpublished drafts; the same ones shown in your Pages panel.

- **Drafts to Review**—Drafts others have sent to you for review.

- **Sent Drafts**—Drafts you have sent out for review by others.

The Draft Console helps you manage drafts in various states of completion.

At first, you'll probably have little need for the Draft Console. But as you send more and more drafts for review, and receive drafts for review from others, you'll find the console a handy way to keep track of your project status.

- To work on any draft listed in the Draft Console, click it.

- To close the Draft Console, click the Back button.

Setting Your Preferences

Although it's available to all users, the **Preferences** dialog box is something you might want to leave alone unless you're a fairly advanced user, or something you might want to fiddle with only with your administrator's guidance. The **Preferences** dialog box enables each user to customize some aspects of the way her copy of Contribute behaves, and understanding these changes requires a little background.

To open the **Preferences** dialog box, choose **Edit**, **Preferences** (or **Contribute**, **Preferences** on a Mac).

The Preferences dialog box enables you to customize Contribute, such as by choosing which other program is used to edit pictures.

Each of the six items in the list on the left side of the dialog box opens a different list of options you can change on the right. For example, clicking **Security** on the left opens options on the right that enable you to set up a username and password that locks others out of Contribute on your

NOTE

If you're not the administrator, even if you feel comfortable changing the **Preferences**, it's probably a good idea to check with your administrator before doing so.

NOTE

To learn in detail how to use each option in the **Preferences** dialog box, see **85** **About Preferences** and **86** **Set Preferences**.

computer so that no one else can edit the content on your computer if you happen to step away and leave it running.

Working Offline

You can edit pages offline, which you might want to do for any of several reasons. For example, you might install Contribute on a notebook PC or PowerBook, and edit pages while on the road and off the network. The next time you're handy to a network connection, you can publish your work. (For more on working offline, **see 4 Work Offline.**)

Undoing and Redoing Recent Actions

Like most document-editing Windows/Mac programs, Contribute offers an **Undo** feature that reverses the last edit you've made to a page.

- To undo an edit, choose **Edit, Undo** or press **Ctrl+Z.** (On the Mac, it's ⌘-**Z.**)

- To redo (reverse an **Undo**, restoring the edit), choose **Edit, Redo** or press **Ctrl+Y** (⌘-**Y** on the Mac).

Printing Pages

You might want to print your Contribute pages for a variety of reasons:

- You find it easier to proofread text and catch mistakes in a printout rather than onscreen.

- You want to proofread your content and mark it up for editing when you don't have access to your computer.

- You want to distribute printouts to others who check your work so they can mark changes and return them to you. (There's a paper-free way to do this, too; **see 76 Send Your Work to Reviewers.**)

To print a page, choose **File, Print.** Note that the printout will be identical whether you're in Edit or Browse mode when you print.

NOTE

If you try to open a page for editing when the network is not available, Contribute will inform you that no connection is available and ask you whether you want to edit the page offline.

NOTE

Printing from Contribute is like printing from any browser. What you get is not an exact representation of what a user sees on the screen, but rather the same content reformatted a little to fit nicely within the shape of a page. Use printouts to evaluate content, but not overall design.

TIP

Choose **File, Page Setup** (Windows only) before printing to change certain aspects of the way the printout will look. For example, you can print in portrait or landscape orientation, or change the look of the header added to the printout that shows the page title.

TIP

There's even more help available than what's in the **Help** facility. If you open the **Help** menu from the menu bar, you'll see items for connecting to online support, taking a tutorial, and viewing a **Quick Start** guide.

Getting Help

The quickest way to get help with a particular task is to use the **How Do I** panel, which was covered earlier in this chapter.

If you want more detail, or if the topic you need help with does not appear in the **How Do I** panel, you can get access to much more help by choosing **Help, Macromedia Contribute Help** from the menu bar.

A full-screen help facility opens, featuring all the **Help** tools available in many other applications: a **Table of Contents**, an **Index** by keyword, a **Search** tab, and a customizable list of **Favorites** (help topics you refer to often). All lead to detailed help text.

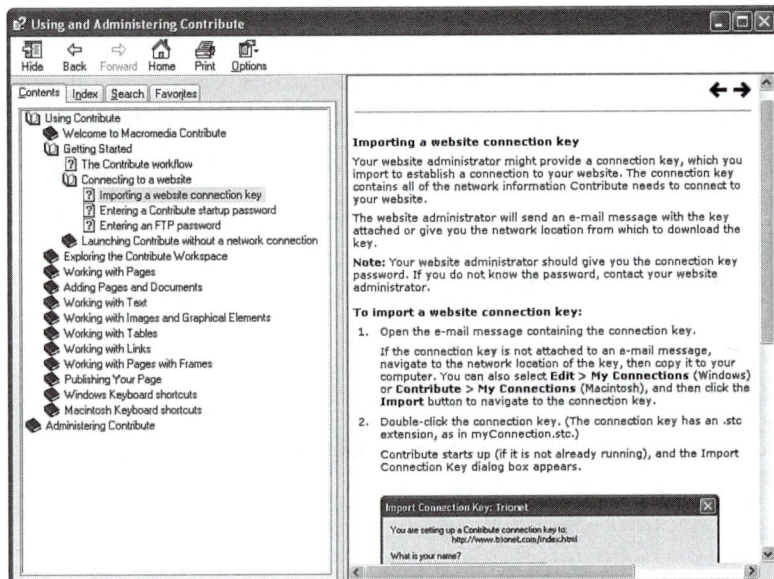

Help, Macromedia Contribute Help opens Contribute's Help facility, where you can browse or search for help text about any Contribute activity.

2

Connecting to a Web Page to Edit It

TIP

You'll also discover in this chapter the first and most important thing you can do when you've first connected to a page: **3** **Locate Editable Regions** to learn which parts of the page you are authorized to edit.

To edit a site, you must *connect* to the copy of it that's currently online. Connecting is one of the security measures in Contribute that enables the administrator to ensure that Web sites are edited only by those authorized to do so. Connections make life easier for contributors, as well, because they automatically take care of the various protocols and passwords required to access the page, making connecting a snap.

Once connected, there are a few other connection-related tasks you need to understand, chiefly working offline and disabling and re-enabling your *connections*.

1 About Connections

KEY TERM

Connection—A set of configuration settings, created and managed by the administrator, that enable a contributor to edit a particular Web site or page.

For each page a contributor is authorized to edit, the administrator will send the contributor a *key* in an email message (or an online address from which to download a key). Using the steps shown in **2** **Import a Connection Key**, the contributor imports each key into his copy of Contribute. After that's done, the contributor no longer needs to fuss with the email message or keys to open the site and edit it; connecting is automatic from then on.

Connecting copies the current online version of a page to the contributor's computer, where it becomes a draft that can be edited or augmented in any way the contributor is authorized. The connection also enables the contributor to publish the page back to the Web, overwriting the old version.

If you edit several sites, after you have imported their keys into Contribute, you might find that over time your connections require some housecleaning. For example, when network settings change (as they might, now and then), your administrator might send you new keys so that you can still connect. However, she might instead send you information about what settings to change in your connections.

TIP

If you are using a Macintosh and have a .Mac account, Contribute detects the .Mac account and asks if you want to create a connection to it.

Finally, you might decide to temporarily disable a connection and re-enable it later (see **6** **Disable Connections** and **7** **Enable Connections**). You might never need to do either, but it's good to know how, just in case. Over time, you might no longer need old or invalid connections, and you might want to delete them (see **5** **Delete a Connection**).

2 Import a Connection Key

Your administrator may provide you with your key(s) in either of two ways:

- In an email message
- As the network address from which you can download the key

Besides the key itself, you'll need a password to open the key. Your administrator should tell you this password—but probably not in the same email message with the key, for security reasons. You learn how to import your keys and connect to Web sites in the steps that follow.

1 Get the Key

Open the email message containing the connection key, or navigate to the address your administrator gave you for downloading the key. Keys are easy to recognize; they're simply files with the extension **.stc**.

2 Open the Key

To open the connection key, double-click it. Contribute opens (if it is not already open), and the **Import Connection Key** dialog box appears.

3 Type Your Identification

Type your name, email address, and the password for the connection key and then click **OK**.

4 View the Result

The main page of the site opens in Contribute's work area in **Browse** mode, ready for your edits. To begin editing, click the **Edit Page** button.

Before You Begin

✔ **1** About Connections

💡 **TIP**

If your administrator gives you a key on a diskette or CD-ROM, copy the key to your computer before opening it as shown in step 2.

💡 **TIP**

You can also navigate to the address containing your keys by choosing **Edit, My Connections** (or on a Mac, **Contribute, My Connections**) and then clicking the **Import** button.

🖐 **NOTE**

The administrator might set your role so that you can open and edit only certain pages on a site to which you have a key. If you can connect to a site, but can't edit a page on that site that you need to edit, contact your administrator.

Macromedia Contribute connection key for Tutorial ...

File   Edit   View   Tools   Message   Help

Reply   Reply All   Forward   Print   Delete   Previous

From: Edward Averill-Snell
Date: Wednesday, September 24, 2003 7:46 PM
To: Edward Averill-Snell
Subject: Macromedia Contribute connection key for Tutorial Website
Attach: TutorialWebsite-Users.stc (733 bytes)

This e-mail contains a connection key to connect Macromedia Contribute to your website so that you can edit website content. To import this connection key:

1. Ensure that Macromedia Contribute is installed on your computer. If it's not installed, contact the sender of this e-mail for instructions, or go to http://www.macromedia.com/contribute.

2. Double-click the connection key e-mail attachment.

1 Get the Key

2 Open the Key

Macromedia Contribute connection key for Tutorial ...

File   Edit   View   Tools   Message   Help

Reply   Reply All   Forward   Print   Delete   Previous

From: Edward Averill-Snell
Date: Wednesday, September 24, 2003 7:46 PM
To: Edward Averill-Snell
Subject: Macromedia Contribute connection key for Tutorial Website
Attach: TutorialWebsite-Users.stc (733 bytes)

This e-mail contains a connection key to connect Macromedia Contribute to your website so that you can edit website content. To import this connection key:

1. Ensure that Macromedia Contribute is installed on your computer. If it's not installed, contact the sender of this e-mail for instructions, or go to http://www.macromedia.com/contribute.

2. Double-click the connection key e-mail attachment.

Import Connection Key: Tutorial Website

Import Connection Key

You are setting up a Contribute connection key to:
file:///...ttings/Application Data/Macromedia/Contribute 2/Configuration/Content/Tutorial/

What is your name?
Ned Snell

What is your e-mail address?
tutorial_user@tutorial.org

What is the connection key password?

Contact the sender of the connection key if you don't know the password.

Help   OK   Cancel

3 Type Your Identification

Stop   Refresh   Home Pages

Go   Choose...

Fictional Company   WELCOME TO TRIONET

News

TrioNet home

Company Directory

Finance

Human Resources

Information Tech

Marketing

Meeting Notes

Product Mgmt.

Org. Charts

Philanthropy

Sales

TrioMotor Supplier Evaluation Project
This project, managed by Derek Bendek, will make sure our company uses the best, customer-focused, part suppliers in the market.
Project Overview

IT Readiness project to start in November 2004
The IT managers have teamed up with ICOM to work on cleaning up the Outlook distribution lists. There are currently over 2000 lists on the Exchange Server...
Read More

How do I know if I have an ergonomics problem in my workplace?
Join us in a 35 minute class to detect ergonomic issues in your workplace. January 23, 2004
Read More

Environmental engineering summit
Come to the anual internal summit to discuss environmental...

Employee Of The Month

Clare Williams
Operations Admin.

With her invaluable help, the operations team managed to put together a comprehensive safer workplace plan

4 View the Result

3 Locate Editable Regions

Because of the synergy between Contribute and the Web authoring environment from the same developer, *Dreamweaver*, many companies using Contribute to manage their Web site maintenance will also be using Dreamweaver to create their Web pages (although there is no requirement to do so; Contribute works with all Web pages, no matter how they were created).

A unique feature of the templates used to define page design in Dreamweaver is the capability to define *editable* and *non-editable* regions on the page.

For example, suppose an author working in Dreamweaver wants to enable Contribute users to edit the general content on a page, but not to edit the title graphic containing the company logo or the button bar along the side of the page that contains links to other pages on the site. That author could use the Dreamweaver template to declare the title and the button bar non-editable regions, to prevent contributors from inadvertently changing content that should never be changed, except by the author.

If the sites you edit were authored in Dreamweaver, odds are you'll come across non-editable regions. The following steps show how to tell the editable from the non-editable. It's really only a matter of watching your pointer.

1 Point Anywhere

In Edit mode, point anywhere on the page and observe what the pointer looks like.

2 Move the Pointer Around

Move your pointer among the various parts of your page. As it passes over pictures, it will appear as your regular arrow pointer. As it passes over text, it will change to a text pointer to show that you can click to position the insertion point for editing text. As it passes over table borders, it will change to a multi-pointed arrow, indicating that you can click and drag the borders to resize the table.

Before You Begin

✔ **1** About Connections

✔ **2** Import a Connection Key

🔍 KEY TERM

Dreamweaver—A full-featured Web authoring program from the same company that produces Contribute (Macromedia), which is often used to create the pages that Contribute users later edit and maintain.

🔍 KEY TERM

Editable region—A portion of a Web page (authored in Dreamweaver) that contributors are permitted to edit.

Non-editable region—Dreamweaver authors may also define regions as *non-editable*, preventing contributors from making any changes to those regions.

💡 TIP

If content you believe you need to change appears in a non-editable region, contact your administrator. The Dreamweaver Web author can make the region editable, and the Contribute administrator can configure permissions to restrict the access of anyone else who should not edit that content.

1 Point Anywhere

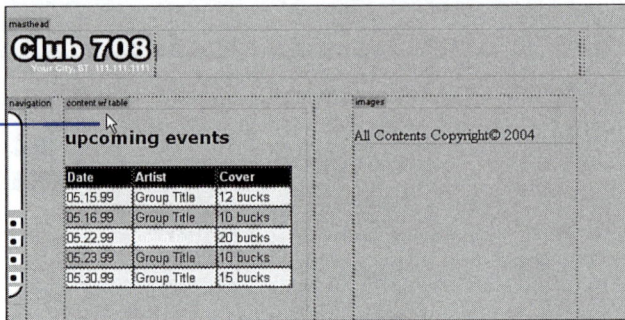

2 Move the Pointer Around

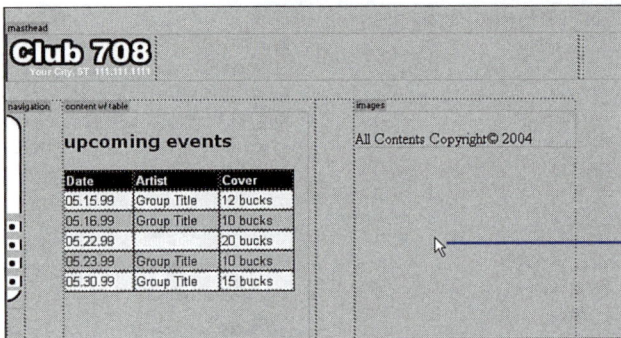

3 Watch for the "Anti" Cursor

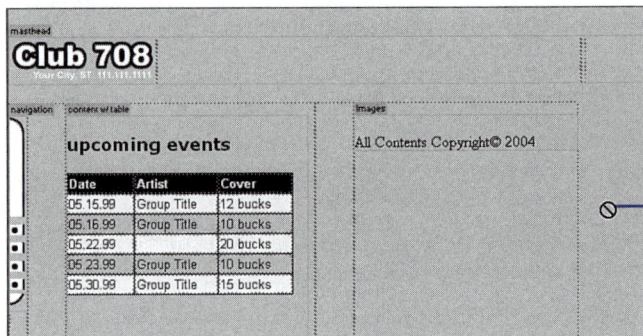

3 Watch for the "Anti" Cursor

If, when you pass over a region, your mouse pointer changes to the "anti" symbol, the region you're pointing to is non-editable.

4 Work Offline

You might want to work *offline*—not actively connected to the site you're editing—for a variety of reasons. First, you might choose to edit a site on a notebook or on other computer running Contribute that's not currently connected to the network. Also, if the site you want to edit is unavailable at startup, Contribute reports that it can't open the connection, offering you the chance to edit the page anyway, offline, using the latest draft of that page currently stored on your computer.

Although this is a handy capability, use it carefully. Contribute won't let two users edit the same page at the same time. When the connection fails, it could be because someone else is editing the site. Moreover, it's possible that someone else has edited the page since you last published the draft on your computer. In either case, if you make changes offline and publish later, you could publish a draft that doesn't contain subsequent changes made by other contributors.

For that reason, working offline is recommended only when you know you are the only contributor who edits the site, or when you are in close enough communication with other contributors to the site that you can avoid overwriting their changes.

1 Open the Site

Open the site you want to edit. If the connection is working, the site will open; if not, Contribute reports that it can't connect.

2 Switch to Offline Mode

Choose **File, Work Offline** (or **Contribute, Work Offline** on a Mac) from the menu bar. If Contribute was unable to connect in step 1, the latest draft of the current page on your computer appears. Otherwise, the version Contribute displayed in step 1—the current online version, at that moment—remains. In Edit mode, a **Work Online** button appears on the toolbar.

When you are ready to edit online again, or ready to publish changes you made offline, click the **Work Online** button on the toolbar or choose **File, Work Online** from the menu bar. Contribute will reconnect to the site, if the connection is available.

Before You Begin

✔ **1** About Connections

✔ **2** Import a Connection Key

TIP

When you're working offline, a **Work Online** button appears on the toolbar in place of the **Publish** button, so you can jump back online in a snap.

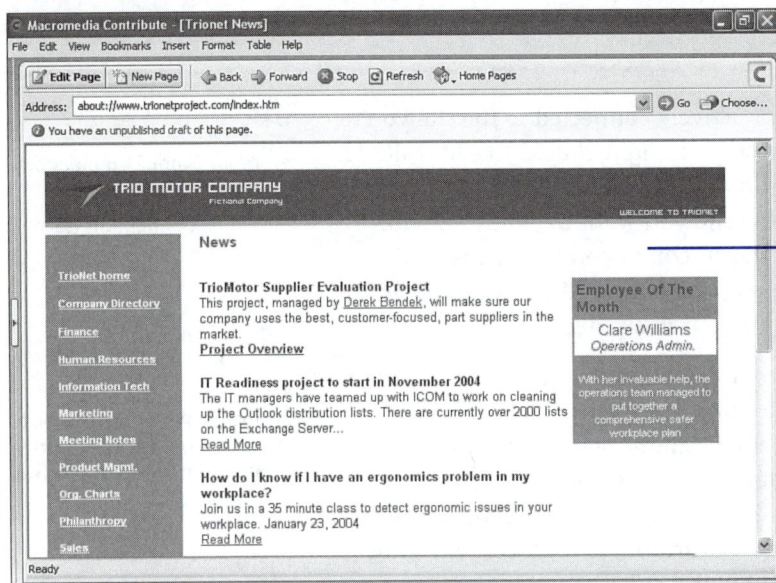

1 Open the Site

2 Switch to Offline Mode

5 Delete a Connection

Before You Begin

✔ **1** About Connections

✔ **2** Import a
Connection Key

Over time, you might accumulate a whole collection of connections. This isn't really a problem, but you'll find that Contribute's performance slows down when you have too many active connections, and you might find connecting to just the site you want more cumbersome if you have old, unused connections lying around. For that reason, it's good to know how to delete connections you no longer need.

Note that deleting a connection does not remove the Web site itself; it just removes the connection information from your computer.

Publish | Save for Later | Cancel ──────── **1** **Close Drafts**

Normal | Default Font | 12

Edit

Undo	Ctrl+Z
Redo	Ctrl+Y
Cut	Ctrl+X
Copy	Ctrl+C
Paste	Ctrl+V
Paste Text Only	Ctrl+Shift+V
Clear	
Select All	Ctrl+A
Find...	Ctrl+F
Preferences...	
My Connections...	
Administer Websites	▶

2 **Open the Connections Dialog Box**

4 **Remove the Connection**

My Connections

Create.. | Import... | Edit.. | Remove | Rename | Disable | Administer..

Website Name	Address	Role	Administrator
Tutorial Website	file:///D|/Documents%20and%20Settings/Snell/Local%20...	Administrator	tutorial_user@t...
Alley Cat Players	http://www.alleycatplayers.org/	Administrator	eaverill@tampa...

3 **Choose a Connection to Delete**

☐ Don't connect to websites at startup [improves Contribute startup time]

Help | Close

1 Close Drafts

Close any open drafts first by clicking the **Cancel** button. You can't delete a connection to a site that's open.

2 Open the Connections Dialog Box

Open the **My Connections** dialog box by choosing **Edit**, **My Connections** (in Windows) or **Contribute**, **My Connections** (on a Mac).

TIP

If multiple connections are slowing down Contribute, but you don't want to delete any, you can temporarily disable connections to speed things up (see **6** **Disable Connections**).

3 **Choose a Connection to Delete**

From the list of connections, click the one you want to delete.

4 **Remove the Connection**

Click the **Remove** button to remove the connection.

---

6 **Disable Connections**

Before You Begin

✔ **1** About Connections

✔ **2** Import a
   Connection Key

NOTE

If Contribute can't connect to a website when you start up, it might disable the connection automatically.

When you start Contribute, it checks all your connections and opens connections to all the sites you edit. If any site is unavailable—which can happen if there's a temporary Web or network problem, or if another contributor is currently editing the site—Contribute will report that it can't open the connection, and prompt you through steps for retrying the connection.

To avoid the prompts for sites you don't need and to improve Contribute's performance, you can disable connections temporarily. When you're ready to edit those sites (and the connection problem is presumably fixed), you can re-enable those sites, as shown in **7** **Enable Connections**.

1 **Open the Connections Dialog Box**

Choose **Edit, My Connections** (in Windows) or **Contribute, My Connections** (on a Mac). The **My Connections** dialog box appears.

2 **Choose a Connection to Disable**

From the list of connections, click the one you want to disable.

3 **Disable It**

Click the **Disable** button. A prompt informs you that the connection has been disabled. Click **OK** to finish disabling and then click the **Close** button to save your changes and close the **My Connections** dialog box.

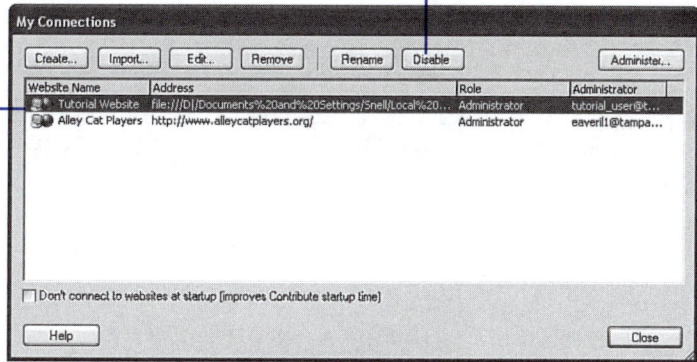

1 Open the Connections Dialog Box

3 Disable It

2 Choose a Connection to Disable

---

7 **Enable Connections**

If Contribute has disabled a connection at startup because the site or network is unavailable, or if you've disabled a connection yourself by following the steps in **6** **Disable Connections**, you'll need to re-enable the connection the next time you want to edit the site.

After a connection has been disabled, Contribute no longer attempts to open the connection automatically at startup, so the following steps are required to get back into that site for editing. After you've enabled a connection, it will open automatically at startup in all future Contribute sessions, until/unless you disable it again.

Before You Begin

✔ **1** About Connections

✔ **2** Import a Connection Key

✔ **6** Disable Connections

Edit

Undo	Ctrl+Z
Redo	Ctrl+Y
Cut	Ctrl+X
Copy	Ctrl+C
Paste	Ctrl+V
Paste Text Only	Ctrl+Shift+V
Clear	
Select All	Ctrl+A
Find...	Ctrl+F
Preferences...	
My Connections...	
Administer Websites	▶

1 Open the Connections Dialog Box

3 Enable It

2 Choose a Connection to Enable

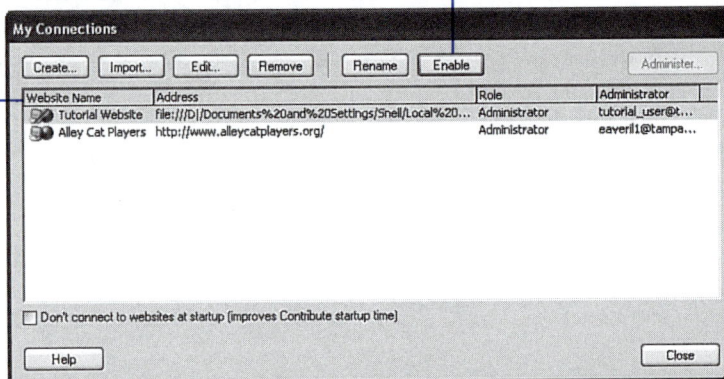

My Connections

| Create... | Import... | Edit... | Remove | | Rename | Enable | | Administer... |

Website Name	Address	Role	Administrator
Tutorial Website	file:///D|/Documents%20and%20Settings/Snell/Local%20...	Administrator	tutorial_user@t...
Alley Cat Players	http://www.alleycatplayers.org/	Administrator	eaverll1@tampa...

☐ Don't connect to websites at startup (improves Contribute startup time)

| Help | | Close |

❶ Open the Connections Dialog Box

Choose **Edit**, **My Connections** (in Windows) or **Contribute**, **My Connections** (on a Mac). The **My Connections** dialog box appears.

❷ Choose a Connection to Enable

From the list of connections, click the disabled connection you want to enable. Disabled connections are easy to spot—they're marked with a red slash.

3 ## Enable It

Click the **Enable** button and then click the **Close** button to save your changes and close the **My Connections** dialog box.

---

8 ## Bookmark Websites You Edit Often

Contribute lets you bookmark sites you visit often, in the same way you can create bookmarks (in Netscape) or Favorites (in Internet Explorer). The bookmarks list provides a handy way to quickly get to pages you edit.

When you pick a site from your **Bookmarks** list, it opens in Browse mode. If you have a connection to that site, you can click **Edit Page** to open it in Edit mode.

1 ### Browse to the Page

In Browse mode, browse to the page you want to add to your bookmarks.

2 ### Open the Bookmarks Dialog Box

Choose **Bookmarks, Add Bookmark** from the menu bar. The **Add Bookmark** dialog box appears.

3 ### Finish Up

Click **OK** to add the page to your bookmarks list.

Before You Begin

✔ **1** About Connections

✔ **2** Import a Connection Key

💡 TIP

You can bookmark any site in Contribute—even those you don't edit and don't have connections to.

💡 TIP

If you want to change the name of the bookmark as it appears in the list, after step 2, type a new name in the **Name** box. If you want to create a separate folder for this bookmark and others like it to keep your bookmarks organized, click **New Folder.**

Macromedia Contribute - [Alley Cat Players]

File Edit View Bookmarks Insert Format Table Help

Edit Page   New Page   Back   Forward   Stop   Refresh   Home Pages

Address: http://www.alleycatplayers.org/   Go   Choose...

1 Browse to the Page

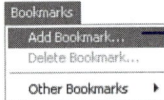

Alley Cat Players

present

Macbeth

Done

Bookmarks

Add Bookmark...
Delete Bookmark...

Other Bookmarks   ▶

2 Open the Bookmarks Dialog Box

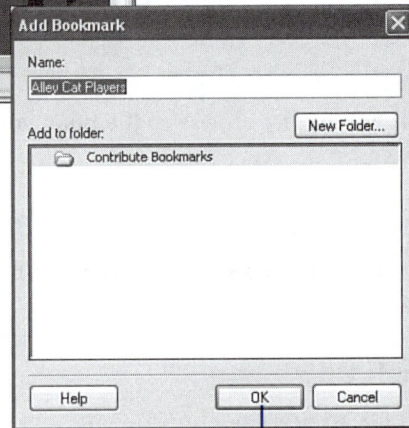

Add Bookmark

Name:

Alley Cat Players

Add to folder: New Folder...

Contribute Bookmarks

Help   OK   Cancel

3 Finish Up

PART II

Editing the Content of a Web Page

3

Editing Text in a Web Page

IN THIS CHAPTER:

TIP

Most of the time when you're editing text, you'll want to change some or all of the words in a region without changing the way the words in that region are formatted—font, color, size, and so on. For this reason, the tasks in this chapter focus on changing text without altering format. Should you choose to change the formatting as well, see Chapter 4, "Changing the Way Text Looks."

If you've ever used any Windows or Mac word processing program, you'll find text editing in Contribute pretty straightforward. Most of the basic text-editing techniques you already know from using these word processors still apply.

A web page, however, is not a word processing document, and there are types of editing and formatting you might expect to be able to do in such a word processor-like program that you really can't do with a web page. Most of the differences have less to do with Contribute than they have to do with long-held, very deliberate restrictions on the way a web page works that limit some types of text editing and formatting. These restrictions exist to ensure that a single web page looks good when viewed through all kinds of browsers, at any resolution, on any size monitor.

If you need text-editing activities to work differently from what you discover—for example, if you need the insertion point to jump down one line instead of two at the end of a paragraph—contact your administrator.

9 About Web Page Text

By design, text and other content elements cannot be as precisely formatted and positioned on a web page as they can be in most word processing programs or desktop publishing programs. Exactly how much control you do have is limited not only by the traditional limitations in web page formatting, but also by options your administrator might have selected.

For example, multiple consecutive spaces typed in a web page by the author typically are recognized and displayed as a single space when the page is viewed through a browser. By default, the same happens in Contribute—if you type multiple spaces in a line, they'll be cut down to one space when the page is browsed. Similarly, pressing the **Enter** key to end a paragraph typically inserts a blank line automatically between paragraphs, as if you'd pressed **Enter** twice in a word processing program.

Both of these restrictions may be overridden by your administrator, who can configure Contribute to accept multiple spaces and display them as typed, or to make the insertion point jump down only one line (instead of two) when you press **Enter**. Your administrator can also set up Contribute to allow or disallow certain kinds of characters. For this reason, I can't always tell you exactly what will happen when you perform certain text-editing activities in Contribute; the best way to find out is to jump in and see what happens.

10 Select Text

Some text-editing activities—and nearly all of the text-formatting activities you'll explore in Chapter 4, "Changing the Way Text Looks,"—require *selecting* text, highlighting it so that whatever you do next affects only what you've highlighted.

If you've ever used a Windows or Mac word processor, you probably already know how to select. But just to cover all the bases, here are the basics of selecting.

1 Point, Click, and Hold

Point to the very beginning of the text you want to select. Click on the spot you pointed to and hold down the mouse button.

2 Drag to Select

Drag the mouse to the right to select characters to the right, or drag down to select large blocks of text.

3 Release

Release the mouse button when the text you want to work on is highlighted. Don't click anywhere else until after you've completed what you want to do to that text—doing so deselects the text.

Before You Begin

✔ **3**   Locate Editable Regions

✔ **9**   About Web Page Text

TIP

You can select an entire paragraph by triple-clicking it. Click fast.

The project goal is to document a complete evaluation of the companies that supply automobile parts to the Trio Motor Company. Each supplier will be evaluated in the following categories: ROI, Service, Responsiveness and Quality.

Meet The Team

Name	Phone	Role
Derek Bendek	x4921	Project Manager
George Woods	x1162	Director, Operations
Diana Smith	x7094	Customer Service

Team list updated: 29-Sep-2004

1   **Point, Click, and Hold**

The project goal is to document a complete evaluation of the companies that supply automobile parts to the Trio Motor Company. Each supplier will be evaluated in the following categories: ROI, Service, Responsiveness and Quality.

Meet The Team

Name	Phone	Role
Derek Bendek	x4921	Project Manager
George Woods	x1162	Director, Operations
Diana Smith	x7094	Customer Service

Team list updated: 29-Sep-2004

2   **Drag to Select**

The project goal is to document a complete evaluation of the companies that supply automobile parts to the Trio Motor Company. Each supplier will be evaluated in the following categories: ROI, Service, Responsiveness and Quality.

Meet The Team

Name	Phone	Role
Derek Bendek	x4921	Project Manager
George Woods	x1162	Director, Operations
Diana Smith	x7094	Customer Service

Team list updated: 29-Sep-2004

3   **Release**

---

11   **Edit and Add Text**

Before You Begin

✔ **3**   Locate Editable Regions

✔ **9**   About Web Page Text

✔ **10**   Select Text

Basic text editing in Contribute is pretty straightforward, just like editing text in any word processor or email program you might have used. Here's a rundown, just to refresh your memory…

1   **Position Your Insertion Point**

Point to the spot where you want to add text and click. The *insertion point*, a flashing vertical bar, appears where you clicked to mark the spot where anything you type will appear.

News

TrioMotor Supplier Evaluation Project
This project, managed by Derek Bendek, will make sure our
company uses the best, customer-focused, part suppliers in the
market.
Project Overview

IT Readiness project to start | ——————————— ① **Position Your Insertion Point**
The IT managers have teamed up with ICOM to work on cleaning
up the Outlook distribution lists. There are currently over 2000 lists
on the Exchange Server...
Read More

How do I know if I have an ergonomics problem in my workplace?
Join us in a 35 minute class to detect ergonomic issues in
workplace.
Read More

News

TrioMotor Supplier Evaluation Project
This project, managed by Derek Bendek, will make sure our
company uses the best, customer-focused, part suppliers in the
market.
Project Overview

IT Readiness project to start in November, 2004| ② **Type Your Text**
The IT managers have teamed up with ICOM to work on cleaning
up the Outlook distribution lists. There are currently over 2000 lists
on the Exchange Server...

News

TrioMotor Supplier Evaluation Project
This project, managed by Derek Bendek, will make sure our
company uses the best, customer-focused, part suppliers in the
market.
Project Overview

③ **Replace Existing Text**

IT Readiness project to begin trials in November, 2004
The IT managers have teamed up with ICOM to work on cleaning
up the Outlook distribution lists. There are currently over 2000 lists
on the Exchange Server...
Read More

How do I know if I have an ergonomics problem in my workplace?
Join us in a 35 minute class to detect ergonomic issues in your
workplace.
Read More

② **Type Your Text**

Type your text. As you type, existing text is pushed to the right to
make room for the new text. The new text takes on the formatting
of the text around it. When you reach the end of a line, keep typing—the insertion point jumps automatically to the next line, just
as in a word processor. If you make a mistake along the way, use
the **arrow** keys, **Backspace** key, and **Delete** key to make repairs.

NOTE

Remember that some
pages might have editable
and non-editable regions.
You'll know a non-editable
region by the "block" cursor
you'll see when you point
to it. If the text you want to
edit is in a non-editable
region, contact your administrator (see ③ Locate
Editable Regions).

TIP

When selecting text to replace, avoid selecting the entire paragraph. Leave at least a character or two at the end of the paragraph unselected, type your text, and then delete the remainder of the text, taking care not to delete the invisible paragraph mark at the very end. This ensures that your new text keeps the formatting of the old.

3 Replace Existing Text

To replace existing text as you type your new text, first select the text you want to replace and then type.

When selecting text to replace, avoid selecting the entire paragraph. Leave at least a character or two at the end of the paragraph unselected, type your text, then delete the remainder of the text, taking care not to delete the invisible paragraph mark at the very end. This ensures that your new text keeps the formatting of the old.

Unlike a word processor, Contribute has no "overtype" mode (where anything you type wipes out what's in front of it). To replace existing text as you type, see step 3.

---

12 Copy or Move Text

Before You Begin

✔ **3** Locate Editable Regions

✔ **9** About Web Page Text

✔ **10** Select Text

See Also

→ **16** Use Find and Replace

→ **65** About Inserting External Documents

TIP

If you want a faster way to perform steps 2 and 4, try the keyboard commands. For step 2, **Ctrl+C** (on a Mac, ⌘**+C**) copies and **Ctrl+X** (on a Mac, ⌘**+V**) cuts (for moving).

Often, editing text on a page is not so much a job of typing new text or replacing old text, but rather juggling bits and pieces of existing content. In such cases, copying and moving text can save you typing time and can also help you avoid adding new typos.

1 Select the Text to Copy or Move

Select the text by placing the mouse pointer at the start of the text you want to select, clicking and holding the mouse button and then dragging to the end of the text. When all the text you want to copy or move is selected, release the mouse button.

2 Choose Edit, Copy or Edit, Cut

If you choose **Edit**, **Cut** or press **Ctrl+X** to cut the text before moving it, the selected text disappears. If you choose **Edit**, **Copy** or press **Ctrl+C**, the selection remains. In both cases, the selected text is placed in the computer's temporary memory. On a Mac, ⌘-C copies text and ⌘-V cuts text.

3 Click the Destination Spot

Click where you want the text to go to position the insertion point there.

PART II: Editing the Content of a Web Page

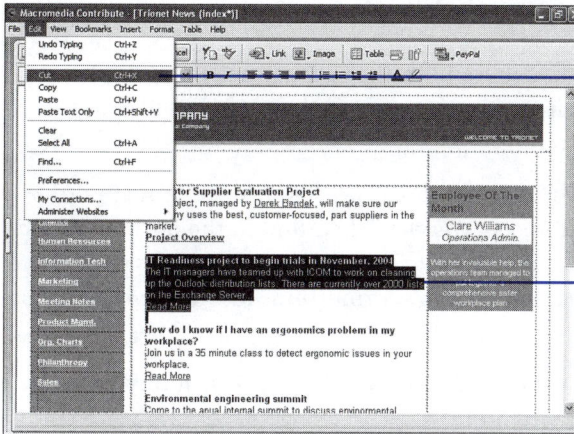

2 Choose Edit, Copy or
Edit, Cut

1 Select the Text to
Copy or Move

3 Click the Destination Spot

4 Choose
Edit, Paste

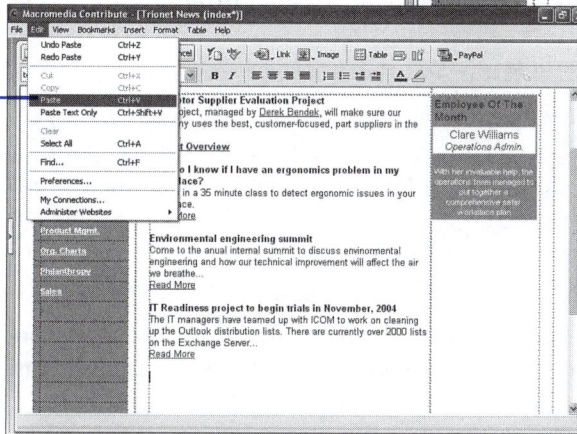

🔦 **TIP**

If the block of text you're copying or moving contains hyperlinks, pictures, or other content besides text, that content is also moved or copied when you choose **Edit, Paste**. If you want to copy or move just the text, leaving out any other content in the selection, paste by choosing **Edit, Paste Text Only**.

4 Choose Edit, Paste

From the menu bar, choose **Edit, Paste**. The text you copied or cut in step 2 appears at the insertion point, moving the existing text to the right to make room.

In this example, you can see that I selected the entire first paragraph under the "Project Overview" heading in the document and moved it (cut it and pasted it) to the bottom of the document. Note that all the original paragraph's formatting was preserved because I selected the entire paragraph.

You can paste the text you copied or moved in step 2 as many times as you want by repeating steps 3 and 4.

13 Insert Special Characters (Symbols)

Before You Begin

✔ **3** Locate Editable Regions

✔ **9** About Web Page Text

See Also

→ **18** Change the Style of Text

→ **20** Change the Font, Size, or Color of Text

→ **75** Preview Your Work

Some of the characters you might need in your text—such as copyright, trademark, or foreign currency symbols—aren't on your keyboard. Such characters are loosely bundled under the name "special characters" or "symbols." To add special characters to your text, use Contribute's **Special Characters** menu and the **Insert Other Character** dialog box.

1 Position Your Insertion Point

Position the mouse pointer at the spot where you want to add a special character and click. The insertion point appears where you clicked to mark the spot where the character you choose will be inserted.

2 Choose Insert, Special Characters

Choose **Insert, Special Characters** from the menu bar. The submenu you see contains most of the commonly used special characters.

3 Choose Your Character

If the character you want appears in the **Special Characters** submenu, choose it from the menu. The menu disappears, and the character appears at the insertion point.

1 Position Your Insertion Point

2 Choose Insert, Special Characters

3 Choose Your Character

4 Or Choose Other

6 View the Result

5 Click the Character and Click OK

4 **Or Choose Other**

If the character you want to insert does not appear in the **Special Characters** submenu, choose **Other** from the bottom of the menu to open the **Insert Other Character** dialog box.

5 **Click the Character and Click OK**

The dialog box contains almost 100 additional special characters. Click the button for the one you want to insert and then click **OK**.

6 **View the Result**

The character you selected in step 3 or 5 appears at the point you clicked in step 1.

Special characters take on the formatting (font, color, and so on) of the characters around them. If you later change the formatting (the font, in particular), the special characters might not display properly. If that happens, reinsert the special characters after you change formatting (**see** **20** **Change the Font, Size, or Color of Text**).

When you add text that contains special characters by importing or copying that text from another program, the special characters might not come out right in Contribute. Carefully check any imported special characters and replace them as necessary (**see** **65** **About Inserting External Documents**).

14 Insert the Date

Before You Begin

✔ **3** Locate Editable Regions

See Also

→ **75** Preview Your Work

Contribute provides a fast and easy way to add a date to a page, and to optionally include the day of the week or the time along with the date.

You can choose to lock in the date/time to the moment you inserted it, or you can configure the date/time so that it will update to the current date and time any time you save the page. This last option provides you with an easy, automatic way to indicate when the page was last updated, or to show when particular content on the page was changed.

1 **Position Your Insertion Point**

Position the mouse pointer at the spot where you want to add the date and click. The insertion point appears where you clicked to mark the spot where the date will appear. As with any text, you can insert the date on a line by itself or within a line of existing text.

2 **Open the Insert Date Dialog Box**

Choose **Insert**, **Date** to open the **Insert Date** dialog box.

News

(Last Updated: |

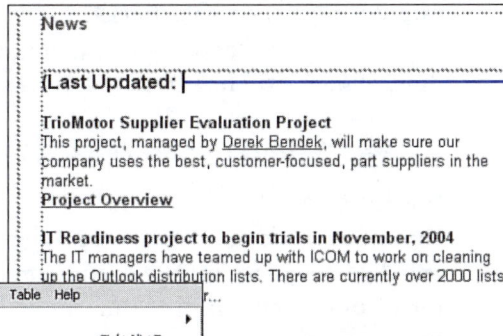

1 Position Your Insertion Point

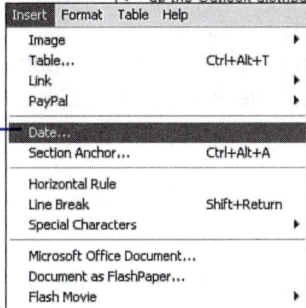

TrioMotor Supplier Evaluation Project
This project, managed by Derek Bendek, will make sure our
company uses the best, customer-focused, part suppliers in the
market.
Project Overview

IT Readiness project to begin trials in November, 2004
The IT managers have teamed up with ICOM to work on cleaning
up the Outlook distribution lists. There are currently over 2000 lists

| Insert | Format | Table | Help |

Image		►
Table...	Ctrl+Alt+T	
Link		►
PayPal		►
Date...		
Section Anchor...	Ctrl+Alt+A	
Horizontal Rule		
Line Break	Shift+Return	
Special Characters		►
Microsoft Office Document...		
Document as FlashPaper...		
Flash Movie		►

2 Open the Insert Date Dialog Box

3 Choose Formats for the Day, Date, and Time

Insert Date

Day format: Thursday,

Date format: March 7, 1974
07-Mar-1974
7-mar-74
03/07/1974
3/7/74
1974-03-07

Time format: [No Time]

☐ Update automatically on save

| Help | OK | Cancel |

4 Choose Whether the Date/Time Update Automatically

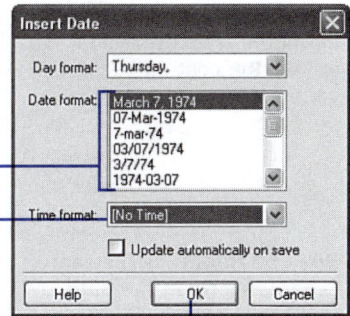

5 Click OK

News

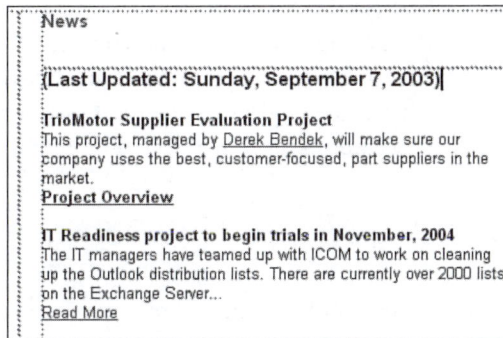

6 Modify the Page and View the Result

(Last Updated: Sunday, September 7, 2003) |

TrioMotor Supplier Evaluation Project
This project, managed by Derek Bendek, will make sure our
company uses the best, customer-focused, part suppliers in the
market.
Project Overview

IT Readiness project to begin trials in November, 2004
The IT managers have teamed up with ICOM to work on cleaning
up the Outlook distribution lists. There are currently over 2000 lists
on the Exchange Server...
Read More

3 Choose Formats for the Day, Date, and Time

Using the lists in the dialog box, choose formats for each part of
the day or time you want to include. For example, if you want the
date to be preceded by the day of the week followed by a comma,
choose **Thursday** from the **Day** list. To choose a date format of

TIP

Don't confuse the date/time you insert here with the kind of date/time that always shows the actual current date and time on some websites. The date and time you insert in Contribute does not update automatically when a visitor views the page online. The date/time you insert can, however, be configured to update whenever you modify the content of the page.

TIP

Don't be thrown by the year (**1974**!) shown in the date formats in step 3. The formats are just examples. You'll get the correct year in the date you see on the page.

mm/dd/yyyy, choose **03/07/1974** from the **Date** list. To omit the day of the week, choose **No Day** from the **Day** list. To omit the time, choose **No Time** from the **Time** list.

4 Choose Whether the Date/Time Update Automatically

To configure the date/time to update each time you save the page, enable the **Update automatically on save** check box. If you leave the box disabled, the date/time on your page will always reflect the moment you performed step 5. If you enable the check box, the date/time on your page will always reflect the last time the page was saved (by you or by anyone else authorized to edit the page).

5 Click OK

When you have selected the formatting and update options in the **Insert Date** dialog box, click **OK**. The new date appears on your page, formatted like the text around it.

6 Modify the Page and View the Result

Observe the date any time you modify and/or publish this page. If you enabled the **Update automatically on save** check box in step 4 and later modify the content of the page, the date is automatically updated to reflect the date on which you modified the page.

---

15 Check Spelling

Before You Begin

✔ **3** Locate Editable Regions

See Also

→ **16** Use Find and Replace

Unlike Microsoft Word and some other word processors and Web authoring programs, Contribute cannot automatically indicate misspelled words as you work on your page. That makes it all the more important to run the spell-checker from time to time—especially right before you publish the page.

Like all spell-checkers, the one in Contribute does not really find misspelled words. It simply compares all the words in your page to its dictionary and calls to your attention any word not in the dictionary. Sometimes, the words it picks are misspellings, but other times, the words the spell-checker picks are correctly spelled words that just aren't in Contribute's dictionary; for example, unusual names are typically caught by the spell-checker. When the spell-checker stops on a word you know to be spelled correctly, it's easy to skip that word.

1 Click the Check Spelling Button

Select **Format, Check Spelling**. The **Check Spelling** dialog box opens and immediately shows the first word it doesn't recognize in the **Word not found in dictionary** box.

2 Address the Word Shown in the Word Not Found in Dictionary Box

If the word shown in the **Word not found in Dictionary** box is in fact spelled correctly, click the **Ignore** button. If the word is misspelled and one suggestion in the **Suggestions** box is the correct spelling, click the suggested word and then click the **Change** button. If the word is misspelled and no correct suggestion appears, type the correct spelling in the **Change To** box and then click the **Change** button.

If you suspect that you might have misspelled the word more than once, you can click **Change All** to make the spell-checker automatically fix that same error (with the same solution) everywhere it finds the error in this spell-check run.

3 Move On to the Next Unrecognized Word

After you perform any of the actions in step 2, the spell-checker moves to the next unrecognized word on the page. Repeat step 2 for each word the spell-checker finds.

4 Finish Up

When the spell-checker has finished checking the whole page or the selection you made before step 1, either of two things will happen:

- If you made a selection before step 1, the spell-checker displays a prompt box asking whether you want to spell-check the rest of the page. Click **Yes** to check the rest of the page or **No** to close the spell-checker.

NOTE

The spell-checker won't help you fix a misspelled word if the misspelling happens to make another correctly spelled word; for example, if you misspell *manager* as *manger*, the spell-checker won't catch it. In addition to running the spell-checker, you should proofread your pages carefully and have others check your work as well (**see 76 Send Your Work to Reviewers**).

TIP

If you want to check the spelling in only a portion of the page, select that portion before performing step 1.

TIP

In step 2, you can click **Ignore All** to make the spell-checker automatically ignore a word everywhere it finds it in this spell-check run. You might click **Ignore All** for a name or unusual word that comes up repeatedly on the page.

TIP

To add an often-used word (such as a name) to the dictionary so that the spell-checker knows it's not an error, click the **Add** button the next time the spell-checker stops on that word.

1 **Select Format, Check Spelling**

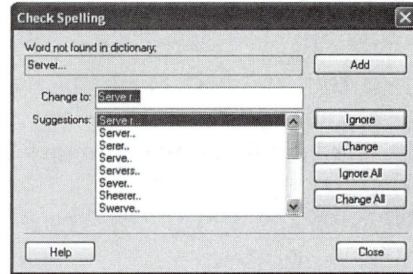

3 **Move On to the Next Unrecognized Word**

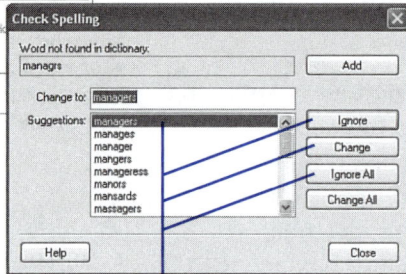

2 **Address the Word Shown in the Word Not Found in Dictionary Box**

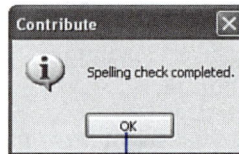

4 **Finish Up**

- If you made no selection before step 1, the spell-checker displays a prompt that spell-checking is complete; click **OK** to close the prompt.

16 Use Find and Replace

Before You Begin

✔ **3** Locate Editable Regions

See Also

→ **15** Check Spelling

Sometimes, you might have to change a particular word or phrase in multiple places. For example, if a product name changes, you need a handy way to make that change everywhere the old product name appears on the Contribute pages you edit. That's when Contribute's **Find and Replace** feature comes in handy.

1 Choose Edit, Find

Open the **Edit** menu and choose **Find** to open the **Find and Replace** dialog box.

2 Type the Word to Replace

In the **Search for** box, type the word or phrase you want to change.

3 Type the Word to Use as a Replacement

In the **Replace with** box, type what you want the text from step 2 changed to.

4 Click Find Next

To choose which instances of the **Search for** text to change, click the **Find Next** button.

You can also replace *all* instances of the **Search for** text with the **Replace with** text in a *global* change. Click the **Replace All** button in the **Find and Replace** dialog box, and all instances of the specified word or phrase—not just in one place, but everywhere that word appears in the page—are replaced, all at once, without stopping for verification at each occurrence.

5 Replace or Skip

Contribute locates the first instance of the text in the **Search for** box on the page. To replace the selected text, click the **Replace** button; click **Find Next** to leave that instance alone and find the next instance.

6 Repeat Step 5 Until Done

When you click **Replace** or **Find Next** in step 5, Contribute automatically moves to the next occurrence of the **Search for** text on the page. Repeat step 5 until all instances of the word or phrase have been handled. When Contribute displays a prompt that the whole document has been searched, click **OK** to close the prompt and then click **Close** on the **Find and Replace** dialog box.

TIP

To change only those instances of the **Search for** text that match the exact capitalization you typed, enable the **Match case** check box in the **Find and Replace** dialog box.

Edit

Undo Typing	Ctrl+Z
Redo Typing	Ctrl+Y
Cut	Ctrl+X
Copy	Ctrl+C
Paste	Ctrl+V
Paste Text Only	Ctrl+Shift+V
Clear	
Select All	Ctrl+A
Find...	Ctrl+F
Preferences...	
My Connections...	
Administer Websites	▶

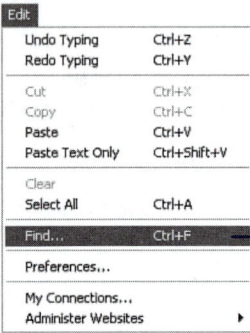

1 **Choose Edit, Find**

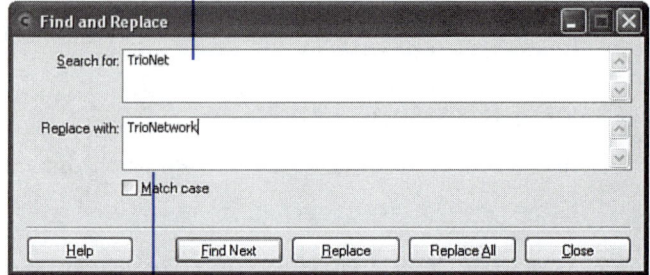

2 **Type the Word to Replace**

Find and Replace

Search for: TrioNet

Replace with: TrioNetwork

☐ Match case

| Help | Find Next | Replace | Replace All | Close |

3 **Type the Word to Use as a Replacement**

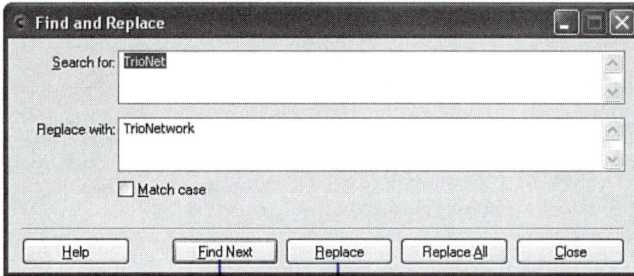

Find and Replace

Search for: TrioNet

Replace with: TrioNetwork

☐ Match case

| Help | Find Next | Replace | Replace All | Close |

Contribute

ⓘ Done. 3 items found, 1 replaced in the current document.

OK

6 **Repeat Step 5 Until Done**

5 **Replace or Skip**

4 **Click Find Next**

4

Changing the Way Text Looks

IN THIS CHAPTER:

As you edit content, you might find that you need all—or none—of the text-formatting techniques in this chapter. A well-designed page will offer you *styles* (**see** **18** **Change the Style of Text**) you can apply to instantly format text in ways that fit the page. If you apply styles carefully and consistently, you may need to do little other formatting.

Still...ya never know, and you can't be satisfied with text unless it looks right to you. The tasks in this chapter give you control of your text's appearance.

17 About Text Formatting

NOTE

Almost everything you learn how to do in this chapter may be enabled or disabled in your role by your administrator. For example, you can change the font of text only if your administrator has configured your permissions to allow font changing.

There are really two different kinds of text formatting:

- **Paragraph formatting**, which always affects whole paragraphs, never just parts of them. Examples of paragraph formatting include styles, alignment, and indents. When you apply paragraph formatting, you don't have to select the paragraph, all you need to do is click within it.

- **Character formatting**, which can affect any group of characters, from a single character to a whole paragraph. Character formatting includes fonts, bold, and italicizing. When you apply character formatting, you must select the exact block of characters to which you want to apply the formatting.

You'll perform both types of formatting in this chapter, but any time you approach text formatting, be judicious in its application. If you edit and add text according to the steps in Chapter 3, "Editing Text in a Web Page," you'll typically preserve the text formatting already defined in the page. Changing formatting carelessly might undermine the design and overall appearance of the site.

Your administrator can help you avoid this by configuring your role to restrict the kinds of formatting you might apply, lessening the chances that you'll inadvertently alter the page's design. However, permissions are no substitute for careful judgment, and it's likely that you *can* do some formatting that you sometimes *shouldn't*. Just be careful.

18 Change the Style of Text

The most important step in controlling the appearance of text is choosing the text's *style*. There are many styles, but the most important are the six different Heading styles (from big Heading 1 to little Heading 6), Normal style (for ordinary, everyday paragraphs), and the List styles (see Chapter 6, "Organizing Content on a Page").

If you edit existing text according to the steps in Chapter 3, "Editing Text in a Web Page," odds are that the text will retain the style already assigned to it by the Web page's author. That's good, because authors can define new styles for a page—available to you in Contribute—so that when you apply them, the appearance of your text matches that of the rest of the site. That's the Contribute way—update the content and preserve the formatting.

However, if you've inadvertently changed the style, or if you are adding substantial new body text or new headings, you'll find it easy to apply styles to those elements so that they match similar or related blocks of text within the page.

1 Choose the Paragraph

Click anywhere within the paragraph you want to format. (You do not need to select the paragraph.)

2 Open the Style List

Click the **down arrow** on the right end of the **Style** box to open the **Style** list.

3 Choose a Style

Click the name of the style you want to apply.

4 View the Result

The paragraph now appears in the style you applied to it.

Before You Begin

✔ **3** Locate Editable Regions

✔ **10** Select Text

KEY TERM

Styles—The principal forms of text formatting on a Web page. Standard styles include six levels of headings, a style for normal text, and several different styles for creating lists. Web authors can create and add additional styles specific to the page or site.

NOTE

You might find styles in your style list different from what you see here. Styles can be created and added to a page by the page's author. Ideally, the only styles you'll see in your list are those specifically designed for the page you're editing, but that's not always the case.

TIP

To apply a style to multiple, consecutive paragraphs all at once, click anywhere in the first paragraph and drag down through the paragraphs to anywhere in the last paragraph. Then choose your style.

1 Choose the Paragraph

Supplier Review Project
Team Lead: Derek Bendek

The project goal is to document a complete evaluation of the companies that supply automobile parts to the Trio Motor Company. Each supplier will be evaluated in the following categories: ROI, Service, Responsiveness and Quality.

Meet The Team

Name	Phone	Role
Derek Bendek	x4921	Project Manager
George Woods	x1162	Director, Operations
Diana Smith	x7094	Customer Service

Team list updated: 29-Sep-2003

2 Open the Style List

text
Normal
copytext
leftLink
Link
quote
subtitles
table
text
titles
Heading 1
Heading 2
Heading 3
Heading 4
Heading 5
Heading 6

3 Choose a Style

Supplier Review Project
Team Lead: Derek Bendek

The project goal is to document a complete evaluation of the companies that supply automobile parts to the Trio Motor Company. Each supplier will be evaluated in the following categories: ROI, Service, Responsiveness and Quality.

Meet The Team

Name	Phone	Role
Derek Bendek	x4921	Project Manager
George Woods	x1162	Director, Operations
Diana Smith	x7094	Customer Service

Team list updated: 29-Sep-2003

4 View the Result

19 Make Text Bold, Italic, or Underlined

Before You Begin

✔ **3** Locate Editable Regions

✔ **10** Select Text

Bold, *italic*, and underlining are valuable tools for making text stand out or for making it match editorial standards (such as setting book titles in italics). They're easy to use, but use them sparingly; too much of this stuff makes text busy and hard to read.

1 Select Your Characters

Select the exact characters you want to format.

🔦 **TIP**

Avoid underlining when you can. Links are generally underlined in Web pages, so underlined text that's not a link might confuse visitors.

George Woods	x1162	D
Diana Smith	x7094	C
Team list updated: 29-Sep-2004		

1 **Select Your Characters**

Format	Table	Help	
Check Spelling...			F7
Bold			Ctrl+B
Italic			Ctrl+I
Underline			Ctrl+U
Other			
Style			▶
Font			▶
Size			▶
Text Color...			
Highlight Color...			
Align			▶
List			▶
Indent			Ctrl+Alt+]
Outdent			Ctrl+Alt+[
Remove Link...			
Table Properties...			
Template Properties...			
Keywords and Description...			Ctrl+Alt+K
Page Properties...			Ctrl+J

2 **Choose the Formatting**

ater | ✖ Cancel | ⏏ Link ✎

✓ 10 ✓ | **B** *I* | ▤ ▤ ▤ ▤

Team Lead: Derek Bendek

The project goal is to document a compl
companies that supply automobile parts
Company. Each supplier will be evaluate
categories: ROI, Service, Responsivenes

Meet The Team

Name	Phone	
Derek Bendek	x4921	Pro
George Woods	x1162	Dire
Diana Smith	x7094	Cus
Team list updated: 29-Sep-2004		

Suppliers List

George Woods	x1162	Direct
Diana Smith	x7094	Custo
Team list updated: 29-Sep-2004		
Suppliers List		

3 **View the Result**

---

2 **Choose the Formatting**

Choose formatting by clicking a button to format the selected characters: the **Bold** button or the **Italic** button. To underline, choose **Format, Underline** from the menu bar. To remove bold, italic, or underlining, repeat the steps for applying the formatting. For example, to de-bold some bold text, select it and click the Bold button.

3 **View the Result**

To see the result, click anywhere to deselect the text. It now shows the character formatting you applied.

💡 TIP

You can combine these kinds of formatting. For example, you can make the selected text both bold and italic by clicking the **Bold** button and then the **Italic** button before deselecting the text.

20 Change the Font, Size, or Color of Text

Before You Begin

✔ **3** Locate Editable Regions

✔ **10** Select Text

The best way to control the appearance of text is to choose an appropriate style. Styles can help you keep your formatting within the fonts, sizes, and colors that are predefined and approved for the site, so that your page maintains the "look" defined by the page's author. But beyond the styles, you can dress up text even more by choosing a particular typeface—or *font*—for it. Just do so carefully—when you apply a font, you're stepping outside the appearance defined in the style.

The style you choose automatically determines the size of the text. Still, you can fine-tune the size of selected text easily when the size chosen by the style isn't exactly what you want.

Text colors are not generally determined by the style; they're applied by the web page author, in hues carefully selected to harmonize with the background color and other text colors and to make the text readable. You might never need to choose text colors, and you should exercise caution when you do, making sure that the color you choose leaves the text clear and legible on the page and goes well with the other colors on the page.

NOTE

Fonts, sizes, and text colors are all forms of character formatting, not paragraph formatting, so they affect only the exact characters you select, not the whole paragraph (unless you select the whole paragraph).

TIP

You can apply any of the formatting shown here without applying the others. For example, after applying a font in step 2, you can skip to step 5 without changing the text's size or color.

1 Select Your Characters

Select the exact characters to which you want to apply a new font.

2 Choose a Font

To choose a new font, locate the **Font** list box on the toolbar. (Note that the box tells the name of the font that's now applied to the text you selected—unless the text selected is the "default" font, in which case no name appears.) Click the arrow on the right side of the box to open the list. Click the name of the font you want to apply. If the **Font** list box shows no font name after you select the text, the block of text you selected contains more than one font. After you apply a font, the selected characters will all show the same font.

3 Choose a Size

To choose a new type size, click the arrow at the right end of the **Font Size** box to open the list. Choose a size, or choose **Default** to allow the style to determine the font size.

1 Select Your Characters

2 Choose a Font

3 Choose a Size

4 Choose a Color

5 View the Result

The numbers in the Font Size list describe "points." In publishing, points measure the height of capital letters (72 pt. = 1 inch), and they're shown to help you estimate size. But they're not meaningful, because the true size of the text depends upon the dimensions and resolution of the screen on which it is viewed.

4 **Choose a Color**

To choose a new color, click the **Text Color** button on the toolbar. The **Text Color** box opens. Click the colored square containing the color you want to apply. (To allow the style to determine the color, click the **Default Color** button on the **Text Color** box.)

5 **View the Result**

To view the result, click anywhere to deselect the text. The text now shows the font, size, and color you applied.

TIP

You should try to stick within the wide range of color choices offered in the **Text Color** box because they represent the 216 "Web-safe" colors that display fairly consistently across a broad range of systems. If you don't see the color you want, click the **System Color** button on the **Text Color** box to open the complete color palette for your system (Windows or Mac), from which you can choose any color. Just keep in mind that colors chosen from the color palette might not appear exactly as you intend on some systems.

21 Apply a Highlight Color to Text

Before You Begin

✔ **3** Locate Editable Regions

✔ **10** Select Text

TIP

You should try to stick within the wide range of color choices offered in the **Highlight Color** box because they represent the 216 "Web-safe" colors that display fairly consistently across a broad range of systems.

TIP

When choosing a highlight color, be careful that the text color contrasts well enough to make the text readable underneath the highlight.

A highlight color lays a bar of transparent color over selected text, creating the same kind of effect you get when you mark printed text with a highlighting marker. Used sparingly, highlight color is a fun and effective way to make text stand out.

1 Select Your Characters

Select the exact characters you want to highlight.

2 Choose a Color

To choose a color, click the **Highlight Color** button on the toolbar. The **Highlight Color** box opens. Click the colored square containing the highlight color you want to apply. To allow the style to determine the color, click the **Default Color** button on the **Highlight Color** box. If you don't see the color you want, click the System Color button on the Highlight Color box to open the complete color palette for your system (Windows or Mac), from which you can choose any color. Just keep in mind that colors chosen from the color palette might not appear exactly as you intend on some systems.

3 View the Result

To view the result, click anywhere to deselect the text. The text now shows the highlight color you applied.

News

~~TrioMotor Supplier Evaluation Project~~
This project, managed by <u>Derek Bendek</u>, will
company uses the best, customer-focused, p
market.

1 **Select Your Characters**

#CCFF33

3

View the Result

2 **Choose a Color**

News

TrioMotor Supplier Evaluation Project
This project, managed by <u>Derek Bendek</u>, will m
company uses the best, customer-focused, par
market.

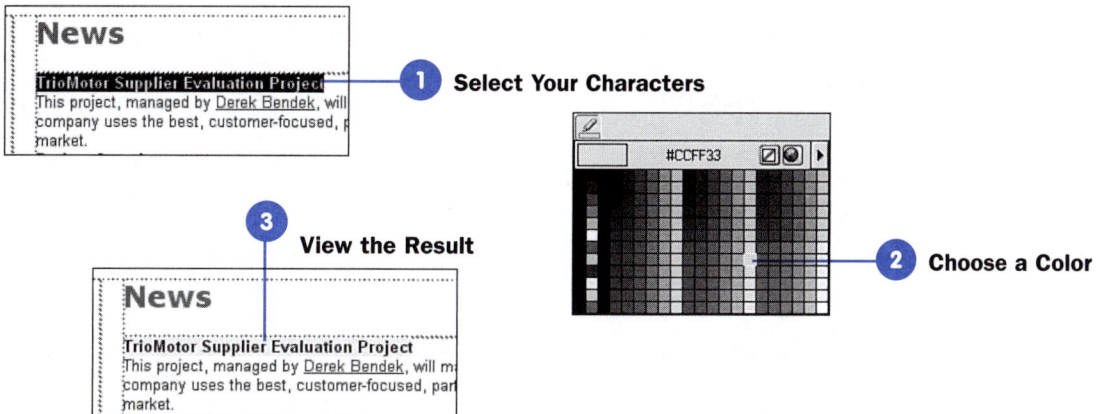

22 Align Text on the Page

You can change the alignment of any paragraph in any of four different ways: tight up against the left side of the page (left alignment), centered on the page (center alignment), hard up to the right side (right alignment), or justified (spread evenly from margin to margin, like a newspaper column).

Note that many web pages control layout by putting all the page content in a large table; you'll know such pages by the dashed lines surrounding each region of the page when in Edit mode. When you align text on such a page, the text will be aligned not within the full margins of the page, but within the table cell in which the text you choose appears.

In other words, the text is in a box. If you choose center alignment for the text, the text will be centered within its box, not centered on the page. If you choose left alignment, the text will line up on the left side of the box, not the page.

Most of the time, left alignment is best. Centering can be nice for large headings (such as Heading 1 or Heading 2 style), especially if they're not used too much. Save right alignment for special needs, such as right-aligning text in a table that's used to format a whole page (**see 63 Use a Table to Arrange the Contents of a Page**). Justified...well, play with it if you want, but it has little use in web pages. Try it and you'll see.

Before You Begin

✔ **3** Locate Editable Regions

✔ **10** Select Text

KEY TERM

Alignment—Term describing the way text, a picture, or a table is aligned on a page. *Left-aligned* objects line up to the left margin, *right-aligned* objects line up to the right margin, and *centered* objects are centered between the left and right margins.

---

2 Choose Your Alignment

News

TrioMotor Supplier Evaluation Project
This project, managed by Derek Bendek, will make sure our company uses the best, customer-focused, part suppliers in the market.
Project Overview

IT Readiness project to start in November 2004
The IT managers have teamed up with ICOM to work on cleaning up the Outlook distribution lists. There are currently over 2000 lists on the Exchange Server...
Read More

1 Choose Your Paragraph

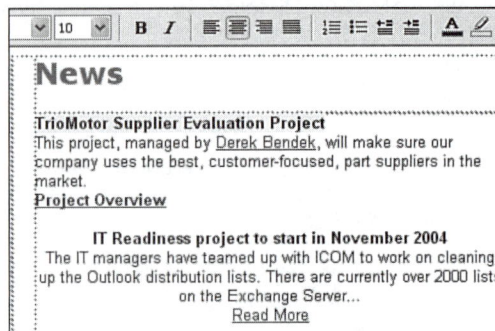

News

TrioMotor Supplier Evaluation Project
This project, managed by Derek Bendek, will make sure our company uses the best, customer-focused, part suppliers in the market.
Project Overview

IT Readiness project to start in November 2004
The IT managers have teamed up with ICOM to work on cleaning up the Outlook distribution lists. There are currently over 2000 lists on the Exchange Server...
Read More

3 View the Result

---

1 **Choose Your Paragraph**

Choose the paragraph you want to align by clicking anywhere within it. You do not need to manually select the entire paragraph.

2 **Choose Your Alignment**

Choose an alignment by clicking one of the four alignment buttons on the toolbar: **Align Left**, **Center**, **Align Right**, or **Justify**.

3 **View the Result**

The paragraph is now aligned as ordered.

---

23 **Indent Paragraphs**

Before You Begin

✔ **3** Locate Editable Regions

✔ **10** Select Text

To *indent* text is to push it inward from the margin to make it stand out on the page and to better show that the indented text is a part of the heading or other text above it. Indenting selected paragraphs can give your page structure and visual variety.

2 Indent the Paragraph

```
[ ] [10 ] | B  I | ☰ ☰ ☰ ☰ | ☷ ☷ ☷ ☷ | A ✎
```

News
....
TrioMotor Supplier Evaluation Project
This project, managed by <u>Derek Bendek</u>, will make sure our
company uses the best, customer-focused, part suppliers in the
market.
Project Overview

News
....
TrioMotor Supplier Evaluation Project
This project, managed by <u>Derek Bendek</u>, will make
sure our company uses the best, customer-focused,
part suppliers in the market.
Project Overview

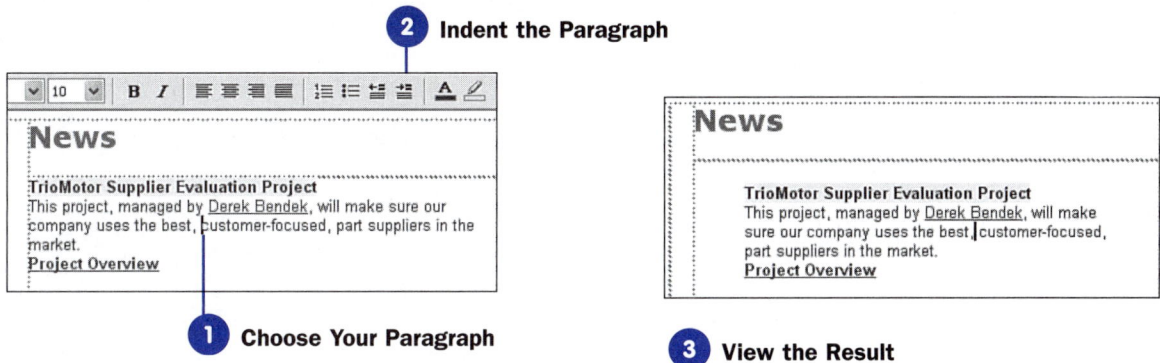

1 Choose Your Paragraph

3 View the Result

1 ## Choose Your Paragraph

Choose the paragraph you want to indent by clicking anywhere within the paragraph.

2 ## Indent the Paragraph

To indent the paragraph, click the **Indent** button on the toolbar. To indent farther, click the **Indent** button multiple times. To remove an indent, click in the indented paragraph and then click the **Outdent** button (to the left of the **Indent** button).

3 ## View the Result

The paragraph now appears indented.

⊗EY TERM

Indent—To shift a paragraph or other page contents to the right, away from the left margin.

♀ TIP

To indent multiple, consecutive paragraphs at once, click anywhere in the first paragraph and drag down through the paragraphs to anywhere in the last paragraph. Then click the **Indent** button.

5

Editing Pictures and Movies

IN THIS CHAPTER:

Updating or adding pictures in a Contribute website is indeed a snap. The only tricky parts are, as always with Contribute, making sure you don't undermine the existing layout while doing it, and making sure that you start off with an image file that's the right type and size for the Web.

24 About Web Images

24 About Web Images

TIP

Windows XP tells you the type of image file by the file icon. GIF images have an icon with a red square, blue circle, and yellow triangle on them. JPEGs have a sailboat at sunset.

TIP

A special sort of GIF file, *animated GIFs*, play simple animations in a browser, such as a pair of clapping hands or a turning wheel. You can find animated GIFs in clip-art libraries, and you can create them in many web graphics programs. For Contribute purposes, you insert, align, and otherwise format an animated GIF image just as you would any other GIF. (You must preview the page in a browser, however, to see the animation play.)

You can tell the type of an image file by its filename extension, and there are plenty of 'em—**.gif**, **.jpg**, **.bmp**, **.tif**, and so on. Not every type of picture file available can be displayed in a web page. As a general rule, you should restrict the images you use to the following types, both of which can be displayed by all graphical browsers:

- **GIF**—an image file with the filename extension **.gif**. GIF files are used most often for highly graphical images such as logos (as opposed to more photographic images). GIF images can be configured to have a "transparent" color in them, so that the Web page background will show through the image's background or any other region of the image in the selected color. Virtually all draw-and-paint programs can save a file in GIF format.

- **JPEG**—an image file with the filename extension **.jpg** or **.jpeg**. JPEG files are used most often for photographic images and backgrounds, and JPEG is the best format to use for scanned photos, photos taken with a digital camera, or any image with a lot of detail or a lot of variation in color or shading. Most draw-and-paint programs and the utility programs that come with scanners and digital cameras can save a file in JPEG format.

Contribute allows you to insert pictures in either GIF or JPEG format, plus several other types: PNG, JFIF, and JPE. Although up-to-date browsers can display these alternative types, there are still browsers out on the Web that can't, and there's no compelling reason to use any of them. Stick with GIF and JPEG and you can't go wrong.

The size of an image file is also an important consideration—not the area it takes up on screen (you can adjust that easily), but rather the amount of data making up the image file, in kilobytes. The larger the image file, the longer it will take to appear on a visitor's screen. High-resolution, high-color photos can easily top one megabyte; through a

56k dial-up connection, a 1-megabyte image could take up to 20 minutes to appear on the screen.

While working with pictures, keep in mind that every picture (including background pictures) lengthens the time it takes the page to fully materialize on a visitor's screen. You know from your own surfing trips how frustrating a slow web page is, especially when it's slow just because it has too many pictures, or the picture files are too large.

You'll learn more about file size in **28** **Prepare an Image for the Web**.

> **TIP**
>
> Image file size is less of a concern when your Contribute page is designed strictly for use over a high-bandwidth company intranet, or for viewing only by users with high-speed connections, such as cable Internet or DSL.

25 Align an Image and Choose Wrapping

A picture can be aligned on a page in most of the same ways text can be: snug up against the left margin (left-aligned), centered on the page (center alignment), or pushed over to the right margin (right alignment). Just as you do for text, you can use the alignment buttons to quickly align a picture in any of these ways (see **22** **Align Text on the Page**).

But a picture isn't text, so aligning a picture brings up another layout consideration: *wrapping*, or the way text relates to the picture. Wrapping comes into play any time you position a picture immediately before, after, or within a block of text, with no paragraph marks between the picture and the text.

You can wrap text to a picture in the following ways:

- **Normal**—The picture acts like its own paragraph, with no text on either side of it.

- **Top**—The first line of text following the picture wraps to the right of the top of the picture. The rest of the text sits beneath the picture.

- **Left**—The picture sits on the left margin of the page, with any text that follows it wrapping to the right of it, and then wrapping under it when the text reaches the bottom of the image.

- **Right**—The picture sits on the right margin of the page, with any text that follows it wrapping to the left of it, and then wrapping under it when the text reaches the bottom of the image.

- **Middle**—The text sits in the middle of the text, with adjacent text wrapping along both sides of it.

> **Before You Begin**
>
> ✔ **24** About Web Images

> **TIP**
>
> If you replace an existing picture as described in **30** **Add or Delete an Image**, the picture you add will automatically be aligned just like the one it replaces.

> **TIP**
>
> Wrapping works only when there are no paragraph marks between the text and the picture. When there are paragraph marks, the picture stands on its own, like a paragraph, with no text to its left or right.

2 Choose Your Alignment

| Normal | Book Antiqua | 12 | **B** *I* | | | | | | | | | | **A** |

Mac Wellman's Swoop, a vampire play far too weird for Bram Stoker, played Oct. 25 to Nov. 9, 2002, at ¡Viva La Frida! Cafe y Galeria. Mina, Lucy, and Dracula debated all things draculean, as well as the merits of housecats and the properties of geezer gas.

1 Select the Picture

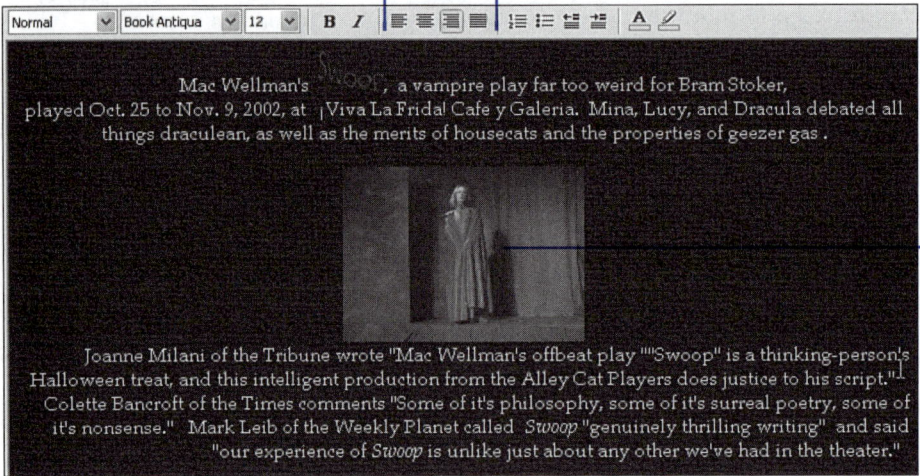

Joanne Milani of the Tribune wrote "Mac Wellman's offbeat play ""Swoop" is a thinking-person's Halloween treat, and this intelligent production from the Alley Cat Players does justice to his script." Colette Bancroft of the Times comments "Some of it's philosophy, some of it's surreal poetry, some of it's nonsense." Mark Leib of the Weekly Planet called *Swoop* "genuinely thrilling writing" and said "our experience of *Swoop* is unlike just about any other we've had in the theater."

3 View the Result

Mac Wellman's Swoop, a vampire play far too weird for Bram Stoker, played Oct. 25 to Nov. 9, 2002, at ¡Viva La Frida! Cafe y Galeria. Mina, Lucy, and Dracula debated all things draculean, as well as the merits of housecats and the properties of geezer gas.

5 View the Result

Hallc
Col
it's

an's offbeat play ""Swoop" is ɛ
he Alley Cat Players does jus
philosophy, some of it's surr
ed *Swoop* "genuinely thrilling
 just about any other we've h

Mac Wellman's Swoop, a vampire
played Oct. 25 to Nov. 9, 2002, at ¡Viva La Frida! Caf
things draculean, as well as the merits of hou

Joanne Milani of the Tr
""Swoop" is a thinking-
production from the Al
Colette Bancroft of the
of it's surreal poetry, so
Planet called *Swoop* "g
experience of *Swoop* is
theater."

Image Properties...
Edit Image
Align   ▶   ✓ Normal
                     Top
Insert Link...   Left
Reset Size   Right
                     Middle
Cut
Copy
Paste

Joanne N   Mac
Halloween tre   tion
Colette Banc   nents "Some
it's nonsense   e Weekly Plar
           "our experience of *Swoop* is

4 Choose Wrapping

Jo Averill-Snell directed, Steve Mountan played Drac
Gallar played Second Mina, and Arrianna Thompson
Ned Averill-Snell designed the set and sound,

1 Select the Picture

To select a picture, click on it. A black border and *handles*—little black squares on the border—appear around the picture to show that it's selected.

2 Choose Your Alignment

To center the picture on the page, click the **Center** button on the toolbar. To right-align it, click the **Align Right** button. To left-align it, click the **Align Left** button.

3 View the Result

The picture immediately takes on the alignment you selected in step 2 and remains selected.

4 Choose Wrapping

Right-click the picture, choose **Align** from the pop-up menu, and choose your wrapping option from the submenu that appears.

5 View the Result

The picture immediately takes on the wrapping you selected in step 4 and remains selected. You can now move on to other picture-formatting tasks that require a selected picture, or click anywhere on the page (except on the picture) to deselect the picture.

26 Reposition an Image

Repositioning (moving) a picture is a no-brainer—it's drag and drop. However, there are things you need to be mindful of when you move an image.

If you want text to wrap along a side of the image (**see 25 Align an Image and Choose Wrapping**), you need to drop it in the text where no paragraph breaks intervene between the picture and the text. Also, after you move an image, it's likely that you might want to adjust the picture's size, alignment, or wrapping after moving it, to make it look just right within the page's layout.

Before You Begin

✔ **24** About Web Images

✔ **25** Align an Image and Choose Wrapping

1 Click and Hold

Sincerity Forever

Arrianna Thompson as Jenue; Alex Wilburn & Clara Haight as Turbella

Sincerity Forever

Arrianna Thompson as Jenue; Alex Wilburn & Clara Haight as Turbella

2 Drag to Where You Want It Moved

3 Release the Mouse Button and View the Result

Sincerity Forever

Arrianna Thompson as Jenue; Alex Wilburn & Clara Haight as Turbella

TIP

After moving a picture, you might want to adjust its alignment and size to fit best in its new spot. See **25** **Align an Image and Choose Wrapping** and **27** **Change the Size of an Image**.

1 **Click and Hold**

Point to the picture you want to move, then click on it and hold down the mouse button.

② Drag to Where You Want It Moved

As you drag, a small rectangular icon follows the pointer to tell you you're dragging something, so you can see where you're going.

③ Release the Mouse Button and View the Result

When the icon is in the spot where you want the picture to be placed, release the mouse button. The picture is moved where you dropped it.

TIP

To drag to a spot below the visible part of the page, drag slowly toward the bottom of the work area. When you see the page begin to scroll, stop dragging, but don't release the button. When the spot where the picture belongs scrolls into view, drag upward slightly to stop the scrolling, point to the spot, and release.

---

27 Change the Size of an Image

After you realign, reposition, replace, or insert a picture, you might feel that it looks too large or too small within the page layout. Changing a picture's size is nothing more than a click and a drag.

Before You Begin

✔ **24** About Web Images

✔ **25** Align an Image and Choose Wrapping

✔ **26** Reposition an Image

① Select the Picture

To select a picture, click on it. A black border and *handles*—little black squares on the border—appear around the picture to show that it's selected.

② Drag a Corner Handle

Click and hold on a corner handle—*not* a side, top, or bottom handle—and drag diagonally toward the picture's center (to shrink it) or away from the center (to enlarge it).

TIP

When you size some pictures—especially photos—the look of the picture might suffer (especially when you enlarge it). If a picture looks lousy right after sizing, click **Undo** to restore its original size.

③ Release the Mouse Button

Release the mouse button when the picture is the desired size.

1 Select the Picture

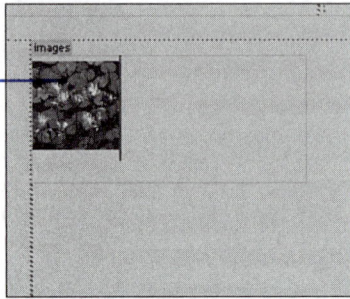

2 Drag a Corner Handle

3 Release the Mouse Button

4 View the Result

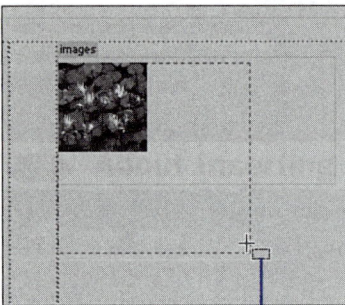

NOTE

Changing the size—the onscreen area—of an image does not affect the file size of the image, so making a small picture larger won't slow your page down, and making a large picture smaller won't speed it up.

4 View the Result

View the result of the image resizing. The picture remains selected after you release the button; you can start over at step 2 to fine-tune the size, perform another task that requires a selected picture, or click anywhere on the page (except on the picture) to deselect the picture.

If you're not careful to drag on a perfect diagonal, you might change the *aspect ratio* of a picture while resizing it, making it look squeezed or stretched. To prevent this, hold down the Shift key while dragging in step 2.

28 Prepare an Image for the Web

Pictures come from many places: You might have a picture file that you copied from the Web or saved in a paint program, one that you scanned, or one that you took with a digital camera and copied into your computer. You might also have access to pictures stored with your pages on the Web specifically for use on your site (such as a company logo).

Whatever the source of the picture, it needs to meet a few requirements to work properly in a web page. You can make sure that the image meets these requirements when saving it in your draw, paint, scanner, or digital camera program, or you can edit an image file in a draw or paint program to make it meet these requirements:

- **Format**—The file should be in GIF (file extension **.gif**) or JPEG (file extension **.jpg**) format. GIF is best for simple, graphical pictures such as cartoons or logos; JPEG is best for photos or other complex images with many colors or shades. (In a draw, paint, scanner, or camera program, you typically choose the file format when saving.)

- **File size**—The bigger the picture file, the longer it will take to appear on your visitors' screens. Try to keep picture files smaller than 50k, and don't forget to add up the size of all the pictures in a page when considering whether it will appear fast enough.

- **Resolution**—The *resolution* of a picture file is the number of dots, or pixels, it takes up per inch of screen space, expressed in *dpi* (dots per inch). The idea of "inches" is approximate, because the same picture will actually appear larger or smaller onscreen depending on the size of the monitor it's displayed on. Higher resolutions give a sharper, clearer picture, but they make the file size larger, too. Choosing resolution is a balancing act of picking the highest resolution (and thus image quality) that still results in a reasonably small file. As a rule of thumb, 72 dpi is fine for both GIF and JPEG files.

- **Color depth**—For some types of images in some programs, you can also choose the *color depth*, the number of different shades displayable, expressed in kilobytes, from 8-bit (256 colors) to 24-bit

Before You Begin

✔ **24** About Web Images

👈 NOTE

You can also pick up image files online, in online clip-art libraries and from other websites. Be very, very careful, however, when using any image that you did not create yourself; doing so could be a violation of someone else's copyright. Always read and obey any copyright or license instructions on the site where you get an image, and when in doubt about an image's copyright status, don't use it.

TIP

Although Windows users can use Paint to convert some image file types to GIF or JPEG, Mac users can use Preview, bundled with Mac OS X.

(millions of colors). Higher color depths cause bigger files. GIF images are limited to 8-bit color, whereas JPEG supports up to 24-bit color for better rendering of photographs.

- **JPEG quality**—JPEG images have a unique setting, which is adjustable in most programs, that lets you choose a "quality" setting to find the best balance between image quality and file size. A quality setting of 100 makes the image look as good as it possibly can, but also begets the biggest file size. A setting of 10 gets you a smaller file, but not as clear or sharp an image.

Ideally, you'll use a draw, paint, camera, or scanner program to prepare your image before inserting it in Contribute, and you can make sure it meets these requirements before saving it.

Just in case you have an image you want to use that's not in the right format and you don't have a program handy to edit it, it's worth knowing that the Paint program that comes with every copy of Windows can convert most image file formats to GIF or JPEG.

1 **Open Paint**

From the Windows XP **Start** button, choose **All Programs**, **Accessories**, **Paint**.

2 **Open the Image File**

Choose **File, Open** from the **Paint** menu bar, then use the **Open** dialog box to navigate to and open your image file.

3 **Choose File, Save As**

Choose **File, Save As** from the **Paint** menu bar to open the **Save As** dialog box. (Give the file a new name or new folder location, if you want to.)

4 **Choose the Format to Save In**

Open the **Save as type** list at the bottom of the **Save As** dialog box and choose **JPEG** or **GIF** from the list.

5 **Click Save**

Click the **Save** button on the **Save As** dialog box and then close Paint. Your image is ready for Contribute.

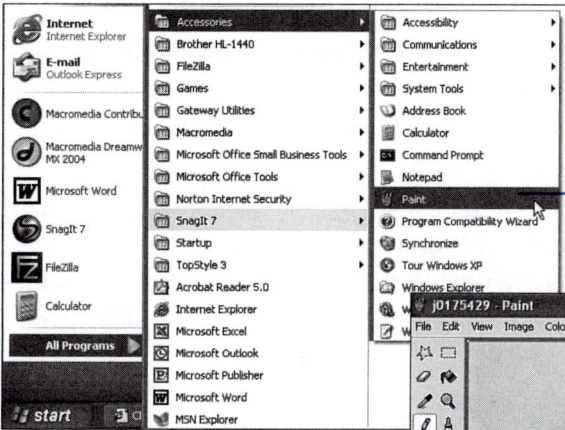

1 Open Paint

2 Open the Image File

3 Choose File, Save As

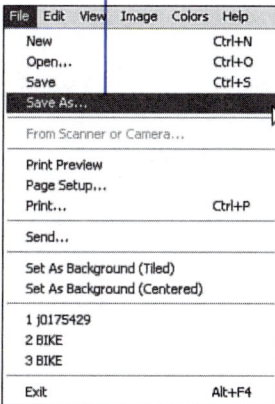

4 Choose the Format to Save In

5 Click Save

29 Replace an Image

It's likely that most of the time when you insert a picture in a Contribute site, you'll be replacing a picture already placed there by the site's original author.

That saves you some time and trouble because the picture you insert will automatically take on the position and alignment of the one you replace, so at most you'll only need to adjust the new picture's size to fit it properly into the existing layout (**see** **28** **Change the Size of an Image**).

1 Select the Existing Picture

To select the picture, click on it. A black border and *handles* appear around the picture to show that it's selected.

2 Click the Image Button

On the **Edit** toolbar, click the **Image** button and then choose either **From My Computer** or **From Website** (at this point, it doesn't matter which you choose). The **Image Properties** dialog box opens.

3 Click Browse

Click the **Browse** button on the **Image Properties** dialog box and choose **From My Computer** (to use an image stored on your computer) or **From Website** (to use an image file already online in the site you're editing, such as a company logo).

4 Navigate to and Select the Image File

Either of two different dialog boxes opens, depending upon your choice in step 3. However, both work the same way: Use the list of files and folders provided to navigate to and select the image file you want to insert. After you've selected it, click the **Select** button (for a file on your computer) or **OK** (for a file on the website). The **Image Properties** dialog box reappears.

5 Type a Description

In the **Description (ALT text)** box, type a brief description of this image.

◤ NOTE

The description you type in step 5 is optional, but important: Vision-impaired people use text-to-speech programs that read aloud the contents of web pages. Your text description enables these programs to describe your picture aloud.

2 Click the
Image Button

3 Click
Browse

1 Select the
Existing
Picture

Image Properties

Image file: nts/My Pictures/Sample Pictures/Water lilies.jpg · Browse...

Width: 187 · Pixels · Reset Size

Height: 182 · Pixels · ☑ Constrain proportions

Horizontal padding: 0 · pixels · Alignment: Default

Vertical padding: 5 · pixels · Border: 0 · pixels

Select Image

Look in: Microsoft Clip Organizer

Preview:

j0175429 · mso345451

600 x 403 JPEG, 29K / 9 sec

4 Navigate to
and Select
the Image
File

File name
Files of ty

Image Properties

Image file: file:///D|/Documents and Settings/Snell/My Doc · Brow

Width: 600 · Pixels · Reset Size

Height: 403 · Pixels · ☑ Constrain proportions

Horizontal padding: 0 · pixels · Alignment: Default

Vertical padding: 5 · pixels · Border: 0 · pixels

Description (ALT text):
Bowl of Cereal

This description is used by tools that read web pages to people with visual disabilities.

Help · OK · Cancel · Apply

5 Type a
Description

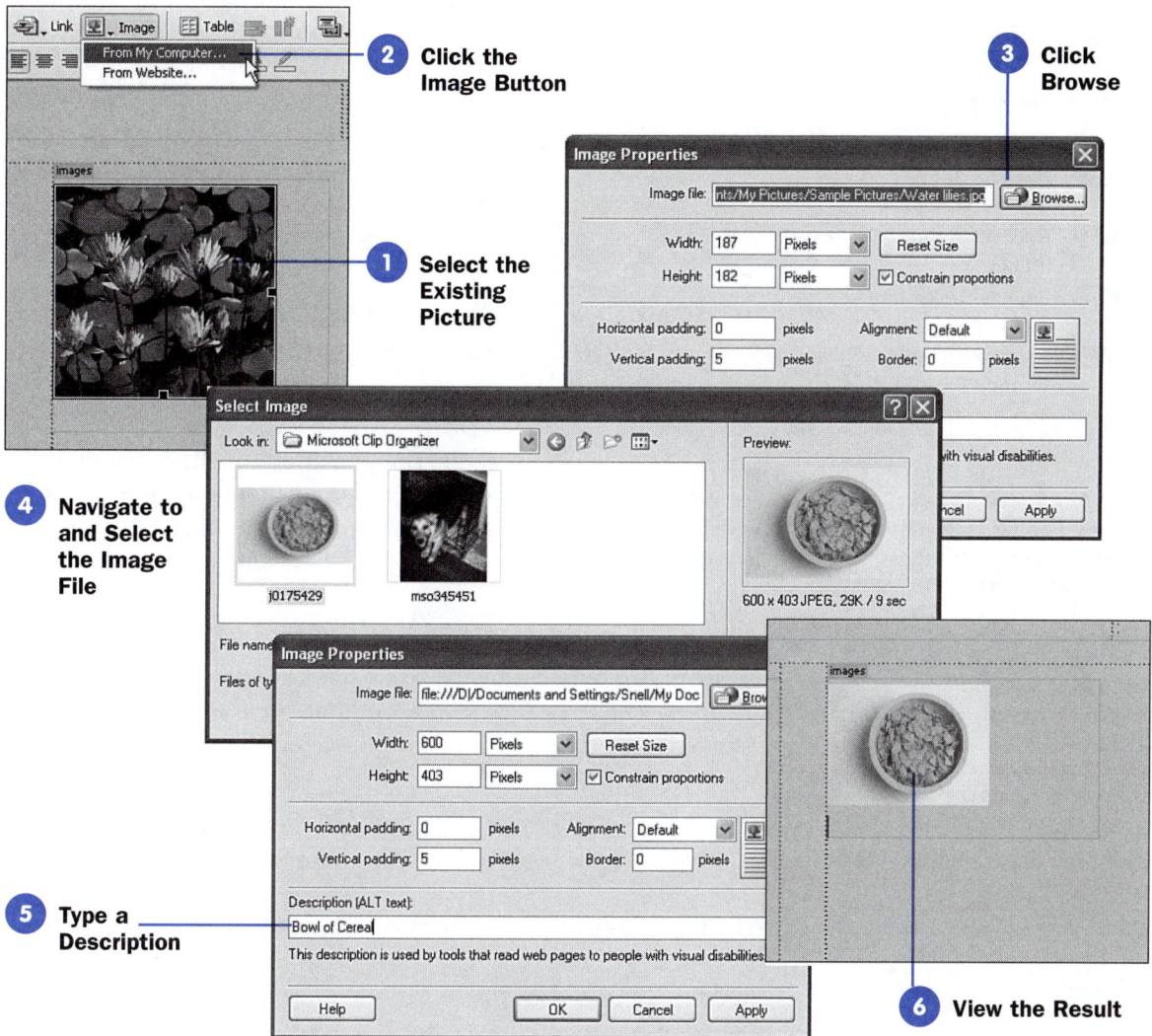

6 View the Result

6 **View the Result**

Click the **OK** button on the **Image Properties** dialog box to close
it. The image you selected appears in the page, in place of the one
you selected in step 1. The new picture is already selected, so you
can go ahead and fine-tune its size, position, or alignment, or click
anywhere on the page (except on the picture) to deselect it.

30 Add or Delete an Image

Before You Begin

✔ **24** About Web Images

✔ **25** Align an Image and Choose Wrapping

✔ **26** Reposition an Image

✔ **27** Change the Size of an Image

✔ **28** Prepare an Image for the Web

🔱 TIP

Deleting an image? You don't need steps for that. Just click the image to select it, and press the **Delete** key.

Adding a new picture to a page is quick and easy. The most important thing is to make sure that the picture you choose is Web-ready before you insert it (**see** **28** **Prepare an Image for the Web**). It's like painting a house—the painting is simple, if you've done the prep work right.

① **Click Where You Want a Picture**

In Edit mode, click the spot in your draft where you want to insert a picture so that the insertion point appears there.

② **Click the Image Button**

On the **Edit** toolbar, click the **Image** button and then choose from the list that appears **From My Computer** (to use an image stored on your computer) or **From Website** (to use an image file already online in the site you're editing, such as a company logo).

③ **Navigate to and Select the Image File**

Either of two different dialog boxes opens, depending upon your choice in step 2. However, both work the same way: Use the list of files and folders provided to navigate to and select the image file you want to insert. After you've selected it, click the **Select** button (for a file on your computer) or **OK** (for a file on the Web site).

④ **View the Result**

The image you selected appears in the page, at the spot you chose in step 1. The new picture is already selected, so you can go ahead and fine-tune its size, position, or alignment, or click anywhere on the page (except on the picture) to deselect it.

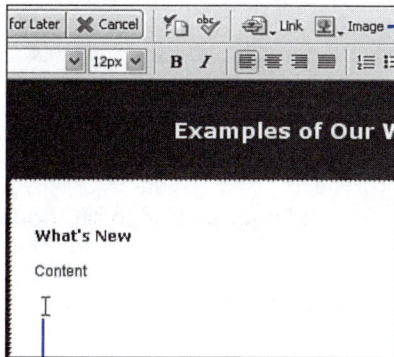

2 Click the Image Button

1 Click Where You Want a Picture

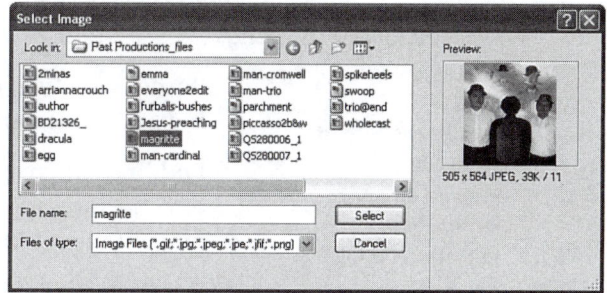

3 Navigate to and Select the Image File

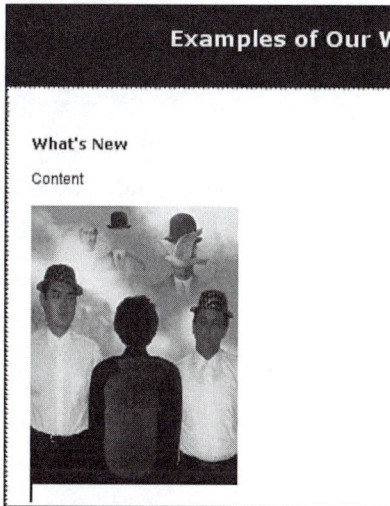

505 x 564 JPEG, 39K / 11

4 View the Result

31 Add a Border or Extra Space Around a Picture

While replacing a picture or at any time later on, you can use the **Image Properties** dialog box to apply a few kinds of additional formatting:

- **Border**—You add a nice black box around your picture to set it off from other elements on the page.

- **Padding**—If your picture seems squeezed too tightly to text or other pictures next to, above, or below it, you can increase the amount of *padding* to add more space around the picture.

- **Description (ALT text)**—Vision-impaired people use text-to-speech programs that read aloud the contents of Web pages. You can add a description for a picture that enables these programs to describe your picture aloud.

TIP

You define borders and padding by typing the number of pixels wide you want the border or padding to be. As a rule of thumb, two pixels make a thin border and add a little padding, and five pixels make a fat border and add a lot of padding.

❶ Open the Image Properties Dialog Box

In Edit mode, right-click the picture and choose **Image Properties** from the pop-up list.

❷ Type a Border Width

In the **Border** box on the **Image Properties** dialog box, type the number of pixels wide you want the border around the picture to be.

❸ Add Padding

In the **Horizontal padding** box on the **Image Properties** dialog box, type the number of pixels of extra space you want to add to the sides (left and right) of the picture. In the **Vertical padding** box, type the number of pixels of extra space you want to add to the top and bottom of the picture.

❹ Type a Description

In the **Description (ALT text)** box, type a brief description of the image.

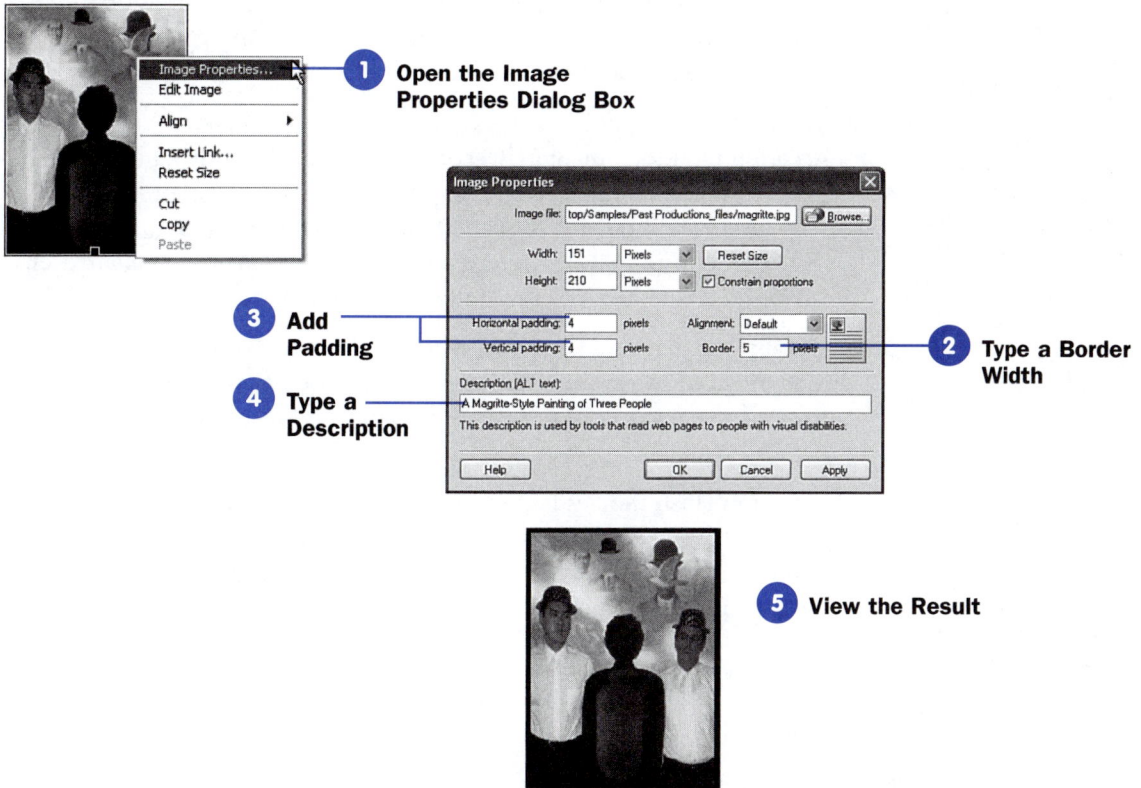

1 Open the Image
Properties Dialog Box

3 Add
Padding

4 Type a
Description

2 Type a Border
Width

5 View the Result

5 View the Result

Click **OK** on the **Image Properties** dialog box to close the box and
see your picture with its added border and padding.

32 About Flash Movies

Flash movies are animated web content created in Macromedia's *Flash*
program. They can be actual "movie" clips, but more often they are animated objects, such as navigation buttons or banners. As a Macromedia
product, Contribute provides simple tools for adding and controlling
Flash movies.

KEY TERM

Flash—A program for creating dynamic Web content, such as movie clips and animated buttons, from the same company that produces Contribute (Macromedia). Flash movies can be inserted in Contribute web pages and viewed online through a Flash-capable browser or a browser equipped with an optional, free Flash player.

TIP

Contribute does create one kind of Flash movie on its own—documents converted to movies by Contribute's FlashPaper utility **(see 68 About FlashPaper)**.

To see your Flash content, your visitors must be using a browser that can display it, or must have installed a free, optional Flash player that's available from Macromedia's website (**http://www.macromedia.com**) for both Windows and Mac.

According to Macromedia, 97% of web users are already equipped to display Flash content, so you can add it with reasonable assurance that your visitors will be able to see it. Still, if the content is essential, it might be better to display it by more traditional means—as web page text or GIF or JPEG graphics—to guarantee that all users can display it.

If you want to create your own new Flash movies, you need Macromedia's Flash program, available by itself or included (along with the Dreamweaver web authoring program) in Macromedia's StudioMX bundle.

Although Flash movies feature some optional settings not available for other pictures, you change the size, position, alignment, borders, and padding of a Flash movie in Contribute exactly as you do for any other picture, as described in the steps in this chapter.

33 **Change the Way a Flash Movie Plays**

Before You Begin

✔ **32** About Flash Movies

After Flash content is in your page, you can alter its play in a few ways. You can choose whether to have the movie play over and over (*loop*) as long as the visitor views the page, or to have it play once and stop. You can also choose whether to make the movie play automatically upon the visitor's arrival or to wait until the visitor chooses to play the movie.

1 Select the Movie

To select the movie, click on its box. A black border and *handles* appear around the movie to show that it's selected.

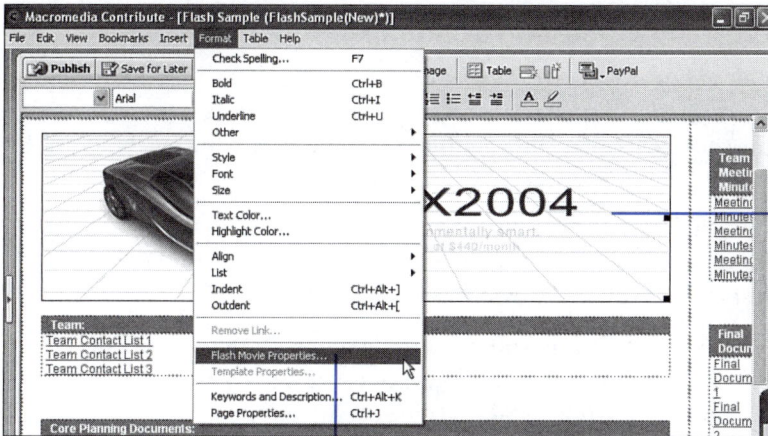

1 Select the Movie

2 Open the Flash Movie Properties Dialog Box

3 Change the Settings for the Movie

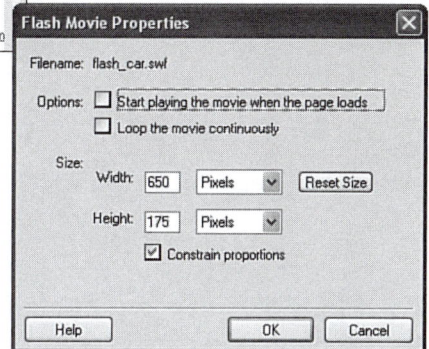

4 View the Result

2 Open the Flash Movie Properties Dialog Box

Choose **Format**, **Flash Movie Properties** from the menu bar. The **Flash Movie Properties** dialog box opens. All of the settings you can change to alter the way the movie plays are in this dialog box.

3 Change the Settings for the Movie

Use the settings in the **Flash Movie Properties** dialog box to change the way the movie plays:

- Select **Start playing the movie when the page loads** if you want the Flash movie to automatically begin playing when the page appears in a visitor's browser. If you don't select this option, the movie appears in a static box when the page opens and doesn't play until the visitor clicks the **Play** button on the movie's controls.

- Select **Loop the movie continuously** if you want the Flash movie to play over and over as long as the page is viewed. If you don't select this option, the movie plays once when the visitor arrives at the page and then stops.

When you're done changing settings, click **OK** in the **Flash Movie Properties** dialog box.

4 View the Result

Publish your page or preview it in a browser to see the Flash movie play with its new settings.

34 Add or Delete a Flash Movie

Before You Begin

✔ **32** About Flash Movies

If you have Flash content you want to add to your page, you'll find that adding it is just like adding any picture, after the first two steps.

1 Click Where You Want to Insert a Movie

In Edit mode, click the spot in your draft where you want the movie to appear.

2 Open the Select File Dialog Box for Movies

Choose **Insert**, **Flash** from the menu bar then choose **From My Computer** or **From Website**. The **Select File** dialog box appears.

3 Make the Dialog Box Display Flash Movie Files

Either of two different dialog boxes opens, depending upon your choice in step 2. Both work the same way: in the **Files of type** list, choose **All Files**.

4 Navigate to the Flash Movie File and Select It

Using the folders and lists provided, navigate to the Flash movie file (with the extension **.swf**) you want to add, and then click **Select** or **OK**.

5 View the Result

The movie appears in the page at the spot you chose in step 1. The movie is already selected, so you can go ahead and fine-tune its size, position, or alignment, or click anywhere on the page (except on the movie) to deselect it.

TIP

You delete a Flash movie just as you would any picture: In Edit mode, click on the movie to select it and then press the **Delete** key.

Publish | **Save for Later** | **Cancel** | Link | Image | Table | PayPal

Normal | Arial | 12px | **B** *I*

1 **Click Where You Want to Insert a Movie**

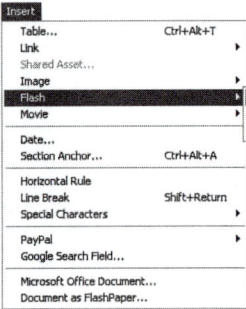

Team:
Team Contact List 1
Team Contact List 2
Team Contact List 3

Insert

Table...	Ctrl+Alt+T
Link	▶
Shared Asset...	
Image	▶
Flash	▶
Movie	▶
Date...	
Section Anchor...	Ctrl+Alt+A
Horizontal Rule	
Line Break	Shift+Return
Special Characters	▶
PayPal	▶
Google Search Field...	
Microsoft Office Document...	
Document as FlashPaper...	

From My Computer...
From Website...
From Shared Assets...

2 **Open the Select File Dialog Box for Movies**

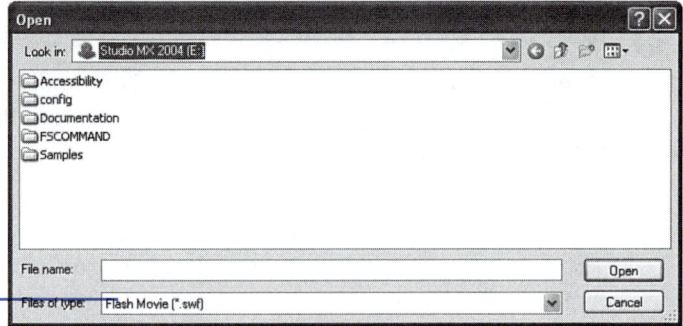

Open

Look in: Studio MX 2004 (E:)

Accessibility
config
Documentation
FSCOMMAND
Samples

File name:

3 **Make the Dialog Box Display Flash Movie Files**

Files of type: Flash Movie (*.swf)

Open
Cancel

Open

Look in: flash

flash_car

4 **Navigate to the Flash Movie File and Select It**

File name:
Files of type:

Publish | **Save for Later** | **Cancel** | Link | Image | Table | PayPal

Arial | 12px | **B** *I*

ZX2004

5 **View the Result**

Team:
Team Contact List 1
Team Contact List 2
Team Contact List 3

6

Organizing Content on a Page

IN THIS CHAPTER:

A web page made up of nothing but paragraphs and pictures would look pretty chaotic. Fortunately, there are a few simple tools for organizing web page content within the layout that also add visual interest and a professional appearance to your page: lists, horizontal rules, and tables.

35 About Lists

In Contribute, you can quickly create two basic kinds of lists:

- Bulleted lists (like this one), in which each list item is preceded by a "bullet" character. Bulleted lists are best when the order of the items listed isn't important.

- Numbered lists, in which each list item is preceded by a number. Numbered lists are best when the order of items is important; for example, when listing the steps in instructions.

Beyond these basic types, Contribute lets you do a little advanced list formatting. For example, you can "nest" one list inside another, as in a hierarchical outline. You can also choose the numbering style for numbered lists (1, 2, 3 or A, B C, for example).

36 Create a List

Before You Begin

✔ **35** About Lists

Basic lists are really a two-step job:

1. Type up your list items, one on each line.

2. Choose a Type: **Bulleted List** or **Numbered List**.

See how effective a list can be?

1 Position Your Insertion Point

In your draft, point to the spot where you want to add the list.

2 Type the List Items

Type the list, pressing the **Enter** key at the end of each list item.

1 Position Your Insertion Point

2 Type the List Items

4 Choose Your List Type

3 Select the List

5 View the Result

3 Select the List

To select the list, click and hold anywhere within the top list item, drag down to anywhere within the last list item, and release the mouse button. (You do not need to select all of the first item, or the last.)

4 Choose Your List Type

Choose your list type. On the **Edit** toolbar, click the button for the type of list you want: **Bulleted List** or **Numbered List**.

5 View the Result

The list items take on the list formatting you selected.

37 Nest Lists Inside One Another

Before You Begin

✔ **35** About Lists

✔ **36** Create a List

A *nested* list is a list within a list, which can be necessary for a complete table of contents or other hierarchically organized items. For example:

1. Oranges

2. Apples

    a. Macintosh

    b. Delicious

    c. Rome

3. Bananas

In the preceding list, the list of apple types is nested within the list of fruits. You can create nested lists of two, three, or as many levels as you want. You can also choose to vary the numbering/lettering scheme for each level.

TIP

To select a different numbering style or starting number for nested portions of your list, select the list as described in step 4, then choose **Format, List, Properties** to open a dialog box in which you can choose a numbering style and starting number.

1 Create the Main List

Using the steps in **36** **Create a List**, create the main list in which you will nest another list.

2 Position Your Insertion Point

In the main list, point to the spot where you want to add the nested list and press the **Enter** key to start a new line.

3 Type the Nested List Items

Type the items for the nested list, pressing the **Enter** key at the end of each list item.

4 Select the List

To select the list, click and hold anywhere within the top item of the nested list, drag down to anywhere within the last item.

5 Choose Your List Type

Choose your list type. On the **Edit** toolbar, click the button for the type of nested list you want: **Bulleted List** or **Numbered List**.

        PART II: Editing the Content of a Web Page

Table of Contents

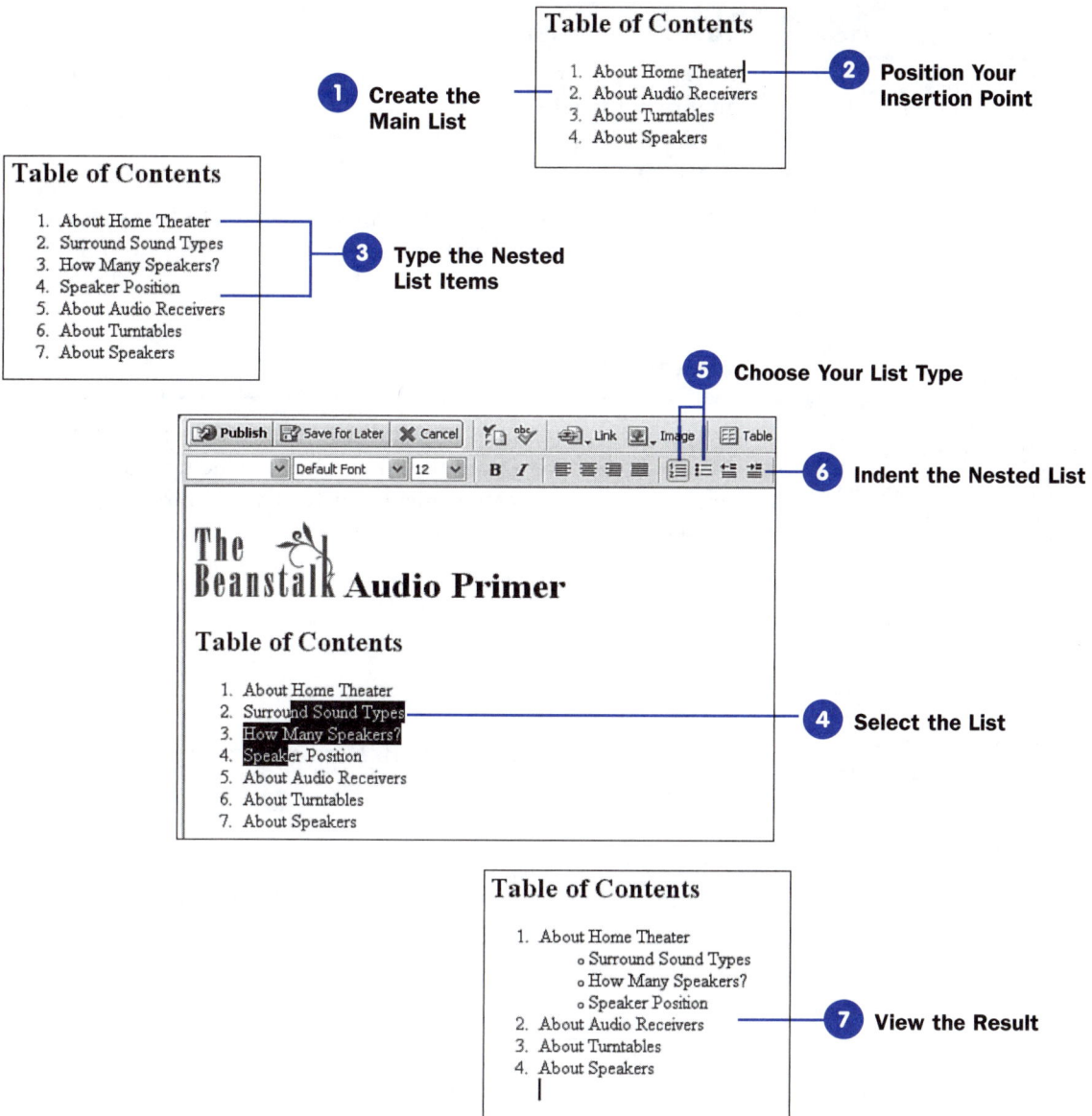

1. About Home Theater
2. About Audio Receivers
3. About Turntables
4. About Speakers

1 **Create the Main List**

2 **Position Your Insertion Point**

Table of Contents

1. About Home Theater
2. Surround Sound Types
3. How Many Speakers?
4. Speaker Position
5. About Audio Receivers
6. About Turntables
7. About Speakers

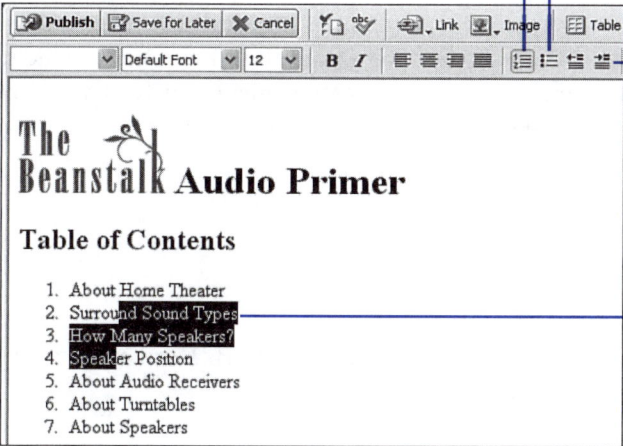

3 **Type the Nested List Items**

5 **Choose Your List Type**

| Publish | Save for Later | Cancel | | Link | Image | Table |

| Default Font | 12 | **B** *I* |

6 **Indent the Nested List**

The
Beanstalk **Audio Primer**

Table of Contents

1. About Home Theater
2. Surround Sound Types
3. How Many Speakers?
4. Speaker Position
5. About Audio Receivers
6. About Turntables
7. About Speakers

4 **Select the List**

Table of Contents

1. About Home Theater
   - Surround Sound Types
   - How Many Speakers?
   - Speaker Position
2. About Audio Receivers
3. About Turntables
4. About Speakers

7 **View the Result**

6 Indent the Nested List

To separate the nested list from the main list, click the **Indent** button on the **Edit** toolbar.

7 View the Result

View the result; the nested list appears indented from the main list, and takes on its own numbering sequence independent from the main list.

38 Add or Delete a Horizontal Rule

KEY TERM

Horizontal rule—**A straight line that divides sections of a Web page horizontally. Also known as a** *horizontal line*.

TIP

Deleting a rule is too simple even for steps; you click the rule to select it, then press the **Delete** key.

A *horizontal rule* (sometimes also called a *horizontal line*) is just a line across the web page (or a part of it). Rules help divide up logical sections of a long page, or set special elements (such as a logo graphic at the top of a page) apart from other page content.

1 Position Your Insertion Point

Point to the spot where you want to insert the horizontal rule.

2 Insert the Rule

To insert the rule, choose **Insert, Horizontal Rule** from the menu bar.

3 View the Result

The rule appears in your page at the spot you selected in step 1.

The Beanstalk Audio Primer

| I

Table of Contents

① Position Your
Insertion Point

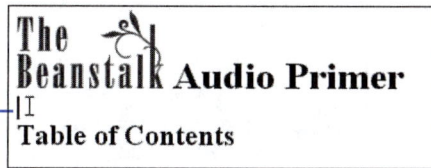

Insert Format Table Help

Image	▶
Table...	Ctrl+Alt+T
Link	▶
PayPal	▶
Date...	
Section Anchor...	Ctrl+Alt+A
Horizontal Rule	
Line Break	Shift+Return
Special Characters	▶
Microsoft Office Document...	
Document as FlashPaper...	
Flash Movie	▶

② Insert the Rule

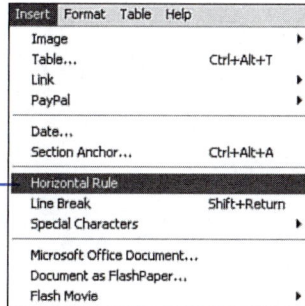

The Beanstalk Audio Primer

Table of Contents

③ View the Result

---

39 Change the Style of a Horizontal Rule

After you've added a rule, you can change its appearance in a variety of ways, making it longer or shorter, thicker or thinner, and 3D or 2D.

① Open the Horizontal Rule Properties

Right-click on the rule and choose **Properties** from the pop-up menu that appears.

② Change the Properties

In the **Horizontal Rule Properties** dialog box, change any settings you want:

* **Width**—The width of the rule in pixels. To define the width of the rule as a percentage of the width of the web page, choose **percent** from the list to the right of **Width**, then enter a percentage instead of pixels (**100** for a rule across the whole page, **50** for a rule half the width of the page, and so on).

* **Height**—The height of the rule in pixels. A height of **2** makes a very fine line; a height of **6** makes a nice, fat line.

Before You Begin

✔ **38** Add or Delete a
Horizontal Rule

TIP

It's usually best to define your rule width as a percentage, not as pixels. Choosing pixels can produce unpredictable results on displays of varying size and resolution.

TIP

If you make the width of your rule less than 100% of the page width, Contribute automatically centers it on the page. You can change that alignment by selecting the rule and clicking an alignment button on the toolbar: **Align Left** or **Align Right**.

The Beanstalk Audio Primer

Cut
Copy
Paste

Properties...

Table of Conten

1. About Home Theater

1 **Open the Horizontal Rule Properties**

Horizontal Rule Properties   [X]

Width: 50   percent ▼

Height: 6   pixels

☑ Use Outline Shading

Help   OK   Cancel

The Beanstalk Audio Primer

Table of Contents

3 **View the Result**

2 **Change the Properties**

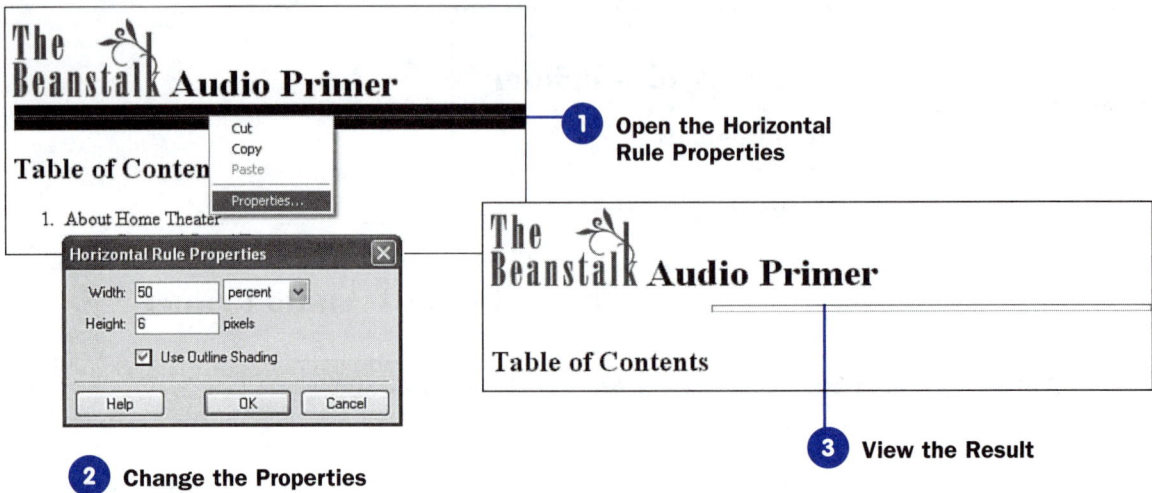

- **Outline Shading**—By default, Contribute puts a gray shadow behind your rule, to make it appear three-dimensional. Clear this check box to remove the shadow.

  When you're done changing the properties, click **OK** on the **Horizontal Rule Properties** dialog box.

3 **View the Result**

The rule takes on the new style in your page.

40 Edit or Add Text in a Table

KEY TERM

Cell—One of the individual boxes that make up a table. One cell appears at each intersection of one row and one column.

Most often in Contribute, you'll probably be editing the contents of a table already inserted in a web page by somebody else. Editing table content is easy, and Contribute gives you plenty of help.

1 **Position Your Insertion Point**

Click in the table *cell* in which you want to enter text, to position the insertion point there.

1 **Position Your Insertion Point**

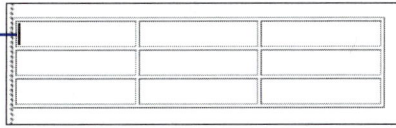

2 **Edit and/or Type Your Text**

Phase 1		

3 **Move On to the Next Cell**

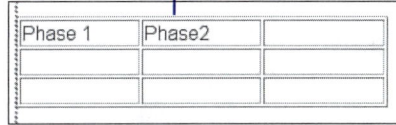

Phase 1	Phase2	

---

2 **Edit and/or Type Your Text**

Type and change away. As you type, you may apply any of the text formatting steps from Chapters 3 and 4.

3 **Move On to the Next Cell**

When finished typing in a cell, press the **Tab** key to jump to the next cell or click in the next cell you want to edit.

To delete the contents of a cell, double-click there to select the whole cell contents and then press the Delete key.

TIP

At any time, you can apply any kind of formatting to text in a table cell by highlighting the text and applying formatting. You may also select whole rows, columns, or tables, and apply text formatting to format all of the text in a table the same way.

---

41 **Edit or Add Pictures in a Table**

Pictures can go in a table as easily as text. Why would you put a picture in a table cell? Well, imagine a table of products and prices that featured a column showing a picture of each product listed. Or imagine a whole Web page whose layout is controlled by one big table, in which case the ability to insert pictures in a table is the only way to add pictures to that page (**see** **63** **Use a Table to Arrange Content of a Page**).

1 **Position Your Insertion Point**

Click in the table cell in which you want to insert a picture, to position the insertion point there.

Before You Begin

✔ **40** Edit or Add Text in a Table

TIP

Most pictures are too big at first to look good in a table, where the size of a cell changes automatically to accommodate the picture. After adding pictures to a table, you can make the pictures smaller (**see** **27** **Change the Size of an Image**).

1 **Position Your Insertion Point**

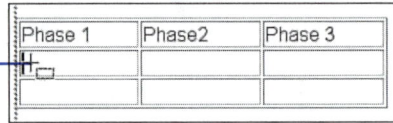

Phase 1	Phase2	Phase 3

2 **Click the Image Button**

Select Image

Look in: Samples

But2	CACTUS4	dnbannerN3
butterfl	CACTUS5	dolphin_
buttrans	camera	earth_ss
Cactus	citynet	eclipse_
CACTUS2	diamond_	egypt_ss
CACTUS3	diamondb	elibrary_logo

Preview.

37 x 33 GIF, 1K / 1 sec

File name: camera

Files of type: Image Files [*.gif;*.jpg;*.jpeg;*.jpe;*.jfif;*.png]

Select

Cancel

4 **View the Result**

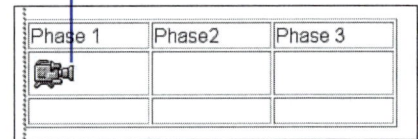

Phase 1	Phase2	Phase 3

3 **Navigate to and Select the Image File**

TIP

You can do anything to a picture in a table cell that you can do to a picture in a page: replace it, change its size, align it within the cell, and so on (see Chapter 5, "Editing Pictures and Movies").

2 **Click the Image Button**

On the **Edit** toolbar, click the **Image** button, and then choose from the list that appears **From My Computer** (to use an image stored on your computer) or **From Website** (to use an image file already online in the site you're editing, such as a company logo).

3 **Navigate to and Select the Image File**

Either of two different dialog boxes opens, depending upon your choice in step 2. However, both work the same way: Use the list of files and folders provided to navigate to and select the image file you want to insert. After you've selected it, click the **Select** button (for a file on your computer) or **OK** (for a file on the website).

4 **View the Result**

The image you selected appears in the table, in the cell you chose in step 1.

42 Add or Delete Rows or Columns

When editing or creating a table, you might find that you need the table to contain more rows or columns than it has at first. At any time, you can add new, empty rows or columns to a table to hold whatever you need to put in them.

1 **Click Above or to the Left**

When adding a new row, click anywhere in the row **above** where you want the new row inserted. When adding a new column, click in any cell in the column to the **left** of where you want the new column inserted.

2 **Add the Row or Column**

On the **Edit** toolbar, click a button: **Table Row** or **Table Column**.

3 **View the Result**

The row or column appears in the table, and the insertion point is in the new row or column, so you can add content right away. You can immediately repeat step 2 to add more rows or columns.

Before You Begin

✔ **40** Edit or Add Text in a Table

✔ **41** Edit or Add Pictures in a Table

💡 **TIP**

To add new rows to the bottom of a table while typing, just press the **Tab** key when the insertion point is in the bottom-right cell of the table.

💡 **TIP**

To delete rows or columns, click in the row or column to delete, choose **Table, Delete**, and then choose **Row** (to delete the row you clicked) or **Column** (to delete the column).

2 Add the Row or Column

3 View the Result

1 Click Above or to the Left

43 ## Change the Dimensions of a Table

Before You Begin

✔ **40** Edit or Add Text in a Table

✔ **41** Edit or Add Pictures in a Table

TIP

It's usually best to define your table width as a percentage, not as pixels. Choosing pixels can produce unpredictable results on displays of varying size and resolution.

To some extent, table dimensions are automatic. Row height changes automatically to fit whatever you put in each row. But to make your table look its best, you might want to take tighter control of your table's width by editing settings on the **Table Properties** dialog box.

1 **Open the Table Properties**

Right-click on the table and choose **Table Properties** from the pop-up menu. The **Table Properties** dialog box opens.

2 **Define the Table's Width**

In the **Table width** box, enter the width for the table, in pixels. To define the width of the table as a percentage of the width of the web page, choose **percent** from the list to the right of **Table width**, then enter a percentage instead of pixels (**100** for a table across the whole page, **50** for a table half the width of the page, and so on).

3 **View the Result**

Click **OK** on the **Table Properties** dialog box to see the changes to your table.

① **Open the Table Properties**

Table Properties

Table | Cell

Phase 1	Phase2	Phase 3	

Table Properties...
Table Cell Properties...

Text Options ▶

Merge Cells
Split Cell...

Insert Row Above
Insert Row Below

Insert Column to the Left
Insert Column to the Right

Insert Multiple Rows or Columns...

Delete Row
Delete Column

Insert Link...

Cut   Ctrl+X
Copy   Ctrl+C
Paste   Ctrl+V

IT Readiness project to
The IT managers have tea
the Outlook distribution lis
the Exchange Server...
Read More

How do I know if I have
workplace?
Join us in a 35 minute cla
workplace. January 23, 20
Read More

Environmental enginee

media Contribu...

Table alignment: Default
Table width: 75   Percent
Border thickness: 1   pixels
Cell padding: pixels between border and content
Cell spacing: pixels between cells

Border color: Background color:

Help   OK   Cancel   Apply

② **Define the Table's Width**

Phase 1	Phase2	Phase 3	

③ **View the Result**

44 Change the Size of Rows and Columns

Row height changes automatically to fit whatever you put in each row, so it's not always necessary to fiddle with sizes. Still, after you've entered and edited all your table content, you might decide the table would look a little better if this column was narrower, this one wider, and so on.

You can make such adjustments simply by dragging the *gridlines*, or internal borders, of the table.

① Point Carefully to a Gridline

Point to a horizontal gridline (to change row height) or to a vertical gridline (to change column width). When you are pointing accurately to a gridline, the pointer changes to a double line.

② Drag the Gridline

Click and hold on the line, and drag until your row or column is the height or width you want.

Before You Begin

✔ **40** Edit or Add Text in a Table

✔ **41** Edit or Add Pictures in a Table

✔ **43** Change the Dimensions of a Table

1 Point Carefully to a Gridline

2 Drag the Gridline

3 View the Result

3 View the Result

Release the mouse button to see your table with its new row or column dimensions.

45 Align a Table on the Page

Before You Begin

✔ **43** Change the Dimensions of a Table

✔ **44** Change the Size of Rows and Columns

TIP

The **Justify** alignment button on the Edit toolbar has no effect on a table. Your table alignment options are Left, Center, or Right.

Some tables will be 100% of the width of the page, in which case alignment is irrelevant. But when a table takes up less than the full width of a page, you can choose its alignment—left, center, or right—just as you would for a paragraph.

Note that the "alignment" referred to here is the way the whole table aligns to the margins of the page, not the way content aligns within cells.

1 Select the Table

To select a whole table, click anywhere on the table, then choose **Table, Select Table** from the menu bar. A black border with handles appears around the table to show that it's selected.

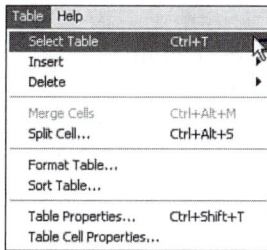

1 Select the Table

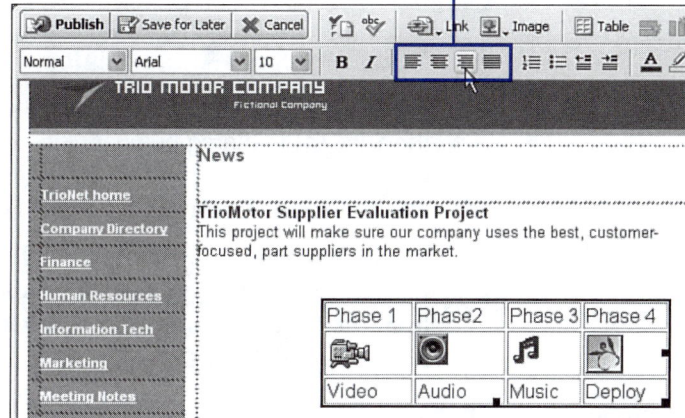

2 Choose Your Alignment

3 View the Result

2 Choose Your Alignment

On the **Edit** toolbar, click an alignment button: **Align Left, Center,** or **Align Right**.

3 View the Result

The table immediately takes on the alignment you chose, and remains selected in case you want to make another change. To deselect the table, click anywhere else on the page.

46 Sort Data in a Table

Contribute can reorganize the content of a table so that it's sorted alphabetically or numerically.

For example, suppose the left-most column of a table is a list of products, followed in other columns by prices, and so on. If you want the products to be listed alphabetically and don't want to take the time to alphabetize the rows yourself, you can have Contribute do it for you by telling it to sort the table on "Column 1" (the left-most column).

Before You Begin

✔ **40** Edit or Add Text in a Table

If you want to get really sorty, you can optionally perform a secondary sort, sorting the whole table first by the contents of one column, and then sorting after that column by the contents of another.

1 Open the Sort Table Dialog Box

Click anywhere in the table, then choose **Table**, **Sort Table** to open the **Sort Table** dialog box.

2 Choose the Column to Sort By

From the **Sort by** list, choose the column to sort by. From the list next to **Order**, choose to sort **Alphabetically** or **Numerically**, and from the list to the right of the **Order** list, choose **Ascending** (A to Z or low to high) or **Descending** (Z to A or high to low).

3 Choose a Secondary Sort Column (optional)

To sort by a second column following the first sort, choose that column in **Then by**. From the list next to **Order**, choose to sort **Alphabetically** or **Numerically**, and from the list to the right of the **Order** list, choose **Ascending** (A to Z or low to high) or **Descending** (Z to A or high to low).

4 Choose Sort Options

Check or clear check boxes to control options for how the table will be sorted:

- Check **Sort includes first row** to include the first row of the table in the sort.

- Check **Sort header rows** to sort header rows using the same criteria as the body rows.

- Check **Sort footer rows** to sort table footer rows using the same criteria as the body rows.

- Check **Leave row colors in original positions** to leave any background colors you've added to rows associated with the same data after the sort.

5 View the Result

Click **OK** to close the **Sort Table** dialog box and see your sorted table.

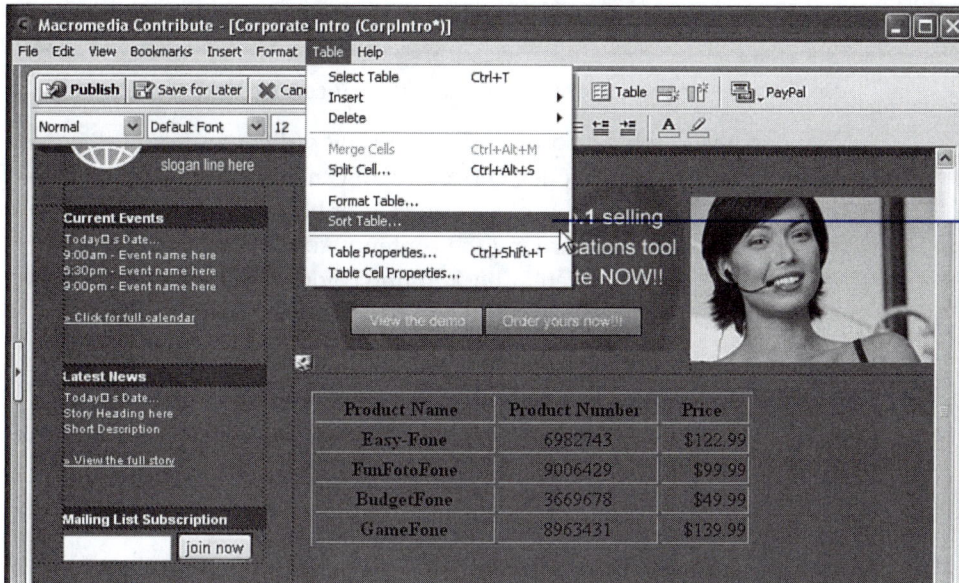

① Open the Sort Table Dialog Box

② Choose the Column to Sort By

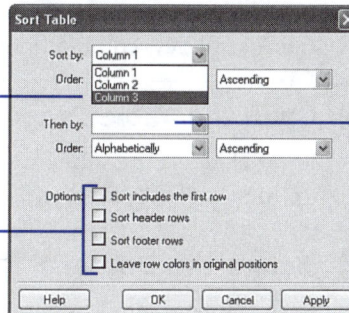

③ Choose a Secondary Sort Column (optional)

④ Choose Sort Options

⑤ View the Result

47 About Table Borders, Colors, Backgrounds, and Spacing

Beyond the basics of tables, there's a lot you can do to dress them up.

You can give a table its own background color (different from the page's background color or image), choose the thickness and color of the table border, and add extra space between cells or between the contents of cells and the cell walls around the contents. You can even give a row or column of a table a different background color than the rest of the table, which is a great way to set off row or column headings.

When choosing border and table background colors, keep a careful eye on how these colors go with the page's background and text colors. It's important for text to contrast with the background it's against, and for the table and its border to stand out from the page background.

48 Choose the Border Thickness and Color

Before You Begin

✔ **40** Edit or Add Text in a Table

✔ **41** Edit or Add Pictures in a Table

✔ **47** About Table Borders, Colors, Backgrounds, and Spacing

💡 **TIP**

For small, simple tables, you can make the border "invisible" by entering **0** (zero) in the **Border** thickness box in step 2. Note that you'll still see dashed lines for the borders in Edit mode, but that's just to show you where the table is.

A bold, colored border can really help a table make a strong statement, and adding a heavy, colored border is easy.

1 Open the Table Properties

Right-click on the table and choose **Table Properties** from the pop-up menu. The **Table Properties** dialog box opens.

2 Define the Border's Thickness

In the **Border thickness** box, enter the width for the table, in pixels. A thickness of 1 or 2 makes a thin, delicate border; a thickness of 4 or 6 makes a heavy, thick one.

3 Click the Border Color Box

Click the **Border color** box to open a pallette of color choices from which you can choose a border color.

4 Choose a Color

From the pallette, click the color box containing the color you want to use for the border.

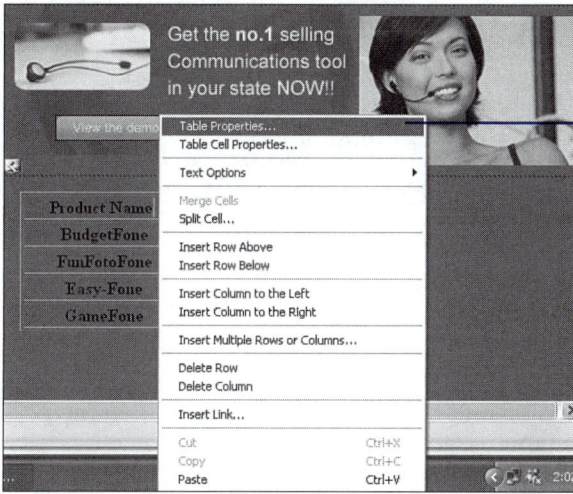

1 Open the Table Properties

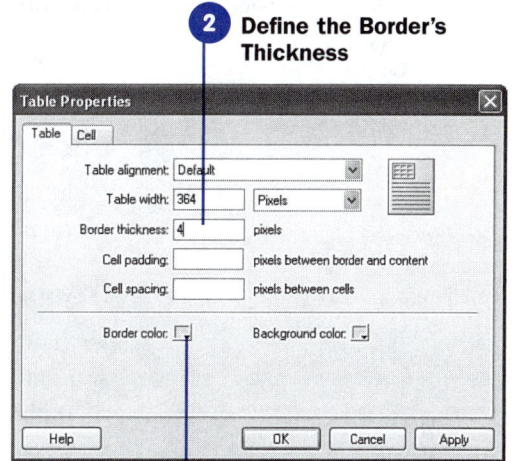

2 Define the Border's Thickness

4 Choose a Color

3 Click the Border Color Box

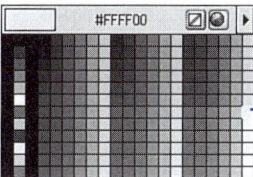

5 View the Result

---

5 **View the Result**

Click **OK** on the **Table Properties** dialog box to see the changes to your table.

49 Change the Spacing Around Cell Contents

Before You Begin

✔ **40** Edit or Add Text in a Table

✔ **41** Edit or Add Pictures in a Table

✔ **47** About Table Borders, Colors, Backgrounds, and Spacing

If your table looks a little cramped and hard to read, you can open up its spacing by changing two simple settings:

- **Cell padding**—The amount of space between the contents of each cell and that cell's borders.

- **Cell spacing**—The amount of space between all cells in the table.

1 Open the Table Properties

Right-click on the table and choose **Table Properties** from the pop-up menu. The **Table Properties** dialog box opens.

2 Define the Cell Padding

In the **Cell padding** box, enter the width of the padding, in pixels. A padding of 1 or 2 opens a little more space around cell contents; a padding of 4 or 6 opens a lot of space.

3 Define the Cell Spacing

In the **Cell spacing** box, enter the width of the spacing, in pixels. A spacing of 1 or 2 opens a little more space between cells; a padding of 4 or 6 opens a lot of space.

4 View the Result

Click **OK** on the **Table Properties** dialog box to see the changes to your table.

1 **Open the Table Properties**

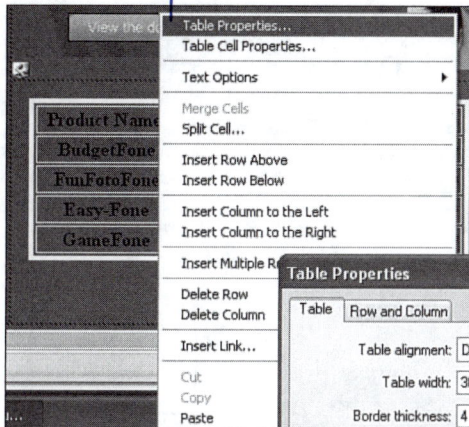

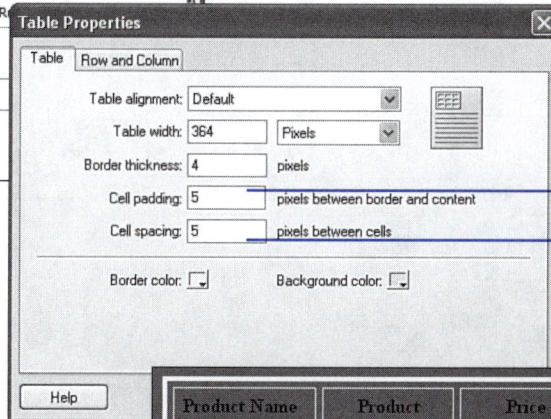

Table Properties...
Table Cell Properties...

Text Options ▶

Merge Cells
Split Cell...

Insert Row Above
Insert Row Below

Insert Column to the Left
Insert Column to the Right

Insert Multiple R...

Delete Row
Delete Column

Insert Link...

Cut
Copy
Paste

Product Name
BudgetFone
FunFotoFone
Easy-Fone
GameFone

Table Properties ☒

Table | Row and Column

Table alignment: Default ▾
Table width: 364 | Pixels ▾
Border thickness: 4 | pixels
Cell padding: 5 | pixels between border and content
Cell spacing: 5 | pixels between cells

Border color: ▾ Background color: ▾

Help

2 **Define the Cell Padding**

3 **Define the Cell Spacing**

Product Name	Product Number	Price
BudgetFone	3669678	$49.99
FunFotoFone	9006429	$99.99
Easy-Fone	6982743	$122.99
GameFone	8963431	$139.99

4 **View the Result**

50 Add a Background Color to a Table

When you specify no background color for a table, the page's background color or image shows through the table, and often, that looks great. But to give your table extra oomph, you can give it its own background color. You can also give parts of the table a different background color than others.

Before You Begin

✔ **47** About Table Borders, Colors, Backgrounds, and Spacing

1 Open the Table Properties

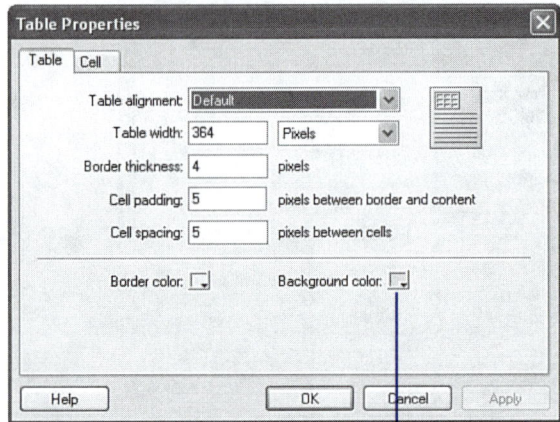

Table Properties

Table | Cell

Table alignment: Default

Table width: 364 Pixels

Border thickness: 4 pixels

Cell padding: 5 pixels between border and content

Cell spacing: 5 pixels between cells

Border color: ☐ Background color: ☐

Help OK Cancel Apply

#999999

3 Choose a Color

2 Click the Background Color Box

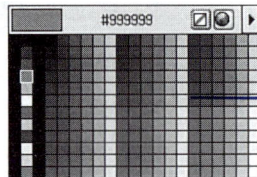

Product Name	Product Number	Price
BudgetFone	3669678	$49.99
FunFotoFone	9006429	$99.99
Easy-Fone	6982743	$122.99
GameFone	8963431	$139.99

4 View the Result

1 Open the Table Properties

Right-click on the table and choose **Table Properties** from the pop-up menu. The **Table Properties** dialog box opens.

2 Click the Background Color Box

Click the **Background color** box to open a pallette of color choices from which you can choose a background color.

When choosing a table background color, keep a careful eye on how the color goes with the page's background and text colors. It's important for text to contrast with the background it's against, and for the table to stand out from the page background.

3 Choose a Color

From the pallette, click the color box containing the color you want to use for the table background.

4 View the Result

Click **OK** on the **Table Properties** dialog box to see the changes to your table.

TIP

To add a background color to just a particular row, column, or cell, select that row (by clicking to the left of it), column (by clicking right above it), or cell (by clicking it) in step 1. Then click the second tab of **Table Properties** and continue with step 2.

51 Create a New Table

Creating new tables in Contribute is a snap, and it's fun, too. After you've created a new table, you can add content to it and format it in all the ways already described in this chapter.

1 Position Your Insertion Point

Point to the spot where you want to add a table and click to position the insertion point there.

2 Open the Insert Table Dialog Box

On the **Edit** toolbar, click the **Table** button to open the **Insert Table** dialog box.

3 Choose the Number of Rows and Columns

In **Number of rows**, type the number of rows for the table, and in **Number of columns**, type the number of columns.

TIP

You can also choose from among a set of predefined table designs in Contribute, to give your table a professional look in a hurry. Right after you create the table, choose **Table, Format Table** and then choose from among the designs presented.

TIP

Don't worry if you're not sure how many rows or columns you need—just take your best guess. You can add rows later by pressing the **Tab** key in the last cell of the table, or choosing **Table, Insert** and then choosing one of the options.

2 **Open the Insert Table Dialog Box**

1 **Position Your Insertion Point**

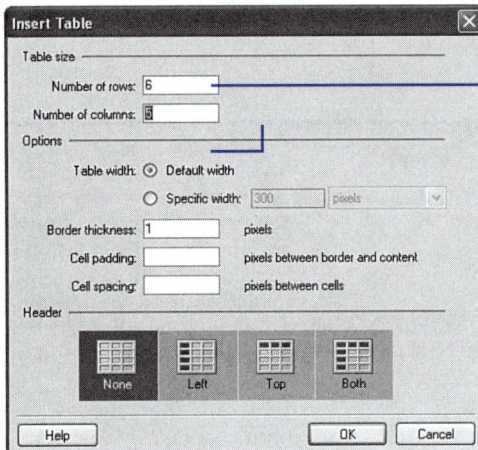

3 **Choose the Number of Rows and Columns**

4 **View the Result**

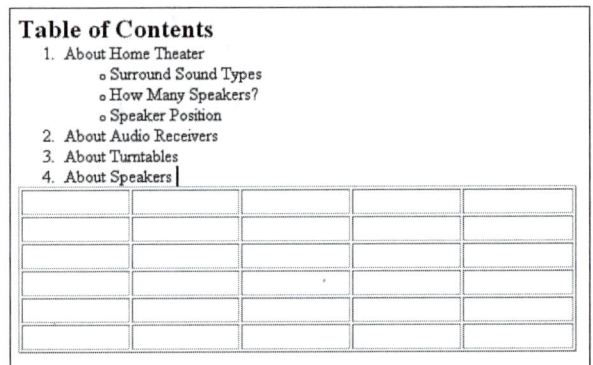

4 **View the Result**

Click **OK** on the **Insert Table** dialog box to see your new table. You may now add content to your table or change it in any of the ways described in this chapter.

7

Linking to Web Pages, Files, and Email

IN THIS CHAPTER:

---

52 About Links

KEY TERM

Link—Short for *hyperlink*, a link is an object in a web page that takes the visitor to another page, downloads a file, or starts some other action.

Many contributors might find that keeping up with *links* is one of the most important content-management activities they perform. Anyone who's spent much time on the Web knows the frustration of clicking on a link only to find that it leads to old content, the wrong content, or no content at all—flashing forth the dreaded "404" error message ("Cannot find…").

Especially in a typical Contribute environment—where multiple authors are changing various web documents daily or weekly—links inevitably need correcting and/or updating. Keeping up with your links is an essential part of keeping a Contribute site looking professional and running smoothly for your visitors.

52 About Links

The only tricky part about links is understanding that they can point to several different kinds of content and that the steps for creating or editing a link differ slightly, depending upon the type of content to which you're pointing. Links created or edited in Contribute can point to the following kinds of content:

KEY TERM

Section anchor—An invisible marker to which a link can point. A link can point not to a whole page, but rather to a particular part of a page. Also known as *targets*, *anchors*, or *bookmarks*.

- Pages in your Contribute website.

- New pages added to your site at the moment you create the link (**see** **58** **About New Pages**).

- Other sites or pages anywhere on the Web.

- *Section anchors*, or specific spots within a page, as when a table of contents at the top of a long page is made up of links that each point to a particular section or heading.

- Email addresses already addressed to someone you have indicated in the link (opening a new message in the visitor's email program).

- Files on your computer, which will download to the visitor's computer when the link is clicked. (Contribute automatically copies those files to the server so that the visitor is actually downloading a copy of the file from the server, not pulling a file straight from your PC.)

Contribute gives you a lot of help with this by making you choose which type of link you're creating before letting you do much else. It then limits the options it displays to just what you need to create the type of link you want.

For example, when you click the **Link** button on Contribute's toolbar, it first shows you a list of things you can link to (as seen in the figure here).

The Link button makes you choose the kind of content you're linking to before showing you a dialog box for creating that link.

After you've selected one of the list options, the **Insert Link** dialog box opens. However, this dialog box will look different depending on which selection you make from the list under the **Link** button.

For example, if you choose **Drafts and Recent Pages**, the **Insert Link** dialog box shows a list of your drafts and recent pages (see figure) so that all you need to do to create the link is pick one. If you choose **E-mail Address**, the dialog displays a simple text box where you can type the email address to which you want to link.

Choosing Drafts and Recent Pages from the list under the Link button displays this version of the Insert Link box, so you can simply click the page to which you want to link.

Choosing E-Mail Address from the list under the Link button displays this version of the Insert Link box, so you can simply type the email address to which you want to link.

> **TIP**
>
> After you reach the **Insert Link** dialog box, you can change your mind. There's a row of buttons along the top of the dialog box (see figure) that let you choose the type of link you're creating.

> **TIP**
>
> The **Browse** button on the **Insert Link** dialog box is handy when you want to link to a page on the Web, but you're not sure about the address. Clicking this button opens a browser window you can use to navigate to that page, and then you can click **OK** to automatically link to the page.

53 Change Where an Existing Link Leads

Before You Begin

✔ **52** About Links

Often, the text or picture a visitor clicks to use a link doesn't need to be changed, but the URL underneath that link does—because the file or page being linked to has been updated and has taken on a new name, or because other edits to the site have made the link invalid. You can quickly change where a link points without having to change or recreate the text or picture for the link that appears in the page.

1 Right-Click the Link

In your draft, point to the link you want to change and then click the right mouse button. A pop-up menu appears.

2 Choose Link Properties

In the pop-up menu, click on **Link Properties**. The **Insert Link** dialog box opens.

3 Choose the Type of Content to Link To

From the row of buttons at the top of the dialog box, click the button that matches the type of link you want to create. The large panel beneath the row of buttons changes to allow you to select the item to which you want to link.

4 Select or Type an Address

Use the panel provided to create the new link address. For example, if you clicked the **E-mail Address** button in step 3, type the email address you want to link to in the **Email address** box provided. If you chose **Drafts or Recent Pages**, click the name of the draft or recent page in the list provided. If you chose **Browse to Web Page**, type the web page's URL in the box provided. Click **OK** in the **Insert Link** dialog box to return to your draft.

TIP

If in step 3 you chose **Browse to Web Page**, you can click the **Browse** button in step 4 to open a browser window you can use to navigate to the page to which you want to link. When that page appears in the browser window, click **OK** in the browser and then continue to step 5.

5 View the Result

To view the result, click on the link; the URL to which the link now points appears in the status bar. To test the link, publish your draft and then switch to Browse mode and click the link.

2 Choose Link Properties

3 Choose the Type of Content to Link To

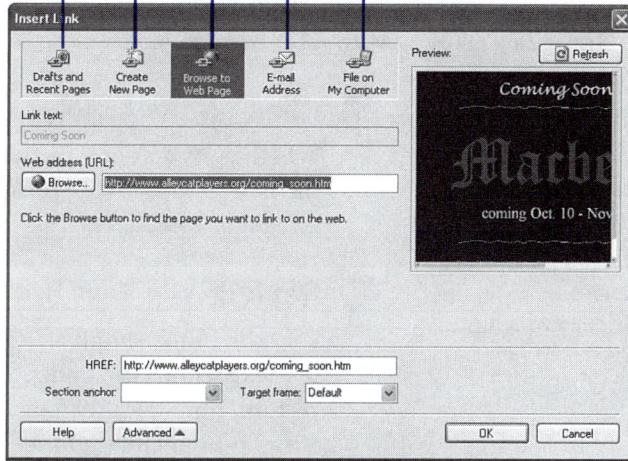

1 Right-Click the Link

4 Select or Type an Address

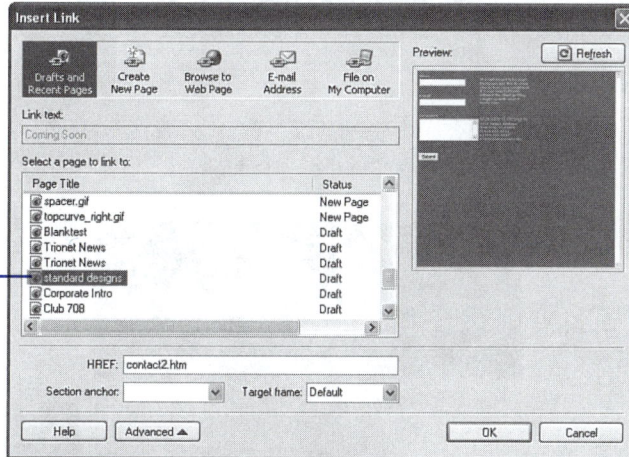

5 View the Result

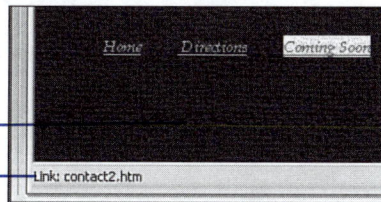

54 Edit an Existing Link's Text or Image

Before You Begin

✔ **52** About Links

✔ **53** Change Where an
Existing Link Leads

TIP

If you follow these steps, it's unlikely that you'll lose the link underlying the text or picture. But if you do, no big deal—just re-create the link using the steps in **55** Add a New Link.

Of course, there may be times when you want to change the text or picture a visitor clicks to activate a link without changing the link underneath so that it still points where it always has. You can do that, too, without having to recreate the link from scratch.

1 Click on the Link

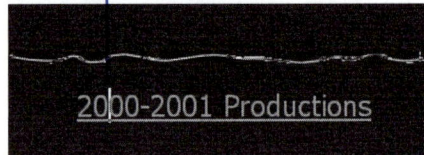

Whether it's text or a picture, click on the link. If it's a text link, the insertion point appears within the text. If it's a picture link, the picture is selected.

2 Replace the Text or Picture

For a text link, simply edit the text. You'll notice as you edit that the text retains the underlining indicating that it's a link. For a picture, right-click the picture and choose **Image Properties** from the pop-up menu and then use the **Image Properties** dialog box to replace the picture as described in **29** Replace an Image.

1 Click on the Link

2000-2001 Productions

2 Replace the Text or Picture

2003-2004 Productions

55 **Add a New Link**

Adding new links is really a two-step process: You add to your web page the text or picture a visitor will click, and then you attach to that text or picture the URL, email address, or filename the link points to.

1 **Add the Text or Image for the Link**

Before creating a new link, type the text for it in your draft or insert the image for the link (**see** **11** **Edit and Add Text** and **30** **Add or Delete an Image**).

2 **Select the Link Text or Picture**

Highlight the text to select it, or click on the picture to select it. (Handles will appear around the picture to show that it is selected.)

3 **Click the Link Button**

Click the toolbar's **Link** button to open a list of items to which you can link.

4 **Choose the Type of Content to Link To**

From the list under the **Link** button, click what you want to link to: one of your drafts or recently edited pages, a page on the Web (**Browse to Web Page**), an email address, and so on. The **Insert Link** dialog box opens, showing options for the type of link you selected.

5 **Select or Type an Address**

Use the options provided in the **Insert Link** dialog box to create the new link address. For example, if you chose **E-mail Address** in step 4, type the email address you want to link to in the **Email** address box provided. If you chose **Drafts and Recent Pages**, click the name of the draft or recent page in the list provided. If you chose **Browse to Web Page**, type the web page's URL in the box provided. When finished, click **OK** in the **Insert Link** dialog box.

Before You Begin

✔ **11** Edit and Add Text

✔ **30** Add or Delete an Image

✔ **52** About Links

TIP

In step 5, instead of typing a web URL, you can click the **Browse** button on the **Insert Link** dialog box to open a window in which you can browse to the page you want to link to. When you get there, click **OK** to copy that page's address into the **Insert Link** dialog box.

Table of Contents

1. About Home Theater
   - Surround Sound Types
   - How Many Speakers?
   - Speaker Position
2. About Audio Receivers
3. About Turntables
4. About Speak

1 Add the Text or Image for the Link

3 Click the Link Button

Publish | Save for Later | Cancel | Link | Image

Normal | Default Font | 12 | B I

The Beanstalk Audio Primer

Table of Contents

1. About Home Theater
   - Surround Sound Types
   - How Many Speakers?
   - Speaker Position
2. About Audio Receivers
3. About Turntables
4. About Speakers

2 Select the Link Text or Picture

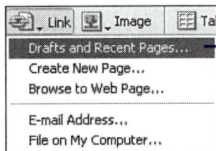

Link | Image | Ta

Drafts and Recent Pages...
Create New Page...
Browse to Web Page...

E-mail Address...
File on My Computer...

4 Choose the Type of Content to Link To

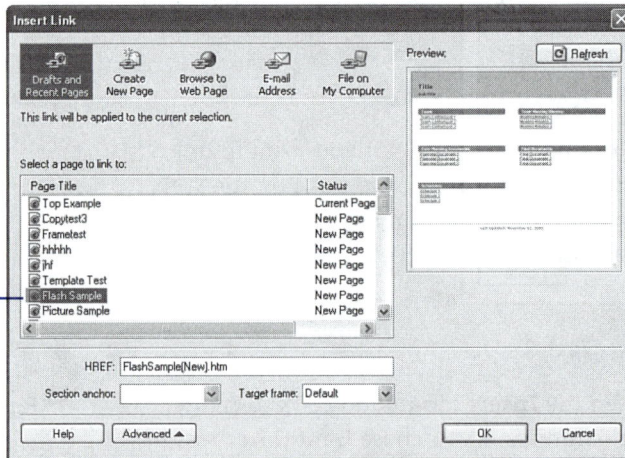

Insert Link

Drafts and Recent Pages | Create New Page | Browse to Web Page | E-mail Address | File on My Computer

This link will be applied to the current selection.

Select a page to link to:

Page Title	Status
Top Example	Current Page
Copytest3	New Page
Frametest	New Page
hhhhh	New Page
jhf	New Page
Template Test	New Page
Flash Sample	New Page
Picture Sample	New Page

HREF: FlashSample(New).htm

Section anchor: | Target frame: Default

Help | Advanced ▲ | OK | Cancel

5 Select or Type an Address

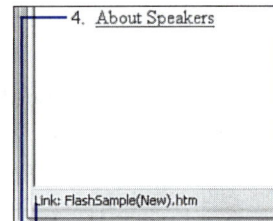

Preview: | Refresh

4. About Speakers

Link: FlashSample(New).htm

6 View the Result

⑥ View the Result

To view the result, click on the link; the URL to which the link now points appears in the status bar. To test the link, publish your draft (to save your changes and switch to Browse mode) and then click the link.

56 Make a Linked Page Open in a New Window

By default, when a visitor clicks on a link that leads to another web page (whether on your own site or elsewhere), the new page replaces the existing page in the same browser window. Under some circumstances, you might want the new page to open in its own new window, leaving the last page open in a separate browser window. This is a good approach when the visitor might want to refer back to the previous page without closing the new page.

Before You Begin

✔ **52** About Links
✔ **55** Add a New Link

1 Right-Click the Link

In your draft, point to the link you want to change and then click the right mouse button. A pop-up menu appears.

2 Choose Link Properties

In the pop-up menu, click on **Link Properties**. The **Insert Link** dialog box opens.

3 Click the Advanced Button

Near the bottom of the **Insert Link** dialog box, you might see list boxes labeled **Section Anchor** and **Target Frame**. If you don't, click the **Advanced** button to display them.

4 Choose "New Window" from Target Frame

Open the list labeled **Target frame** and choose **New Window**. When the link is clicked by a visitor, the content it points to will open in a new browser window, leaving the current page open and active in a separate window. Click **OK** to close the **Insert Link** dialog box.

5 View the Result

To view the result, click on the link; the URL to which the link now points appears in the status bar. To test the link, publish your draft (to save your changes and switch to Browse mode) and then click the link to watch the new window open to display the content.

Table Properties...
Table Cell Properties...

Text Options ▶

Merge Cells
Split Cell...

Insert Row Above
Insert Row Below

Insert Column to the Left
Insert Column to the Right

Insert Multiple Rows or Columns...

Delete Row
Delete Column

Link Properties...
Remove Link

Cut   Ctrl+X
Copy   Ctrl+C
Paste   Ctrl+V

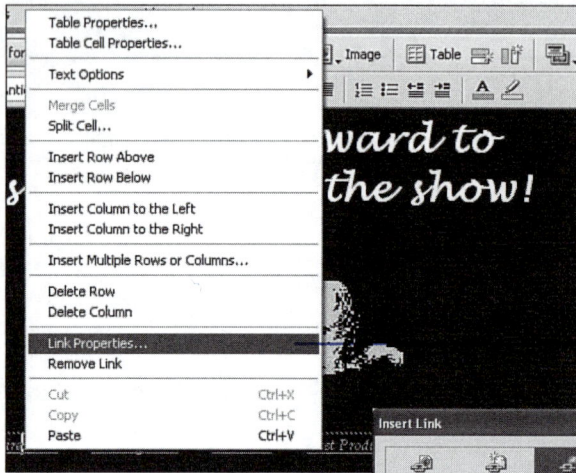

1 **Right-Click the Link**

2 **Choose Link Properties**

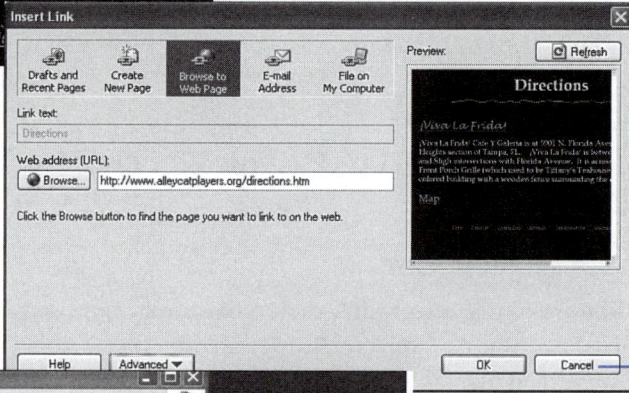

Image | Table

ward to
the show!

Insert Link

Drafts and Recent Pages | Create New Page | Browse to Web Page | E-mail Address | File on My Computer

Preview: | Refresh

Link text:
Directions

Web address (URL):
Browse... | http://www.alleycatplayers.org/directions.htm

Click the Browse button to find the page you want to link to on the web.

Help | Advanced ▼

OK | Cancel

Directions

¡Viva La Frida!

¡Viva La Frida! Cafe Y Galeria is at 5901 N. Florida Ave...
Heights section of Tampa, FL. ¡Viva La Frida! is betwe...
and Sligh intersections with Florida Avenue. It is acros...
Front Porch Grille (which used to be Tiffany's Teahous...
colored building with a wooden fence surrounding the...

Map

3 **Click the Advanced Button**

HREF: | http://www.alleycatplayers.org/directions.htm

Section anchor: | | Target frame: | Default

Help | Advanced ▲

Default
Entire Window
New Window

4 **Choose "New Window" from Target Frame**

Alley Cat Players - Microsoft Internet Explorer
File Edit View Favorites Tools Help
Back | Search | Favorites | Media
Address http://www.alleycatplayers.org | Go Links Web assistant SnagIt

Directions - Microsoft Internet Explorer
File Edit View Favorites Tools Help
Back | Search | Fa
Address http://www.alleycatplayers.org/directions.htm

Directions

Directions

¡Viva La Frida!

¡Viva La Frida! Cafe Y Galeria is at 5901 N. Florida Avenue in t
Heights section of Tampa, FL. ¡Viva La Frida! is between the l
and Sligh intersections with Florida Avenue. It is across the str

Norton Internet Security

SnagIt 7

Internet

5 **View the Result**

57 Link to a Particular Spot Within a Page

If you've ever browsed a lengthy online FAQ (frequently asked questions) file, you've probably come across *anchors*—markers within a web page that enable you to link to particular spots within the page, instead of just linking to the page itself at the top.

Anchors are commonly used for long pages with many sections. An anchor appears at the start of each new section, and a table of contents appears at the top of the page; each item on the TOC is a link to one of the anchors. You can also link from one page to anchors in another when you want to take your visitor directly to a specific part of another page.

❶ Choose the Spot for a Section Anchor

In your draft, click a spot on the page to which you'd like a link to point. You can click on text or select a picture, if that's where you want the link you're going to create later to point.

❷ Insert the Anchor

From the menu bar, choose **Insert, Section Anchor**. The **Section Anchor** dialog box opens.

❸ Name the Anchor

Type a name (or number) for this anchor. It can be anything you want (visitors to your page won't see your anchor names), but every anchor within a page must have its own unique name or number. After typing a name, click **OK** on the **Section Anchor** dialog box. (You may repeat steps 1 through 3 to add all the anchors you need.)

❹ Create and Select the Link Text or Picture

Just as you would when creating any new link, add (if necessary) the text or picture for the link and select it.

Before You Begin

✔ **52** About Links
✔ **55** Add a New Link

NOTE

In Edit mode, your anchors will appear as little flag icons wherever you've inserted them so you know where they are. The flags won't appear in Browse mode or online.

TIP

If you see little flag icons in your page in Edit mode, the page's author or another contributor has already added anchors you might want to use. To learn the name of an anchor, right-click on it and choose **Anchor Properties**.

5 Click the Link Button

Click the toolbar's **Link** button to open a list of items to which you can link.

6 Choose Drafts and Recent Pages

From the list under the **Link** button, choose **Drafts and Recent Pages** (because the pages to which you just added section anchors will be among those pages). The **Insert Link** dialog box opens.

7 Choose Your Page

From the list of pages in the box under **Select a page to link to**, choose the page to which you added the section anchors.

8 Click the Advanced Button

Near the bottom of the **Insert Link** dialog box, you might see list boxes labeled **Section Anchor** and **Target Frame**. If you don't, click the **Advanced** button to display them.

9 Choose an Anchor to Link To

Open the list labeled **Section anchor** and choose the name of the anchor to which you want this link to point. Click **OK** to close the **Insert Link** dialog box. (If you created more than one anchor at the beginning of this task, repeat steps 4 through 9 to create links to your other anchors.)

10 View the Result

To view the result, click on each link; the URL to which the link now points appears in the status bar, followed by a pound symbol (#) and the name of the anchor to which it points. To test the link, publish your draft (to save your changes and switch to Browse mode) and then click the link.

1 Choose the Spot for a Section Anchor

| Insert | Format | Table | Help |

Image
Table...   Ctrl+Alt+T
Link
PayPal

Date...
Section Anchor...   Ctrl+Alt+A

Horizontal Rule
Line Break   Shift+Return
Special Characters

Microsoft Office Document...
Document as FlashPaper...
Flash Movie

2 Insert the Anchor

Image   Table

Phase 3 Phase 4

Music   Deploy

IT Readiness project to start in November 2002
The IT managers have teamed up with ICOM to work on cleaning up
the Outlook distribution lists. There are currently over 2000 lists on
the Exchange Server...
Read More

Section Anchor   [×]

Section Anchor Name: News1

Help   OK   Cancel

3 Name the Anchor

5 Click the Link Button

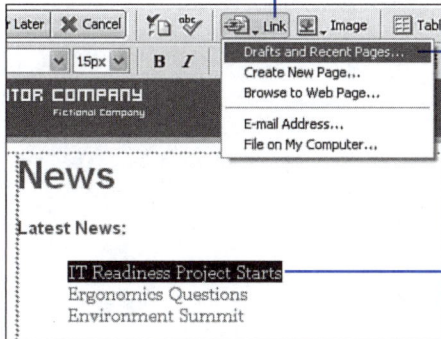

Later   Cancel   Link   Image   Table

15px   B I

Drafts and Recent Pages...
Create New Page...
Browse to Web Page...

E-mail Address...
File on My Computer...

6 Choose Drafts and Recent Pages

ITOR COMPANY
Fictional Company

News

Latest News:

IT Readiness Project Starts
Ergonomics Questions
Environment Summit

4 Create and Select the Link Text or Picture

7 Choose Your Page

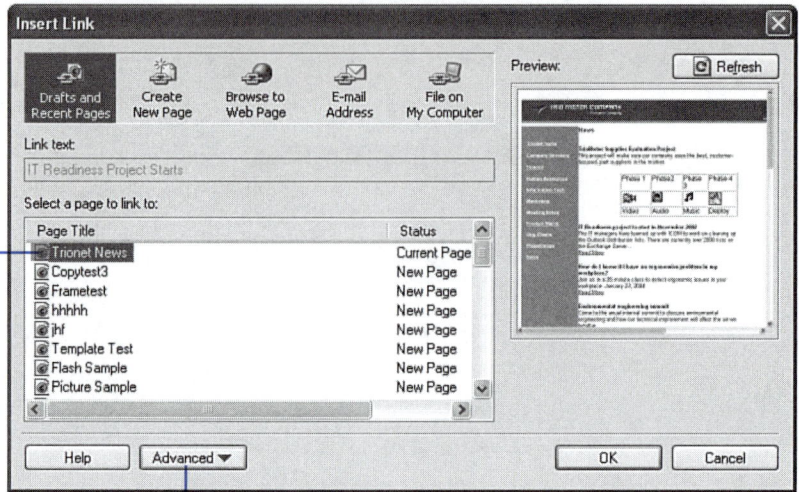

Insert Link

Drafts and Recent Pages | Create New Page | Browse to Web Page | E-mail Address | File on My Computer

Link text:
IT Readiness Project Starts

Select a page to link to:

Page Title	Status
Trionet News	Current Page
Copytest3	New Page
Frametest	New Page
hhhhh	New Page
jhf	New Page
Template Test	New Page
Flash Sample	New Page
Picture Sample	New Page

Preview:

Help | Advanced ▼ | OK | Cancel

8 Click the Advanced Button

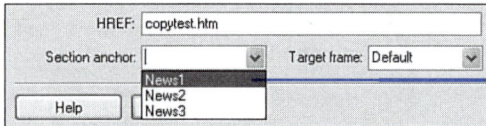

HREF: copytest.htm

Section anchor: [ ] Target frame: Default

News1
News2
News3

Help

9 Choose an Anchor to Link To

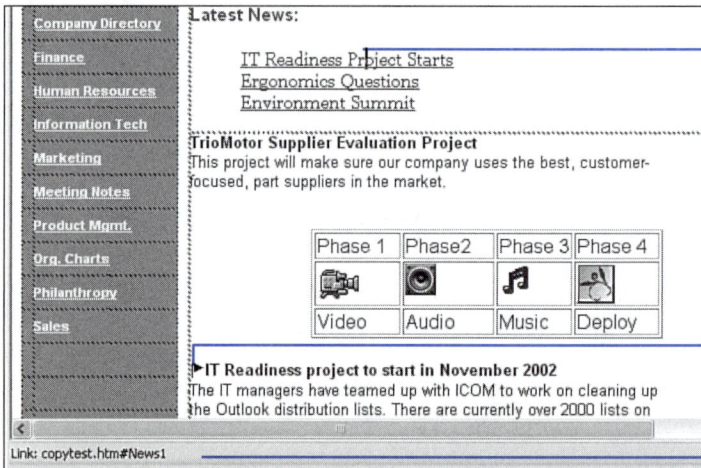

Company Directory

Finance

Human Resources

Information Tech

Marketing

Meeting Notes

Product Mgmt.

Org. Charts

Philanthropy

Sales

Latest News:

IT Readiness Project Starts
Ergonomics Questions
Environment Summit

TrioMotor Supplier Evaluation Project
This project will make sure our company uses the best, customer-focused, part suppliers in the market.

Phase 1	Phase2	Phase 3	Phase 4
Video	Audio	Music	Deploy

IT Readiness project to start in November 2002
The IT managers have teamed up with ICOM to work on cleaning up the Outlook distribution lists. There are currently over 2000 lists on

Link: copytest.htm#News1

10 View the Result

PART III

Creating New Web Page Content

8

Working with New Pages

IN THIS CHAPTER:

New pages are easy to add to a Contribute website, but you must do so carefully. In most companies that use Contribute, the website author will have defined approved corporate colors, fonts, copyrights, disclaimers, and other formatting that you'll be expected to preserve in any page you add.

58 About New Pages

NOTE

For these reasons, among others, your administrator might configure your role so that you cannot add new pages. If the options you need for adding new pages appear grayed out, you'll need to see your administrator to add pages.

Although you can add a completely blank page to a Contribute site, it's often best to add new pages through two other techniques described in this chapter: **59** Copy an Existing Page to Make a New Page (so your new page starts out with all the basic formatting used elsewhere on the site) and **60** Use a Template to Make a New Page (so that your new page incorporates formatting supplied to you by your administrator or the website's author specifically for use in new pages).

Finally, as the tasks show, always make sure that, at the same time you create any new page, you also create one or more links on existing pages that connect to the new page. Doing so will not only ensure that visitors to the site can access the page, but will make it easy for you to access the page if you happen to forget its title or filename.

59 Copy an Existing Page to Make a New Page

Before You Begin

✔ **52** About Links
✔ **58** About New Pages

NOTE

You can't copy (or add, for that matter) a Contribute page that includes *frames*, those individual panels that each contain their own content and (sometimes) scrollbars. For more, **see** **70** About Frames.

An easy way to create a new page that fits the style of the rest of the site is to browse to a page that's a close match for the one you want to add and to copy that page as a new page on the site. Then you can edit that page's content (preserving the formatting) so that it says what you need it to say.

1 Browse to the Page

In Browse mode, navigate to the existing page you want to copy.

2 Click the New Page Button

On the Browser toolbar, click the **New Page** button, or choose **File**, **New Page**. The **New Page** dialog box opens.

2 **Click the New Page Button**

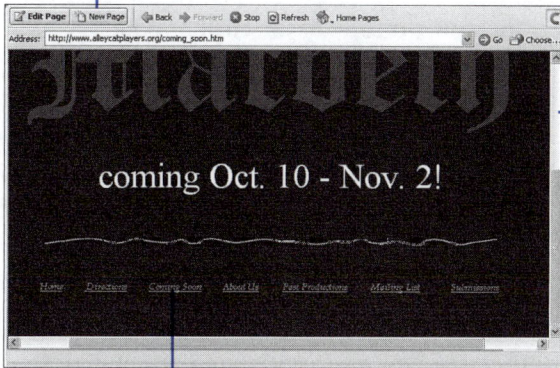

1 **Browse to the Page**

3 **Click Copy of Current Page**

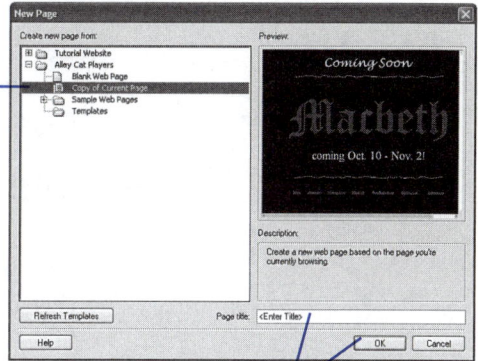

9 **Test the Link**

5 **Open the Page to Link From**

7 **Click the Link Button and Choose Drafts and Recent Pages**

4 **Title the Page and Click OK**

6 **Select the Link Text or Picture**

8 **Click the Title of the New Page**

3 Click Copy of Current Page

Under **Create new page from**, click **Copy of current page**. The **Preview** box to the right shows a copy of the current page.

4 Title the Page and Click OK

Next to **Page title**, type a title for your new page. (Make sure the title is different from that of the page you are copying.) Click **OK** to display the new page in Edit mode. (Don't publish yet!)

5 Open the Page to Link From

Use the **Pages** panel or **Browser** to open (in Browse mode) a page that will contain a link to the new page and then click the **Edit Page** button to switch to Edit mode.

6 Select the Link Text or Picture

In the page you opened in step 5, find (or create) the text or picture for the link to the new page. Highlight the text to select it or click on the picture to select it. Handles will appear around the picture to show that it is selected.

7 Click the Link Button and Choose Drafts and Recent Pages

Click the toolbar's **Link** button to open a list of items to which you can link and click **Drafts and Recent Pages**. The **Insert Link** dialog box opens, showing a list of drafts and recently edited pages.

8 Click the Title of the New Page

In the list, find the title of the new page you created in steps 1–4 and select it. Then click **OK** in the **Insert Link** dialog box.

9 Test the Link

Publish your open drafts (to save your changes and switch to Browse mode). Open the page containing the link to the new page and click it to make sure that the link opens the new page.

NOTE

Remember that it's important to give your page a title that is brief, clear, and descriptive, and that the "title" is not the same thing as the filename of the page's HTML file. When you publish the page, a prompt will show you a suggested filename based on the title, but you can change that when you see it to anything you prefer.

TIP

You can change a page's title at any time by changing the page properties, as described in **62** Choose a Background Color and Other General Settings.

---

60 Use a Template to Make a New Page

The quickest way to get a professional-looking page is usually to use a template. Ideally, your Web site's author or your Contribute administrator will have created templates for your use (already containing all the formatting required to match the rest of the site) and will have set these templates up in Contribute so that you can use them as described in this task.

1 Open the Page to Link From

In Edit mode, open a page that will contain a link to the new page.

2 Select the Link Text or Picture

Find or create the text or picture for the link to the new page. Highlight the text to select it, or click on the picture to select it. Handles will appear around the picture to show that it is selected.

3 Click the Link Button and Choose Create New Page

Click the toolbar's **Link** button to open a list of items to which you can link and click **Create New Page**. The **Insert Link** dialog box opens, showing a list of template options under **Create new page from**.

4 Choose a Template

In the **Create new page from** list, you'll see a list of folders. You can open any folder to see the templates it contains by clicking the plus sign (+) next to the folder. To see what any template looks like, click its name in the list; a preview of that template's layout appears in the **Preview** panel to the right.

When the **Preview** panel shows the template you want to use, move on to step 5.

5 Title the Page and Click OK

Next to **New page title**, type a title for your new page. Click **OK** to display the new page in Edit mode.

Before You Begin

✔ **58** About New Pages

✔ **52** About Links

See Also

✔ **91** Set General Role Settings

⊕KEY TERM

Template—A web page file that's all formatted and ready to go, except that it has no content, or contains "dummy" content you can replace. All you need to do is add and edit the content.

TIP

If no templates have been provided for your new pages, the best way to create a new page that matches the formatting of the rest of the site is to use the steps described in **60** **Copy an Existing Page to Make a New Page**.

NOTE

The folders and templates listed will differ depending upon how your administrator has set up your templates. The **Sample Web Pages** and **Calendars** folders contain handy templates that come with Contribute. The **Templates** folder at the bottom of the list will usually contain the specific templates for your company and site.

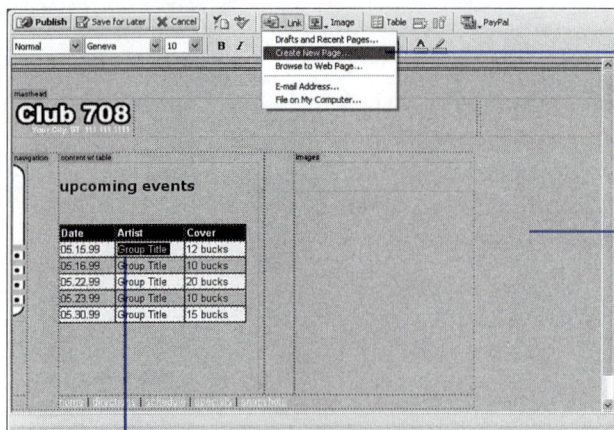

3 Click the Link Button and Choose Create New Page

1 Open the Page to Link From

2 Select the Link Text or Picture

4 Choose a Template

5 Title the Page and Click OK

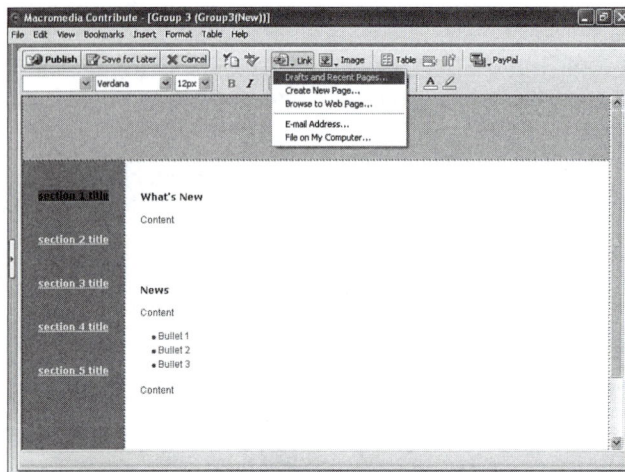

6 Edit the New Page

6 Edit the New Page

Having successfully created and linked to a new template-based page, edit and customize that page any way you like.

61 Create a New Blank Page

There might be times when no template or existing page is remotely like the one you want to add, and in such cases you might want to simply start a completely blank new page you can format and fill in however you like. As always, however, it's important to create a link back to a page in the main site as part of creating your new page.

1 Open the Page to Link From

In Edit mode, open a page that will contain a link to the new blank page.

2 Select the Link Text or Picture

Find or create the text or picture for the link to the new page. Highlight the text to select it, or click on the picture to select it. Handles will appear around the picture to show that it is selected.

3 Click the Link Button and Choose Create New Page

Click the toolbar's **Link** button to open a list of items to which you can link and click **Create New Page**. The **Insert Link** dialog box opens, showing a list of options under **Create new page from**.

4 Click Blank Web Page

In the **Create new page from** list, choose **Blank Web Page**.

5 Title the Page and Click OK

Next to **New page title**, type a title for your new page. Click **OK** to display the new page in Edit mode.

6 Create Your Content

Having successfully created and linked to a new blank page, fill it in with your content any way you like.

7 Test the New Page

Publish your open drafts (to save your changes and switch to Browse mode). Open the page containing the link to the new page and click the link to make sure that it opens the new page.

Before You Begin

✔ **52** About Links
✔ **58** About New Pages
✔ **60** Use a Template to Make a New Page

TIP

When you start with a blank page, you might want to know how to define those general options for how the page will look: Background image (or color), text color, and so on. You'll discover these in **62** Choose a Background Color and Other General Settings.

TIP

When you publish, Contribute will offer a file-name for the new page based on the page's title. You can change the file-name to anything you want without affecting the title.

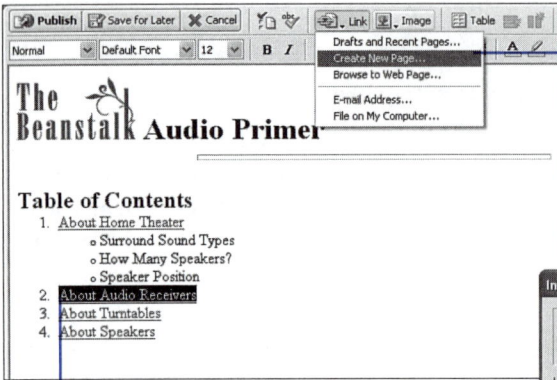

3 Click the Link Button and Choose Create New Page

1 Open the Page to Link From

The Beanstalk Audio Primer

Table of Contents
1. About Home Theater
   o Surround Sound Types
   o How Many Speakers?
   o Speaker Position
2. About Audio Receivers
3. About Turntables
4. About Speakers

Drafts and Recent Pages...
Create New Page...
Browse to Web Page...
E-mail Address...
File on My Computer...

2 Select the Link Text or Picture

4 Click Blank Web Page

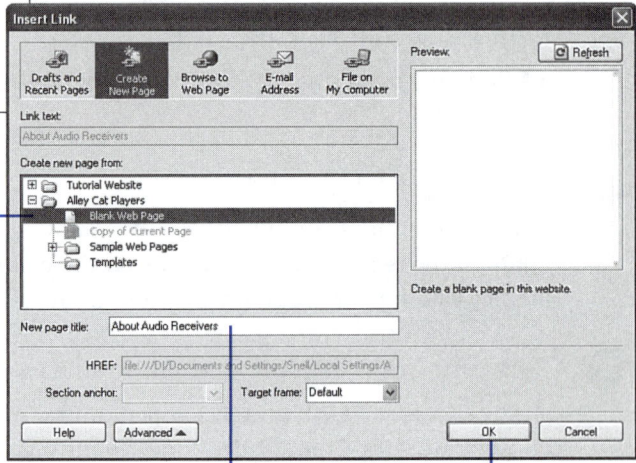

Insert Link

Drafts and Recent Pages | Create New Page | Browse to Web Page | E-mail Address | File on My Computer

Preview: Refresh

Link text:
About Audio Receivers

Create new page from:
⊞ 🗀 Tutorial Website
⊟ 🗀 Alley Cat Players
      Blank Web Page
      Copy of Current Page
   ⊞ 🗀 Sample Web Pages
      🗀 Templates

Create a blank page in this website.

New page title: About Audio Receivers

HREF: file:///D\Documents and Settings/Snell/Local Settings/A

Section anchor: | Target frame: Default

Help | Advanced ▲ | OK | Cancel

5 Title the Page and Click OK

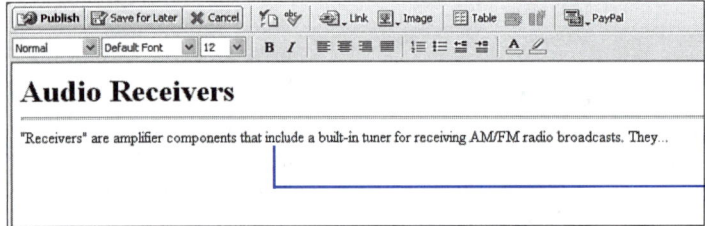

Publish | Save for Later | Cancel | Link | Image | Table | PayPal
Normal | Default Font | 12 | B I

Audio Receivers

"Receivers" are amplifier components that include a built-in tuner for receiving AM/FM radio broadcasts. They...

6 Create Your Content

About Audio Receivers - Microsoft Internet Explorer

File Edit View Favorites Tools Help

Back | Search | Favorites | Media

Address http://www.alleycatplayers.org/AboutAudioReceive_MMtmp6dad/AboutAudi | Go | Links | Web assistant

Audio Receivers

"Receivers" are amplifier components that include a built-in tuner for receiving AM/FM radio broadcasts. They...

7 Test the New Page

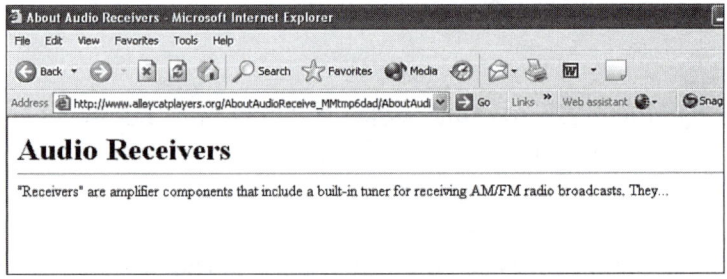

62 Choose a Background Color and Other General Settings

When you add a page based on an existing page or template, the background image (or color), text colors, and other general settings for how the page looks have already been defined for you. However, when you start with a blank page, you need to define these "page properties" yourself.

When choosing page properties, keep the following in mind:

- Background images should be in GIF or JPEG format and should meet all other web image requirements (**see** **24** **About Web Images**).

- Background images trump background colors. If you define both, what you'll see is the image, not the color.

- Tables and table cells can have their own background colors (**see** **50** **Add a Background Color to a Table**). If you define a background color for a table, that color appears there regardless of the page's background color. If you define no background color for a table, the page's background color shows through the table.

- Make sure that any choices you make for text color contrast well with the background (and table background, if any), so the text will be legible. That applies not only to the default text colors you choose in page properties, but also to any specific text colors you may add to selected text (**see** **20** **Change the Font, Size, or Color of Text**).

- If you go with a picture background, make sure it's not so busy that it makes the text appearing over it hard to read.

- Popular browsers let the user elect to reject "custom" colors specified in the page properties and instead display a set of "default" colors configured in the browser. Few folks use this option, but it's worth remembering that not everyone will see exactly the colors you specify.

Before You Begin

✔ **20** Change the Font, Size, or Color of Text

✔ **24** About Web Images

✔ **50** Add a Background Color to a Table

✔ **58** About New Pages

✔ **61** Create a New Blank Page

TIP

You can, of course, change such page properties as the background image or color for any page you can edit (if your administrator has given you permission to do so) by following steps 2–4 of this task. However, you should resist doing so, because those properties might have been defined as the "approved" properties for the site.

KEY TERM

Tiled—A background image that's repeated across the whole background. Some images designed for backgrounds are made to be tiled so that when repeated they form a pattern, such as a marbled texture.

➊ Open the Page in Edit Mode

Browse to the page for which you want to change properties and click the **Edit Page** button to switch to Edit mode.

➋ Choose Format, Page Properties

From the menu bar, choose **Format**, **Page Properties** (or click the **Page Properties** button on the toolbar). The **Page Properties** dialog box for the page you're editing opens, showing the current properties for that page.

➌ Choose Your Properties

Move among the tabs to choose your properties. To add a background image, open the **Appearance** tab, click the **Browse** button and browse to the image file you want to use. Alternatively, you may choose a color for the background by clicking the box next to **Background color** and choosing a color from the grid of color choices that appears.

Click the other "color" boxes beneath **Background color** if you want to choose the basic color for **Text**, the color of the **Link** text, the color of **Visited links**, or the color of of **Active links**.

Finally, you can vary the amount of blank space around all the content on your page by typing the number of pixels of space to add in the four **margin** boxes. A higher number adds more space around your content. (The exact amount of space, in inches, will vary with the visitor's monitor size and resolution.)

Click **OK** on the **Page Properties** dialog box to finish up.

➍ View the Result

View the result. If you're not happy with the results, simply return to step 2 and change the properties again.

The Beanstalk Audio Primer

Table of Contents

1. About Home Theater
   o Surround Sound Types
   o How Many Speakers?
   o Speaker Position
2. About Audio Receivers
3. About Turntables
4. About Speakers

Format

Check Spelling...	F7
Bold	Ctrl+B
Italic	Ctrl+I
Underline	Ctrl+U
Other	▶
Style	▶
Font	▶
Size	▶
Text Color...	
Highlight Color...	
Align	▶
List	▶
Indent	Ctrl+Alt+]
Outdent	Ctrl+Alt+[
Remove Link...	
Object Properties...	
Template Properties...	
Keywords and Description...	Ctrl+Alt+K
Page Properties...	Ctrl+J

Page Properties

Category: Title/Encoding, Appearance, Links, Headings

Appearance

Page font: Default Font **B** *I*

Size:

Text color:

Background color:

Background image: #EFEBDE Browse

Left margin:

Top margin:

Help   OK   Cancel   Apply

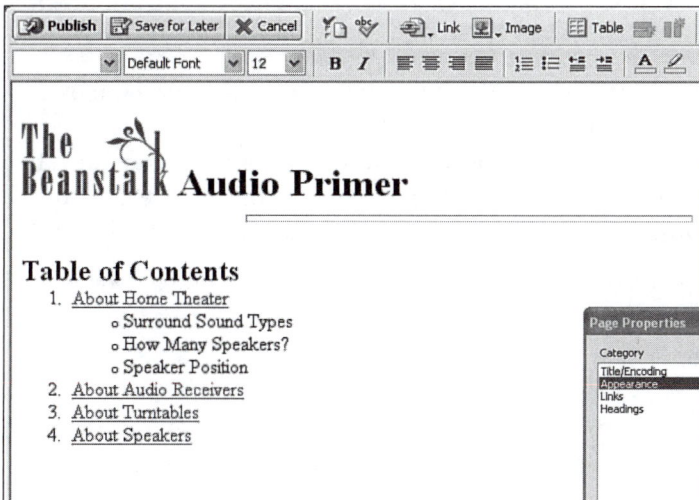

1 Open the Page in Edit Mode

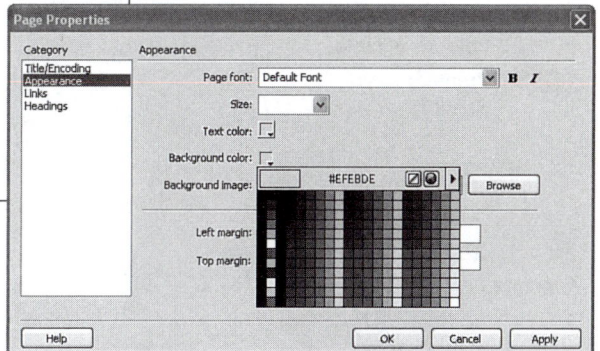

2 Choose Format, Page Properties

3 Choose Your Properties

4 View the Result

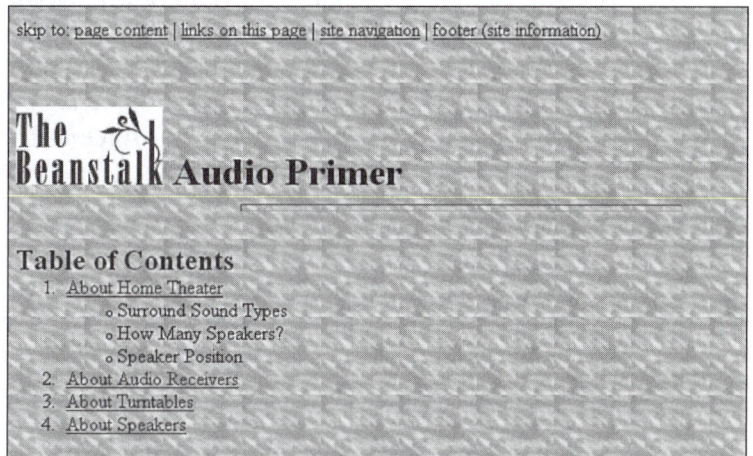

skip to: page content | links on this page | site navigation | footer (site information)

The Beanstalk Audio Primer

Table of Contents

1. About Home Theater
   o Surround Sound Types
   o How Many Speakers?
   o Speaker Position
2. About Audio Receivers
3. About Turntables
4. About Speakers

63 Use a Table to Arrange the Contents of a Page

Before You Begin

✔ **40** Edit or Add Text in a Table

✔ **41** Edit or Add Pictures in a Table

✔ **44** Change the Size of Rows and Columns

✔ **50** Add a Background Color to a Table

✔ **61** Create a New Blank Page

In some web pages, even some you might find among your templates, the overall layout of the page is defined by a table that takes up the entire page, with the position of each part of the content determined by which table cell it's in. You won't always know at first glance that this is the case because most such pages use tables with "invisible" borders.

Table-based pages are easy to make and edit, and provide a good way to take a new blank page quickly from an empty slate to a well ordered presentation.

1 Start with a New Blank Page

Follow the steps in **61** Create a New Blank Page to create a new page to fill in with your table.

2 Click Table

In Edit mode, click the **Table** button to open the **Insert Table** dialog box.

3 Format the Table

Begin by making the table the full width (100%) of the page: Next to **Table width**, click the option **Specific width**; in the box to the right of **Specific width**, type **100** and then choose **percent** from the list box to the right of that. You can use solid borders when laying out a page as a table, but in most cases, such tables have invisible borders. To make the borders invisible, delete any number you see in **Border thickness**. When finished, click **OK** on the **Insert Table** dialog box.

4 Fine-Tune the Layout

Fine-tune the layout by dragging the table gridlines (**see** **44** **Change the Size of Rows and Columns**) as desired. Alternatively, skip to step 5 to insert your content first and then drag the gridlines to fit the content into the most pleasing design.

5 Add your Content

Insert the text and pictures of your page into the table cells, as described in **40** **Edit or Add Text in a Table** and **41** **Edit or Add Pictures in a Table**.

> **TIP**
>
> Your table-based page's appearance may vary somewhat when viewed through monitors at different resolutions. For best results, format your page while viewing it at 800×600 resolution and test your page at a variety of resolutions. **See** **76** **Preview Your Work**.

> **NOTE**
>
> After you click **OK** in step 3, your new table will appear to have a solid border around it and dashed gridlines within, even if you cleared the **Border thickness** box. These are just guidelines to help you format the table; they won't show up online.

2 Click Table

| Publish | Save for Later | Cancel | | Link | Image | Table | | | PayPal |

| Normal | Default Font | 12 | **B** *I* | | | | | |

1 Start with a New Blank Page

Insert Table

Table size
Number of rows: 5
Number of columns: 2

Options
Table width: ○ Default width
● Specific width: 100   pixels
pixels
percent
Border thickness: 0   pixels
Cell padding: pixels between border and content
Cell spacing: pixels between cells

Header

None   Left   Top   Both

Help   OK   Cancel

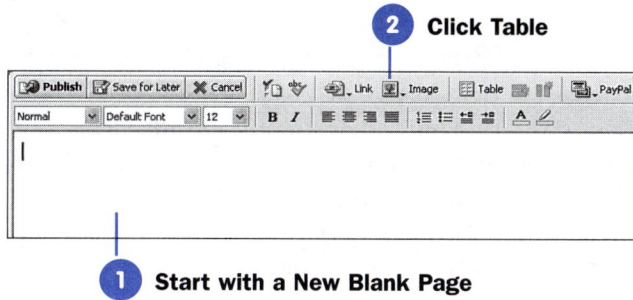

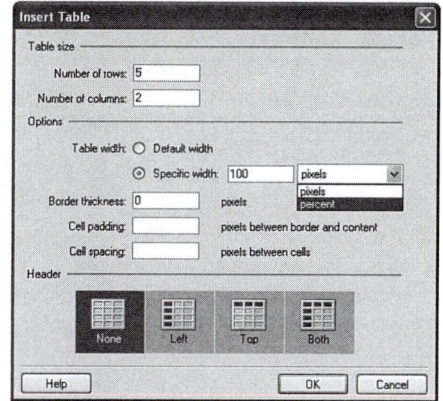

3 Format the Table

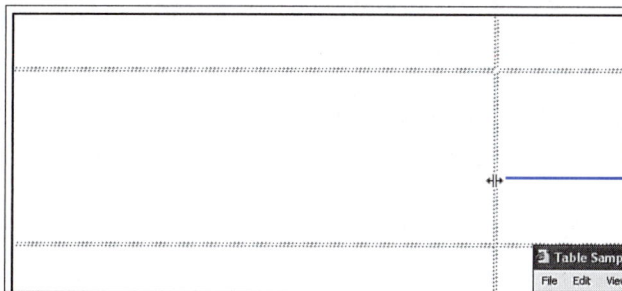

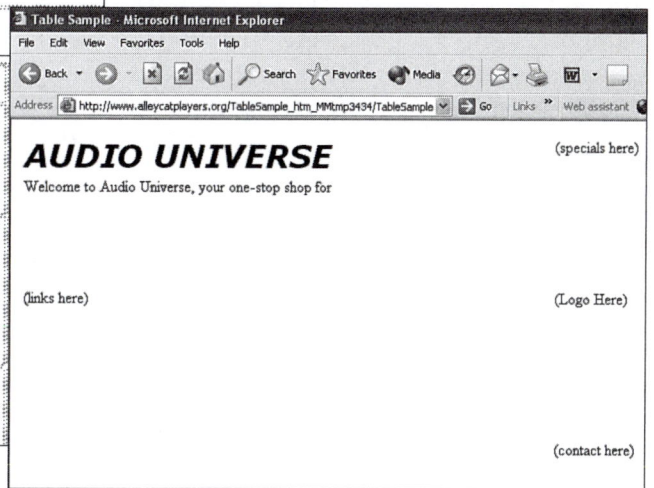

4 Fine-Tune the Layout

AUDIO UNIVERSE
Welcome to Audio Universe, your one-stop shop for

(links here)

Table Sample - Microsoft Internet Explorer

File   Edit   View   Favorites   Tools   Help

Back ▼   ▼   Search   Favorites   Media

Address http://www.alleycatplayers.org/TableSample_htm_MMtmp3434/TableSample   Go   Links   Web assistant

AUDIO UNIVERSE   (specials here)
Welcome to Audio Universe, your one-stop shop for

(links here)   (Logo Here)

(contact here)

5 Add Your Content

6 View the Result

6 View the Result

To view the result, publish your page and see how it looks in
Browse mode or view it through your browser. Return as necessary
to Edit mode to make any further changes.

64 Delete Pages

Before You Begin

✔ **58** About New Pages

Sure, you can delete pages from your site, and doing so is easy. The only caveat is that, for obvious reasons, many administrators deny contributors permission to delete pages from the site. If you need to delete a page and discover in step 2 that **Delete Page** is grayed out, you do not have permission to delete that page. Ask your administrator to delete it for you or to give you permission to do it yourself.

1 Browse to the Page to Delete

In Browse mode, open the page you want to delete.

2 Choose File, Action, Delete Page

From the menu bar, choose **File**, **Delete Page**. A message appears asking whether you're sure you want to delete the page.

3 Click Yes

To delete the page, click **Yes**.

1 Browse to the Page to Delete

3 Click Yes

2 Choose File, Actions, Delete Page

9

Inserting Documents in Word, Excel, and Other Formats

IN THIS CHAPTER:

KEY TERM

Microsoft Office—Catchall term for a family of application programs from Microsoft. Office programs are available individually or in a variety of "suites" that usually include the word processing program Word and the spreadsheet program Excel, and may also include the slideshow maker PowerPoint, the database program Access, and others.

Often, the content you need to add to your Contribute Web site already exists in another document form. A staff directory, for example, might already exist in Word or in another Microsoft Office file format. A listing of products, for example, and prices might exist in an Excel spreadsheet.

You can save yourself a lot of typing—and reduce the chances that you'll introduce an error—if you take advantage of Contribute's built-in document conversion features to copy such content directly into your Contribute pages.

65 About Inserting External Documents

KEY TERM

FlashPaper—A utility in the Windows version of Contribute that lets you insert content from almost any Windows program into your Contribute pages. For more, see **68** About FlashPaper.

Contribute offers two ways to copy existing content into your pages:

- **Insert Microsoft Office Document**—If your document is in Word or Excel format (Office 2000 or later versions), you can pull it directly into your Contribute Web site in a few simple steps.

- **FlashPaper**—Any other type of document you might have can be copied into your page with Contribute's FlashPaper utility. However, FlashPaper forces a few compromises on the content while doing so and should generally be used only as a last resort.

These two options enable you to insert external documents into your pages quickly. However, there is another way to add almost any kind of content to your page—inserting a link to the file containing the content. When you do this, the content does not appear automatically in your page, but will appear whenever a visitor clicks the link. This approach has a number of advantages, as you'll discover in **67** Link to a Word or Excel File.

66 Insert a Word or Excel File into a Web Page

You can insert virtually any Word or Excel file into a Contribute Web page as long as:

- The file is in Office version 2000 or higher format.

- The file is smaller than 300KB. (If you try to insert a larger file, Contribute displays a dialog box reporting that the file is too large and offers other options for inserting it, such as FlashPaper.)

When you insert a file this way, Contribute converts the file's contents to HTML (Web page format) in the web page, preserving as much of the original formatting as possible in HTML. (Word files come over as formatted text, and Excel files come over as web page tables.) In your page, you may edit and format the content as you would any other Contribute content.

1 Open the Page to Add the Content To

In Contribute, open in Edit mode (or create) the web page to which you want to add Word or Excel content.

2 Click Where You Want to Add Content

Click at the spot within your draft where you want to insert the content so that the insertion point appears there.

3 Choose Insert, Microsoft Office Document

From the menu bar, choose **Insert, Microsoft Office Document**. The **Open** dialog box appears.

4 Navigate to the File and Choose Open

Using the **Open** dialog box, navigate to the folder containing the Word or Excel file you want to use. Click the file's name in the list and then click the **Open** button. The **Insert Microsoft Office Document** dialog box opens.

Before You Begin

✔ **65** About Inserting External Documents

💡 TIP

If you want to insert only a portion of a Word or Excel document and not the whole thing, make a copy of the file in Word or Excel, edit the copy down to just the portion you want to use, and then insert the edited copy in your Web page as described in this task. You can also use standard copy-and-paste techniques to copy portions of Office documents from an Office document into a Contribute page.

My Resume

2 Click Where You Want to Add Content

1 Open the Page to Add the Content To

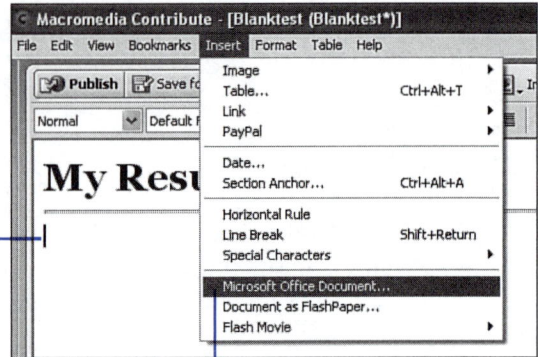

3 Choose Insert, Microsoft Office Document

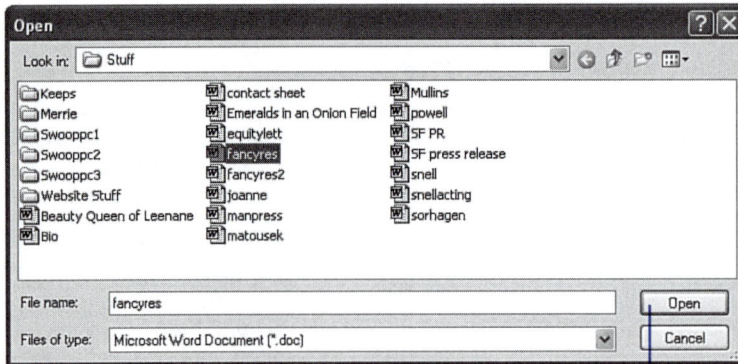

5 Choose Insert the Contents of the Document into This Page

4 Navigate to the File and Choose Open

6 View the Result

My Resume

SAG/AFTRA   Height: 5' 9"
555-555-5555| Green Eyes, Brown Hair

Pato, *BEAUTY QUEEN OF LEENANE,* Jobsite Theater, Tampa, FL. Dir: Paul Potenza
Sir Thomas More, *A MAN FOR ALL SEASONS* , Alley Cat Players, Tampa, FL. Dir: Jo Averill
Ralph, *A CHRISTMAS STORY* , American Stage, St. Petersburg, FL. Dir: Van Huff
Marc, *ART* , Tampa Bay Performing Arts Center, Tampa, FL. Dir: Wendy Leigh
Starling, *CAMPING WITH HENRY & TOM* , American Stage, St. Petersburg, FL. Dir: Wendy Leigh
Terry, *SIDE SHOW,* Gorilla Theatre, Tampa, FL. Dir: Brett Smock
All Roles, *ABOUT THE AUTHOR...* , Alley Cat Players, Tampa, FL. Dir: Self
Ensemble, *A THURBER CARNIVAL,* Gorilla Theatre, Tampa, FL. Dir: Steve Mountan

5 **Choose Insert the Contents of the Document Into This Page**

On the **Insert Microsoft Office Document** dialog box, choose **Insert the contents of the document into this page** to indicate that you want to copy the entire contents of the file as new web page content into your page and then click **OK**.

6 **View the Result**

The contents of the Word or Excel document appear in your draft.

NOTE

After you insert Word or Excel content, it's disconnected from the original document. Changes you make to that content in your page are not reflected in the original file and vice versa. If you want the web page content to change whenever the original document changes, try **67** **Link to a Word or Excel File.**

67 Link to a Word or Excel File

Instead of copying the full content of a Word or Excel file into your page, you can insert a link to that content. Contribute automatically uploads the Word or Excel file to your web server when you publish the page, and when a visitor clicks the link, the file downloads and displays on the visitor's computer.

This approach comes in handy in several situations, such as the following:

- The content is too long to display in a web page of a reasonable length.

- The file is too large (larger than 300KB) to convert in Contribute.

- The file contains content that only some visitors are likely to want to see, so there's no point in showing it to everybody. (Keep in mind that linking to the file in no way hides it—it's still on the Net and can still be seen by anyone who wants to see it.)

- The file is one that's updated and changed often. In such situations, all you need to do is republish the page containing the link each time the file is changed to make the latest information available.

Before You Begin

✔ **54** Edit an Existing Link's Text or Image

✔ **65** About Inserting External Documents

✔ **66** Insert a Word or Excel File into a Web Page

1 Open the Page to Add the Content To

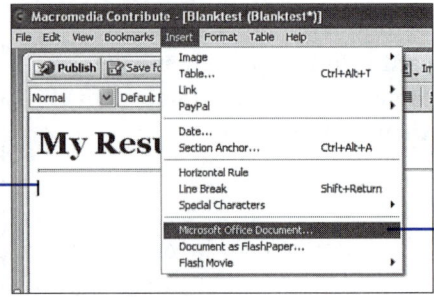

2 Click Where You Want the Link

3 Choose Insert, Microsoft Office Document

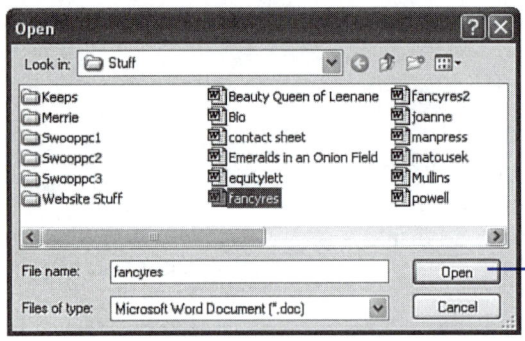

4 Navigate to the File and Choose Open

5 Choose Create a Link To the Document

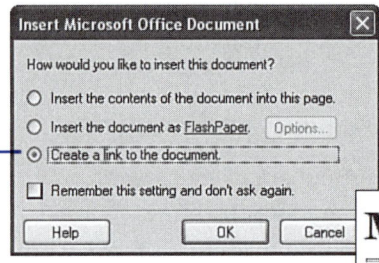

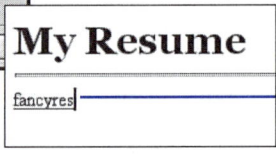

6 Edit the Link Text

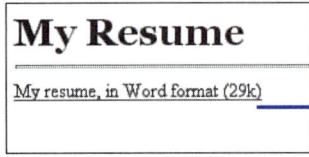

My Resume

fancyres

7 Test Your New Link

My Resume

My resume, in Word format (29k)

Of course, there are drawbacks to this approach as well. When you convert Word or Excel files as described in **66** **Insert a Word or Excel File into a Web Page**, the content is converted to HTML, viewable through any browser. When you link to a file as described here, the visitor can't view the content unless his browser and/or computer are configured for viewing Word or Excel files. Most folks are set up to view these files, so it's not a huge concern, but it is one worth keeping in mind.

1 Open the Page to Add the Content to

In Contribute, open in Edit mode (or create) the web page to which you want to add Word or Excel content.

2 Click Where You Want to Insert the Link

Click the spot within your draft where you want to insert the link so that the insertion point appears there.

3 Choose Insert, Microsoft Office Document

From the menu bar, choose **Insert, Microsoft Office Document**. The **Open** dialog box appears.

4 Navigate to the File and Choose Open

Using the **Open** dialog box, navigate to the folder containing the Word or Excel file you want to use. Click the file's name in the list and then click **Open**.

5 Choose Create a Link To the Document

On the **Insert Microsoft Office Document** dialog box, choose **Create a link to the document** to indicate that you want to insert a link in your page that downloads and displays the document and then click **OK**.

6 Edit the Link Text

In your web page, a new link appears, using the filename of the document you selected in step 4 as the link text. You might want to edit that text to something more descriptive or replace the link text with a picture, as described in **54** **Edit an Existing Link's Text or Image**.

NOTE

As long as the original Word or Excel file's location on disk or its filename are not changed when the file gets updated, you can make the latest version available online simply by republishing the page that links to it. If either the filename or location are changed, however, you must re-create the link to match.

TIP

It's good practice to edit the link text so that it reports the format of the file (Word or Excel) and the size of the file (in kilobytes). That way, your visitors can determine whether they can display the file and whether they want to wait through the download of a file of that size before clicking the link.

7 **Test Your New Link**

To test your new link, publish the page and then click the link. The Word or Excel document should download and display.

68 About FlashPaper

See Also

✔ **32** About Flash Movies

FlashPaper is an unusual utility (although a handy one), and it requires a little explaining.

When you install Contribute, FlashPaper automatically adds a new print driver to Windows. When you use Contribute to add content to your site through FlashPaper, Contribute sends that content to the FlashPaper printer driver, as if it were going to be printed. However, instead of actually printing the content, FlashPaper captures the content and converts it into a Flash movie, which it then inserts it into a Flash window in your page.

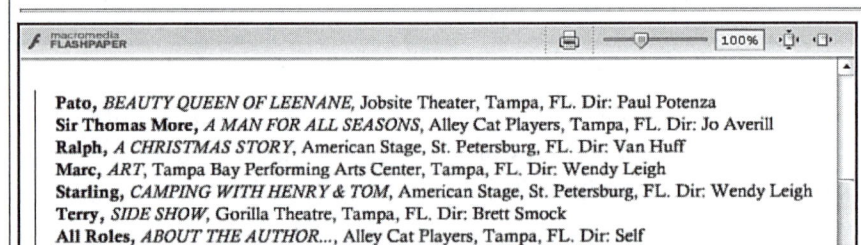

My Resume

macromedia FLASHPAPER | 100%

Pato, *BEAUTY QUEEN OF LEENANE,* Jobsite Theater, Tampa, FL. Dir: Paul Potenza
Sir Thomas More, *A MAN FOR ALL SEASONS,* Alley Cat Players, Tampa, FL. Dir: Jo Averill
Ralph, *A CHRISTMAS STORY,* American Stage, St. Petersburg, FL. Dir: Van Huff
Marc, *ART,* Tampa Bay Performing Arts Center, Tampa, FL. Dir: Wendy Leigh
Starling, *CAMPING WITH HENRY & TOM,* American Stage, St. Petersburg, FL. Dir: Wendy Leigh
Terry, *SIDE SHOW,* Gorilla Theatre, Tampa, FL. Dir: Brett Smock
All Roles, *ABOUT THE AUTHOR...,* Alley Cat Players, Tampa, FL. Dir: Self

FlashPaper converts any printable content into a Flash movie so it can be displayed in your website.

The Flash window displays a set of standard controls above the document: a printer icon for printing the document, a slider for zooming in or out, buttons for orienting the document within the window, and page buttons for moving through the pages of the document (if it contains more than one page). These same controls will appear in the browser of any visitor who displays this page after it's published.

Because FlashPaper functions as a print driver, virtually any file that can be printed can be picked up by FlashPaper and displayed in your Contribute website, no matter what program created it originally. That's a powerful convenience—but there are a few minor limitations to keep in mind before using FlashPaper.

- First and foremost, your visitors can display the content you insert through FlashPaper *only* if their browser is equipped to play Flash movies or if they've installed a Flash player. There's so much Flash content on the Web these days that most folks can watch Flash movies (97% of Internet-enabled desktops worldwide, according to Macromedia), but not all can, or want to.

- Secondly, content displayed in a Flash movie can't be copied as text by the visitor. Sometimes, you want your visitors to be able to make use of what they find on your site.

For these reasons, it's best to carefully consider other options (such as converting a file to Word or Excel format and then inserting it) before resorting to FlashPaper.

69 Use FlashPaper to Insert a Document in Any Format

FlashPaper is your solution when content you want in your page (but don't want to re-create) exists in some format other than Word or Excel. Before starting the steps, make sure you know the folder and filename of the file you want to use.

Before You Begin

✔ **65** About Inserting External Documents

✔ **68** About FlashPaper

1 Open the Page to Add the Content To

In Contribute, open in Edit mode (or create) the web page to which you want to add FlashPaper content.

2 Click Where You Want to Add Content

Click at the spot within your draft where you want to insert the FlashPaper content.

3 Choose Insert, Document as FlashPaper

From the menu bar, choose **Insert, Document as FlashPaper**. The **Open** dialog box appears.

1 Open the Page to Add the Content To

Macromedia Contribute - [Blanktest (Blanktest*)]

File   Edit   View   Bookmarks   Insert   Format   Table   Help

Publish   Save fo

Image   ▶
Table...   Ctrl+Alt+T

Normal   Default F

Link   ▶
PayPal   ▶

Press Relea

Date...
Section Anchor...   Ctrl+Alt+A

2 Click Where You
Want to Add Content

Horizontal Rule
Line Break   Shift+Return
Special Characters   ▶

Microsoft Office Document...

Document as FlashPaper...

Flash Movie   ▶

3 Choose Insert,
Document as
FlashPaper

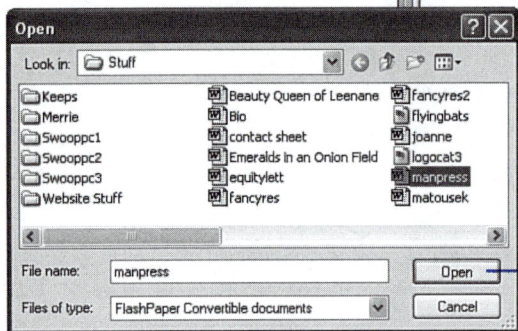

Open

Look in: 📁 Stuff   ▼ ◎ 👤 📂 🎛▾

📁 Keeps   📄 Beauty Queen of Leenane   📄 fancyres2
📁 Merrie   📄 Bio   📄 flyingbats
📁 Swooppc1   📄 contact sheet   📄 joanne
📁 Swooppc2   📄 Emeralds in an Onion Field 📄 logocat3
📁 Swooppc3   📄 equitylett   📄 manpress
📁 Website Stuff   📄 fancyres   📄 matousek

File name: manpress   Open

Files of type: FlashPaper Convertible documents ▼   Cancel

5 Choose Your FlashPaper Options

FlashPaper Options   ✕

ⓘ The document you're inserting will be displayed on the web page as
   FlashPaper. The following options control the appearance of the
   document:

Page orientation: ⊙ 🄰 Portrait

                   ○ 🄰 Landscape

Page size: ⊙ Standard: Letter   ▼

            ○ Custom: 4   x   6   inch ▼

Help   OK   Cancel

4 Navigate to the File and Choose Open

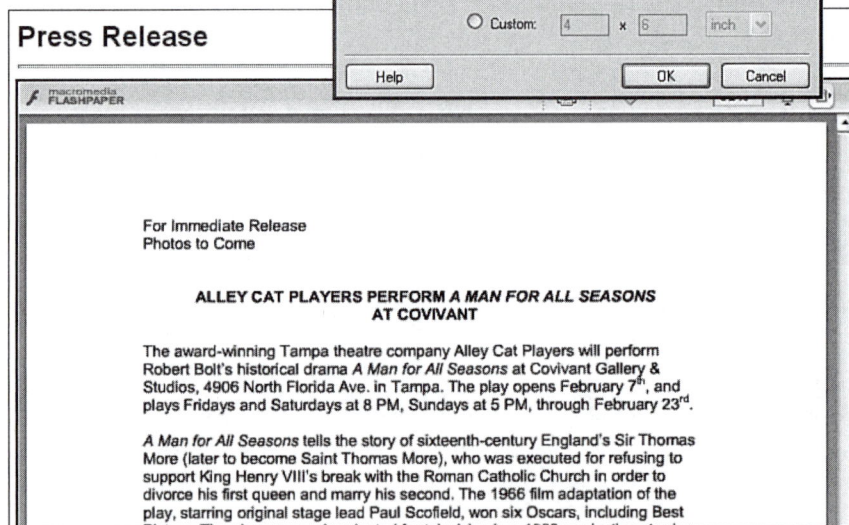

Press Release

macromedia
FLASHPAPER

For Immediate Release
Photos to Come

**ALLEY CAT PLAYERS PERFORM *A MAN FOR ALL SEASONS*
AT COVIVANT**

The award-winning Tampa theatre company Alley Cat Players will perform
Robert Bolt's historical drama *A Man for All Seasons* at Covivant Gallery &
Studios, 4906 North Florida Ave. in Tampa. The play opens February 7th, and
plays Fridays and Saturdays at 8 PM, Sundays at 5 PM, through February 23rd.

A Man for All Seasons tells the story of sixteenth-century England's Sir Thomas
More (later to become Saint Thomas More), who was executed for refusing to
support King Henry VIII's break with the Roman Catholic Church in order to
divorce his first queen and marry his second. The 1966 film adaptation of the
play, starring original stage lead Paul Scofield, won six Oscars, including Best

6 View the Result

4 Navigate to the File and Choose Open

Using the **Open** dialog box, navigate to the folder containing the file you want to insert. Click the file's name in the list and then click **Open**. The **FlashPaper Options** dialog box appears.

5 Choose Your FlashPaper Options

In the **FlashPaper Options** dialog box, select among options controlling how the Flash movie will appear in your web page:

- Page Orientation—Choose **Portrait** to display the document in a window that's taller than it is wide (as you would for a typical printed document) or choose **Landscape** to display the document in a window that's wider than it is tall (as you would for a slide).

- Page Size—Choose a standard paper size from the list or choose the **Custom** option and enter dimensions for the window in which the document will appear.

After choosing your options, click **OK**.

6 View the Result

Contribute converts the document to FlashPaper and inserts it in the draft; this may take a minute or two, during which Contribute displays a message informing you that it is "carefully" converting the document to FlashPaper.

When you see the Flash window in your page displaying the document, you can publish the page or continue editing it.

10

Editing Content in Pages That Are Divided Into Frames

IN THIS CHAPTER:

By design, Contribute doesn't let you do much with pages based on frames. However, if you have a frames-based page among those you edit, there are a few ways you can change its content and behavior.

These capabilities not only help you with changes you might need to make, but also have the added benefit of helping you understand how a frames-based page works so that if you move on to a more elaborate web-authoring program some day, you'll find working with frames a snap.

70 About Frames

KEY TERM

Frames–Multiple panes in a browser window, each of which displays a different web page file. Web authors design frames pages to enable visitors to use the frames together as a single, multilevel web page.

NOTE

Frames-based pages are not always as easy to identify as the one shown in the figure. Web authors can create frames-based pages with no borders between panels or no scrollbars.

As you can see in the figure, frames-based pages are divided onscreen into two or more panels, or _frames_. Unlike most web pages, frames-based pages are made up of multiple web page (HTML) files.

The content of a frames-based page is contained in separate web page files, one or more for each frame. Within its frame, each file operates independently; it can be scrolled up or down, or replaced by another file, without affecting other files in other panels. Often, a link in a file in one panel will open a new file in the same frame or in a different frame. In the page shown in the figure, clicking each link in the file displayed in the left panel opens a different file in the right panel.

Because frames are tricky business, Contribute doesn't let you do much with them. You can't create a frames-based page in Contribute, even by copying an existing frames-based page on your site. You can't make any changes that require edits to the frameset file. However, there are a few things you _can_ do when you need to make changes to a frames-based page:

- Edit any of the individual content files that appear in the frames, just as if they were standalone web pages.

- Replace the entire file that appears in a frame with a different one.

- Create links in a file in one panel that open a file in a different panel.

Frameset URL   Frameset

Web page file   Web page file

Frames-based pages are divided up into two or more frames, each containing a separate web document.

71 Edit the Content in One Frame Within a Page

Editing the content in the separate content files that make up a frames-based page is just like editing any page in Contribute. The only added steps are to get the file open for editing. After the file is open in Edit mode, you are free to change it in any way described in this book. When you publish, your changes to individual files will be reflected in the frames that appear online.

Keep in mind that while you're editing the file, it occupies the whole screen, but when it appears online, it will be squeezed into only a portion of the screen. For this reason, keep an eye on the size of the area occupied by any pictures you add, and preview your work often to make sure that what looks good while you're editing still looks good when boxed into a frame.

Before You Begin

✔ **70** About Frames

Edit Page | New Page | Back | Forward | Stop | Refresh | Home Pages | C

Address: http://alleycatplayers.org/UntitledFrameset-2.htm | Go | Choose...

The Beanstalk

About Our Products

Staff Directory

Ordering Information

Mailing List

About Beanstalk Products

Lorem ipsum dolor sit amet, consetetur sadipscing elitr, sed diam nonumy eirmod tempor invidunt ut labore et dolore magna aliquyam erat, sed diam voluptua. Lorem ipsum dolor sit amet, consetetur sadipscing elitr, sed diam nonumy eirmod tempor invidunt ut labore et dolore magna aliquyam erat, sed diam voluptua. Lorem ipsum dolor sit amet, consetetur sadipscing elitr, sed diam nonumy eirmod tempor invidunt ut labore et dolore magna aliquyam erat, sed diam voluptua. Lorem ipsum dolor sit amet, consetetur sadipscing elitr, sed diam nonumy eirmod tempor invidunt ut labore et dolore magna aliquyam erat, sed diam voluptua.

Where Shall We Go?

Done

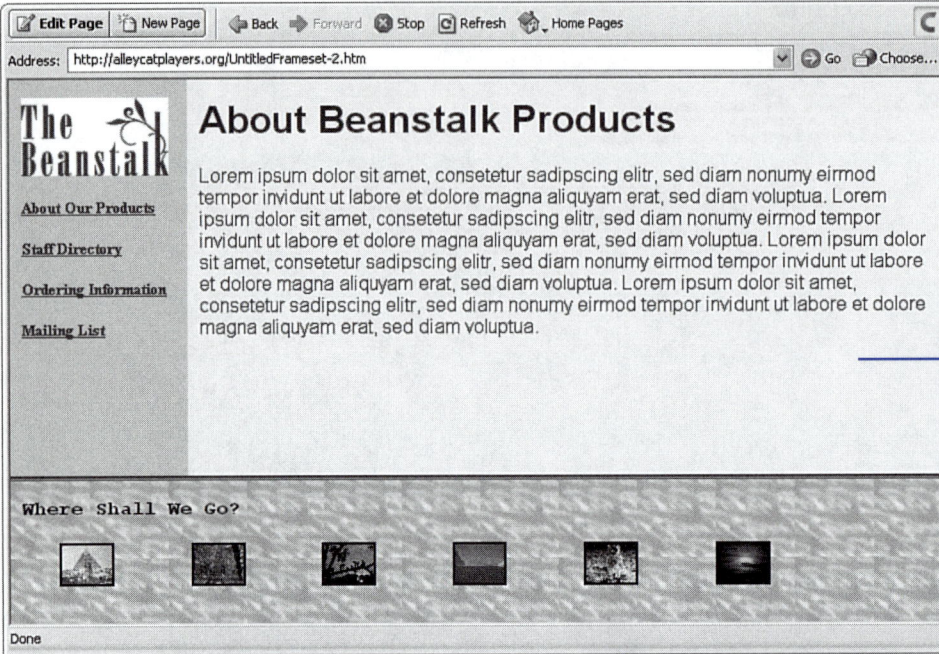

1 Open the Frames Page

4 Click Edit Page

About Beanstalk P

Lorem ipsum dolor sit amet, consetetur s
tempor invidunt ut labore et dolore magn
ipsum dolor sit a
invidunt ut labore
sit amet, conset
et dolore magna
consetetur sadip
magna aliquyam

Back
Forward

Save Background As...
Set as Background
Copy Background
Set as Desktop Item...

Select All
Paste

Create Shortcut
Add to Favorites...
View Source

Encoding ▶

Print
Refresh

Properties

Go?

2 Open the Properties for the Frame to Edit

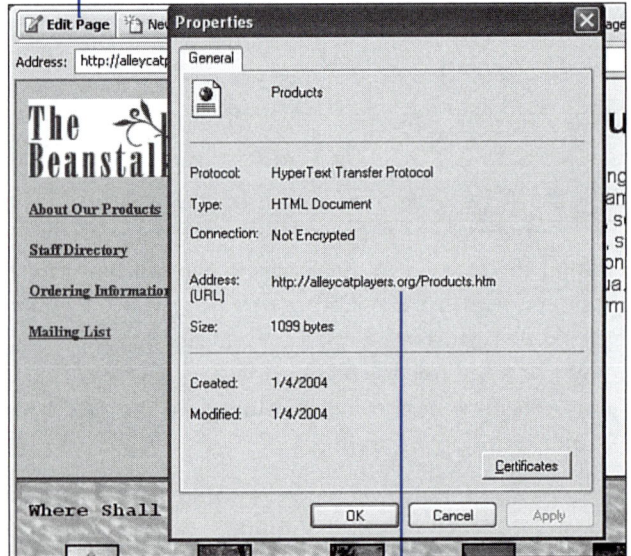

Edit Page | New | age

Address: http://alleycatp

The Beanstal

About Our Products

Staff Directory

Ordering Informatio

Mailing List

Where Shall

Properties ☒

General

Products

Protocol: HyperText Transfer Protocol

Type: HTML Document

Connection: Not Encrypted

Address: http://alleycatplayers.org/Products.htm
(URL)

Size: 1099 bytes

Created: 1/4/2004

Modified: 1/4/2004

Certificates

OK | Cancel | Apply

3 Note the Full Address of the Frame Content

Select a Frame to Edit

(i) The web page you want to edit consists of multiple pages called frames.

Select the frame you want to edit:

Link Panel - http://alleycatplayers.org/Links.htm
Products - http://alleycatplayers.org/Products.htm
Samples - http://alleycatplayers.org/Samples.htm

Note: When you select a frame, Contribute highlights that frame in the browser.

[Help]   [Edit]   [Cancel]

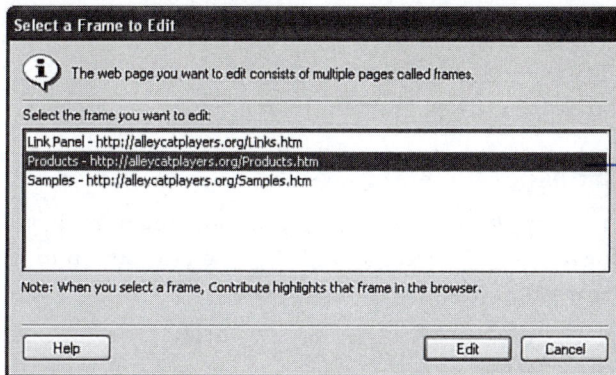

⑤ Choose Your File

☑ Edit Page   ⬚ New Page   ◀ Back   ➡ Forward   ⊗ Stop   ↻ Refresh   🏠 Home Pages

Address: http://alleycatplayers.org/Products.htm   ☑ ⊕ Go 📂 Choose...

About Beanstalk Products

Lorem ipsum dolor sit amet, consetetur sadipscing elitr, sed diam nonumy eirmod tempor invidunt ut labore et dolore magna aliquyam erat, sed diam voluptua. Lorem ipsum dolor sit amet, consetetur sadipscing elitr, sed diam nonumy eirmod tempor invidunt ut labore et dolore magna aliquyam erat, sed diam voluptua. Lorem ipsum dolor sit amet, consetetur sadipscing elitr, sed diam nonumy eirmod tempor invidunt ut labore et dolore magna aliquyam erat, sed diam voluptua. Lorem ipsum dolor sit amet, consetetur sadipscing elitr, sed diam nonumy eirmod tempor invidunt ut labore et dolore magna aliquyam erat, sed diam voluptua.

⑥ Edit Away

① Open the Frames Page

In Browse mode, open the frames-based page containing the frame content you want to edit.

② Open the Properties for the Frame to Edit

Point anywhere in the frame you want to edit (except to a link or picture) and right-click to display the pop-up menu. Choose **Properties** from the pop-up menu to display the **Properties** dialog box for the frame you clicked.

③ Note the Full Address of the Frame Content

In the **Properties** dialog box, the **Address** line shows the full URL of the file in that frame. Jot down the URL and then click **OK** to close the **Properties** dialog box.

4 **Click Edit Page**

Click the **Edit Page** button. Contribute displays a list of the files that appear in the frames of the frameset you're viewing.

5 **Choose Your File**

In the list, find the file whose full URL matches the one you jotted down in step 3, select it, and click the **Edit** button on the **Select a Frame to Edit** dialog box.

6 **Edit Away**

You can now edit the frame content any way you want. Publish the frames-based page or preview it to see your changes.

---

72 **Choose What Content Appears Within a Frame**

Before You Begin

✔ **60** Use a Template to Make a New Page

✔ **61** Create a New Blank Page

✔ **70** About Frames

The frameset lists by filename the file(s) that appear in each frame. You can't edit the frameset, so to completely replace the contents of a frame, you need to trick the frameset by replacing the file in a frame with a new one that has the *exact same name* and *is stored in the exact same location*, both online and off. Doing this requires a little digging to learn the filename of the file you're replacing, but stick to the steps and you'll do fine.

1 **Open the Frames Page**

In Browse mode, open the frames-based page containing the frame content you want to replace.

2 **Open the Properties for the Frame to Replace**

Point anywhere in the frame in which you want to replace the content (except to a link or picture) and right-click to display the pop-up menu. Choose **Properties** from the pop-up menu to display the **Properties** dialog box for the frame you clicked.

③ Note the Full Address of the Frame Contents

In the **Properties** dialog box, the **Address** line shows the full URL of the file in that frame. Jot down the URL, paying special attention to the file's filename—it's the very end portion of the URL, after the last slash (/), usually ending in **.htm** or **.html**. Click **OK** to close the **Properties** dialog box.

④ Click Edit Page

Click the **Edit Page** button. Contribute displays a list of the files that appear in the frames of the frameset you're viewing.

⑤ Choose Your File

In the list, find the file whose full URL matches the one you jotted down in step 3, select it, and click the **Edit** button on the **Select a Frame to Edit** dialog box.

⑥ Delete the Page

Choose **File, Actions, Delete Page** to delete the page.

⑦ Add a New Page

Create your new page, using any of the new page creation steps shown in Chapter 8, "Working with New Pages."

⑧ Publish and Name the File

Click **Publish** to publish your new page. The **Publish As New Page** dialog box appears. In **Filename**, type the exact filename (jotted down in step 3) of the page you deleted in step 6 and then click the **Publish** button on the **Publish As New Page** dialog box.

⑨ View the Result

To view the result, browse back to the original frameset page you opened in step 1. Your new file appears in the frame where the file you deleted once appeared.

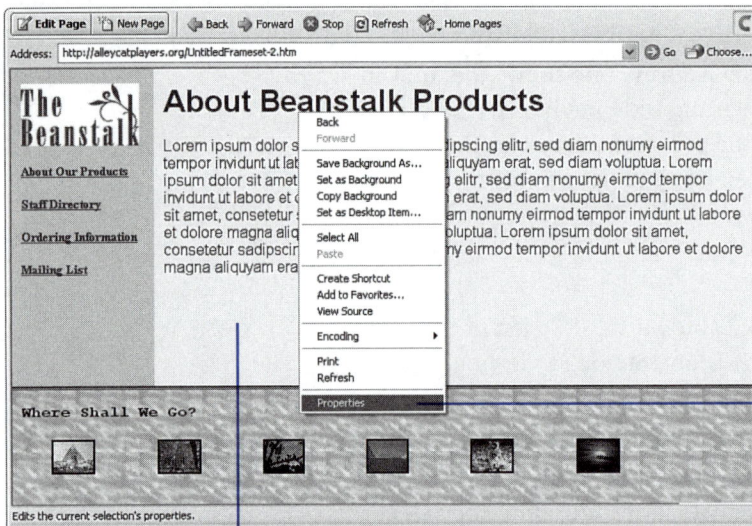

1 Open the Frames Page

2 Open the Properties for the Frame to Replace

4 Click Edit Page

5 Choose Your File

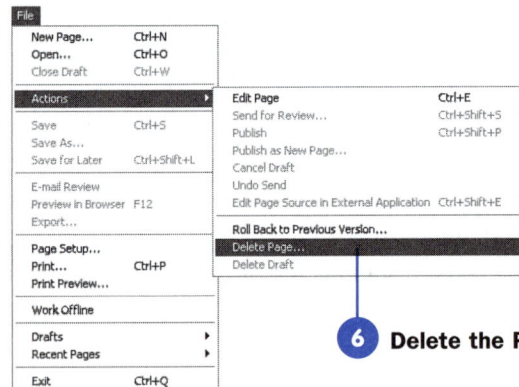

3 Note the Full Address of the Frame Contents

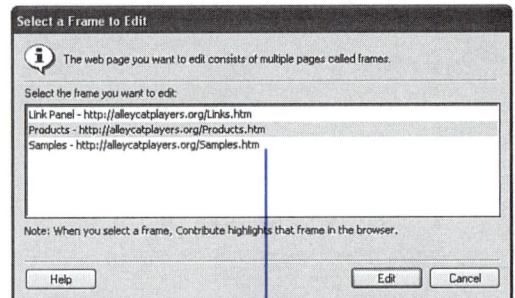

6 Delete the Page

7 Add a New Page

Publish As New Page

Please enter a filename for this new page. The filename will become part of the page's web address on your website.

Page title: standard designs

Filename: Samples.htm   Choose Folder...

Web address: http://www.alleycatplayers.org/Samples.htm

Help   Publish   Cancel

8 Publish and Name the File

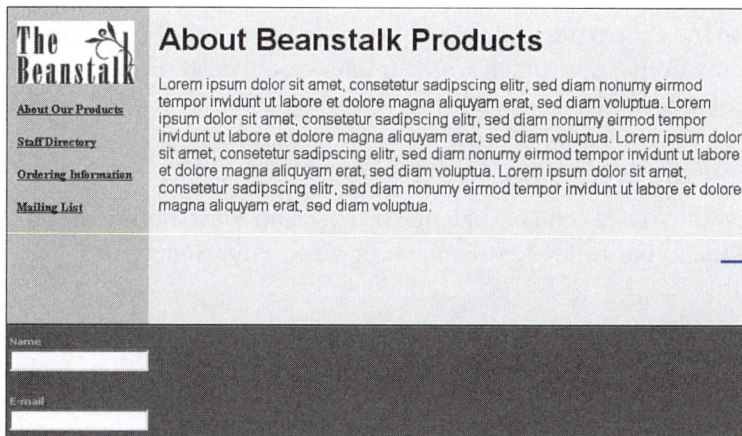

About Beanstalk Products

The Beanstalk

About Our Products

Staff Directory

Ordering Information

Mailing List

Lorem ipsum dolor sit amet, consetetur sadipscing elitr, sed diam nonumy eirmod tempor invidunt ut labore et dolore magna aliquyam erat, sed diam voluptua. Lorem ipsum dolor sit amet, consetetur sadipscing elitr, sed diam nonumy eirmod tempor invidunt ut labore et dolore magna aliquyam erat, sed diam voluptua. Lorem ipsum dolor sit amet, consetetur sadipscing elitr, sed diam nonumy eirmod tempor invidunt ut labore et dolore magna aliquyam erat, sed diam voluptua. Lorem ipsum dolor sit amet, consetetur sadipscing elitr, sed diam nonumy eirmod tempor invidunt ut labore et dolore magna aliquyam erat, sed diam voluptua.

Name

E-mail

9 View the Result

73 Create a Link That Points to a Particular Frame

By default, any link in a frame that opens a new page opens that page in the same frame, replacing in the frame the file containing the link. However, you can edit links so that a link in one frame opens a file in a different frame. This is a handy technique when you want one panel to serve as a directory of links, each of which opens a new file in another panel.

① **Edit the Frames Page**

Browse to the frames-based page and click the **Edit Page** button.

② **Preview the Page**

Choose **File**, **Preview in Browser** to open the page in your default web browser.

③ **Note the URL for Each Frame**

For each frame, point anywhere in the frame and right-click to display the pop-up menu. Choose **Properties** from the pop-up menu to display the **Properties** dialog box for the frame you clicked.

In the **Properties** dialog box, the Address line shows the full URL of the file in that frame. Jot down the URL and then click **OK** to close the **Properties** dialog box. When finished, you'll know which file (by name) appears in which frame—you'll need this information later.

④ **View the HTML Source Code**

View the source code of the page by choosing **View**, **Source** from the menu bar in Internet Explorer or **View**, **Page Source** in Netscape.

⑤ **Find the Name of the Frame**

The source code will contain a group of lines that begins with **frame name=**. These are the lines that determine the names of the frames. The word immediately to the right of **frame name=** in each line is the name of the frame. Find the **frame name=** line containing the name of the file that now resides in your target frame.

6 Return to Contribute

Return to the frameset page in Contribute, click **Edit Page** to switch to Edit mode, and open the list of files appearing in the frames.

7 Choose Your File

In the list, find the file in which you want to add or edit the link that will open a file in a different frame, select it, and click the **Edit** button on the dialog box.

8 Add the Text or Image for the Link

If the page does not already contain the link text or picture you want to use for the link, type the text for it in the page or insert the image for the link.

9 Select the Link Text or Picture

Highlight the text to select it or click on the picture to select it. Handles will appear around the picture to show that it is selected.

10 Click the Link Button

Click the toolbar's **Link** button to open a list of items to which you can link and choose **Drafts and Recent Pages**. The **Insert Link** dialog box opens.

11 Choose the File to Which You Want to Link

In the list under **Select a page to link to**, click the name of the file that the link will open in a frame.

12 Click the Advanced Button

Near the bottom of the **Insert Link** dialog box, you might see list boxes labeled **Section Anchor** and **Target Frame**. If you don't, click the **Advanced** button to display them.

13 Choose Your Target Frame

In the **Target Frame** box, type the name of the frame (from step 5) in which you want this file to open. Don't include any quote symbols (") you might have seen around the frame name in step 5. Click **OK** to close the **Insert Link** dialog box.

TIP

In step 13, instead of specifying a target frame by name, you can select **New Window** from the **Target Frame** list to open the file in a new browser window with no frames, leaving the frames page open in a separate window, or **Entire Window** to clear the frameset from the window and replace it with the file.

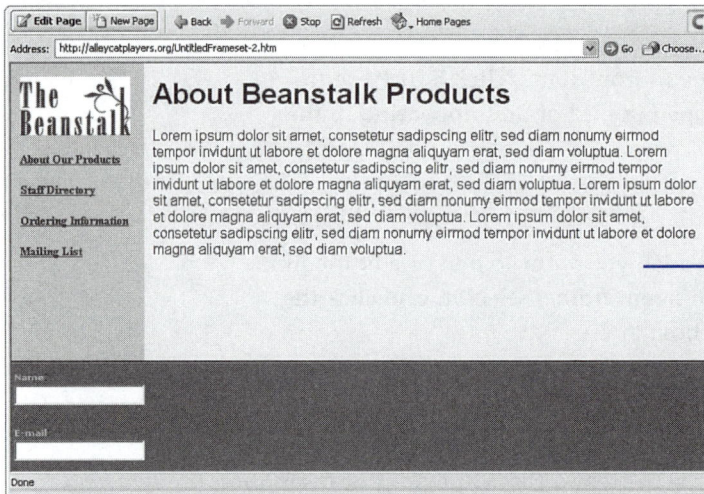

1 Edit the Frames Page

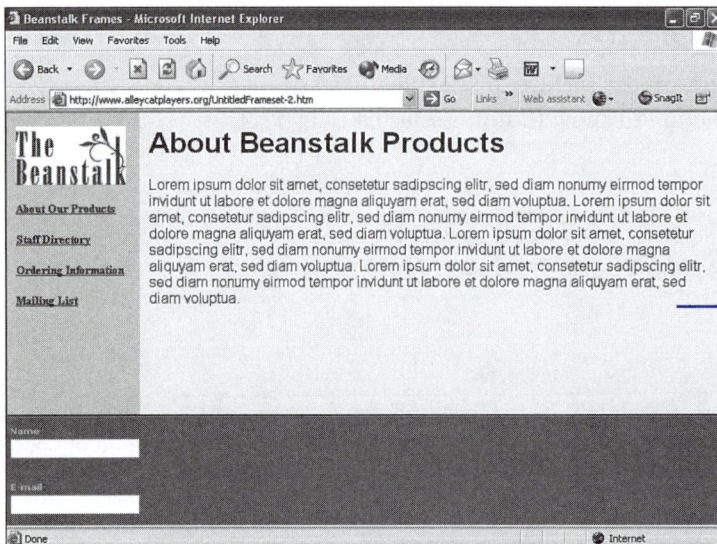

2 Preview the Page

3 Note the URL for Each Frame

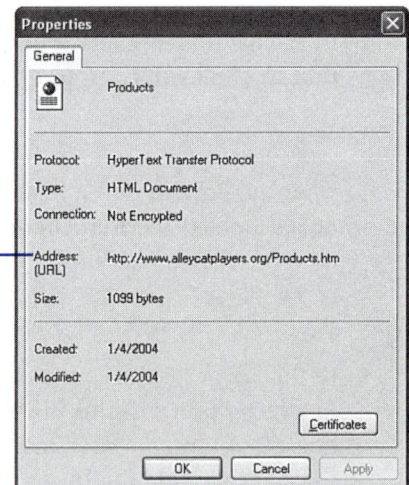

UntitledFrameset-2[1] - Notepad

File   Edit   Format   View   Help

```
<!DOCTYPE HTML PUBLIC "-//W3C//DTD HTML 4.01 Frameset//EN" "http://www.
<html>
<head>
<title>Beanstalk Frames</title>
<meta http-equiv="Content-Type" content="text/html; charset=iso-8859-1"
</head>

<frameset rows="*,121" cols="*" framespacing="2" frameborder="yes" bord
  <frameset rows="*" cols="146,*" framespacing="0" frameborder="NO" bor
    <frame src="Links.htm" name="leftFrame" scrolling="NO" noresize>
    <frame src="Products.htm" name="mainFrame">
  </frameset>
    <frame src="Samples.htm" name="bottomFrame" scrolling="NO" noresize >
</frameset>
<noframes><body>
</body></noframes>
</html>
```

View   Favorites   Tools

Toolbars ▶
✓ Status Bar
Explorer Bar ▶

Go To ▶
Stop   Esc
Refresh   F5

Text Size ▶
Encoding ▶

Source
Privacy Report...
Full Screen   F11

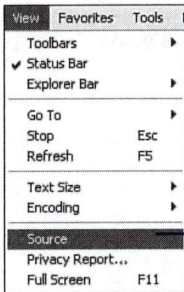

5 Find the Name of the Frame

4 View the HTML Source Code

6 Return to Contribute

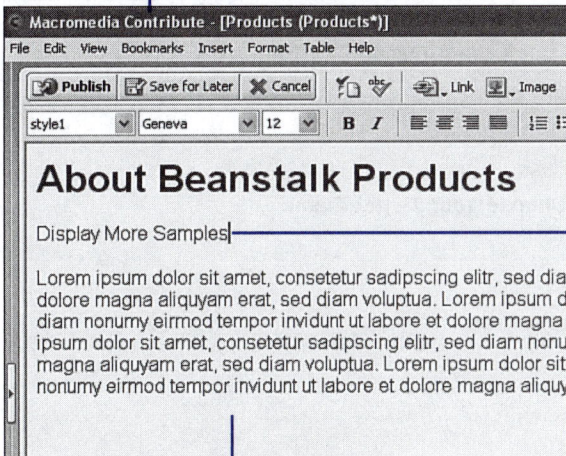

Macromedia Contribute - [Products (Products*)]

File   Edit   View   Bookmarks   Insert   Format   Table   Help

Publish   Save for Later   Cancel   Link   Image

style1   Geneva   12   **B**   *I*

About Beanstalk Products

Display More Samples

Lorem ipsum dolor sit amet, consetetur sadipscing elitr, sed diam
dolore magna aliquyam erat, sed diam voluptua. Lorem ipsum d
diam nonumy eirmod tempor invidunt ut labore et dolore magna
ipsum dolor sit amet, consetetur sadipscing elitr, sed diam nonu
magna aliquyam erat, sed diam voluptua. Lorem ipsum dolor sit
nonumy eirmod tempor invidunt ut labore et dolore magna aliquy

8 Add the Text or Image for the Link

7 Choose Your File

10 Click the Link Button

Publish   Save for Later   Cancel   Link   Image   Tabl

style1   Geneva   12   **B**   *I*

Drafts and Recent Pages...
Create New Page...
Browse to Web Page...

E-mail Address...
File on My Computer...

About Beanstalk Pro

Display More Samples

Lorem ipsum dolor sit amet, consetetur sadipscing elitr, sed diam nonu
dolore magna aliquyam erat, sed diam voluptua. Lorem ipsum dolor sit
diam nonumy eirmod tempor invidunt ut labore et dolore magna aliquyan
ipsum dolor sit amet, consetetur sadipscing elitr, sed diam nonumy eirm
magna aliquyam erat, sed diam voluptua. Lorem ipsum dolor sit amet, c
nonumy eirmod tempor invidunt ut labore et dolore magna aliquyam erat

9 Select the Link Text or Picture

11 Choose the File to Which You Want to Link

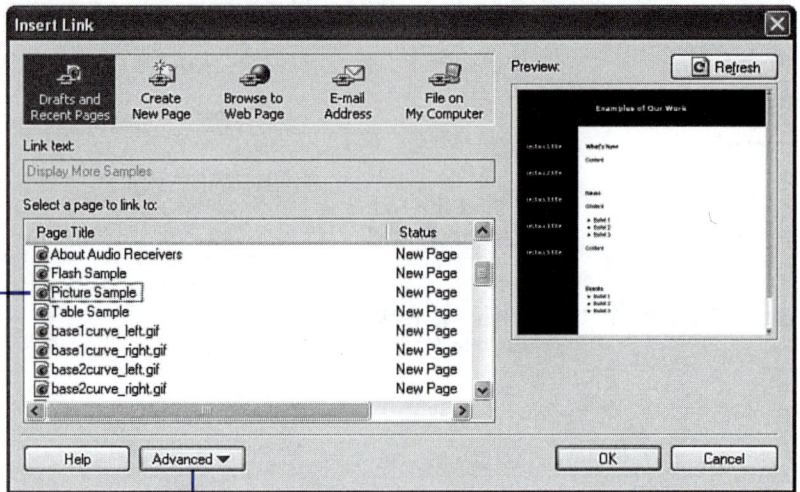

12 Click the Advanced Button

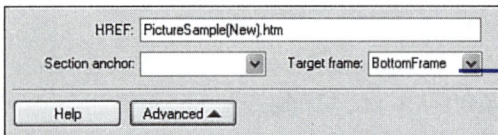

13 Choose Your Target Frame

11

Publishing Pages

IN THIS CHAPTER:

Perhaps Contribute's best quality is how easy it makes publishing. In most cases, when you've simply edited an existing page and haven't added any brand new pages to the site, publishing is literally a one-click job—click the Publish button, and it's done.

However, sometimes there's a little more to publishing than that. In this chapter, you learn how to address all sorts of publishing situations—including "rolling back" a published page to a previous version, which is a great way to recover from a published mistake.

74 About Publishing

KEY TERM

Uploading—The act of sending files from one computer to another, as when you publish web page files from your computer to the server. You're *uploading* when you initiate the sending of files *away* from you, and you're *downloading* when you initiate the sending of files to you. The terms are used another way, by some, relative to the size of the computers—uploading would mean sending from a smaller computer to a larger one. However, this meaning is falling from use.

Publishing is the act of **uploading** copies of your web page files from your computer to a web server, where they become available to anyone on the Web (or intranet, if you publish to a company intranet server).

Note that when you publish, you're not just sending the basic HTML files that make up your pages. You're also uploading picture files, external files you've linked to (such as Word or Excel files), and Flash movies—everything that appears in your pages must travel to the server to appear online.

When you update an existing page, publishing that page replaces—*overwrites*—the previous version on the server, just as if you'd saved a newly edited version of a word processing file over the old.

Publishing pages actually involves a bucket of technical information and settings, such as server addresses, usernames, passwords, and communications protocols, but your administrator has configured all of that information into Contribute so that you needn't fuss with it.

75 Preview Your Work

Before You Begin

✔ **74** About Publishing

The Achilles' heel in the way Contribute makes publishing so simple is that it's too darn easy to make a few quick changes and click Publish without first carefully checking your work.

Never forget that to help you edit effectively, Contribute's Edit mode shows you a version of your page that isn't exactly what you'd see online, whereas Browse mode can only show you pages that are already published.

To find out how your page will look before publishing, you need to use Contribute's Preview in Browser feature. This feature publishes your page—but instead of overwriting the current version of that page online (if there is one), the feature uploads the page to a temporary directory online (leaving any official published version intact), safe from the general public. It then opens the default web browser on your computer and shows you the page, exactly as it would appear if it had been published.

After previewing the page this way, you can jump back into Contribute to make any further edits, repair any mistakes you discover, or publish the page if it's ready to go.

❶ Open the Page in Edit Mode

Preview in Browser works only from Edit mode. You can use it at any time while you are working on a draft. To preview a page you're not currently editing, open the page and switch to Edit mode before moving on to step 2.

❷ Choose File, Preview in Browser

From the menu bar, choose **File**, **Preview in Browser**. The default web browser on your computer opens and displays the draft as it currently stands.

❸ Evaluate the Page

Evaluate the page in the browser carefully and make sure to test any links in the page by clicking them. After you've completed your evaluation, choose the Contribute button on your Windows taskbar to return to Contribute to continue editing or to publish the page.

TIP

Besides previewing your work, it's a good idea to have your work double-checked by others (**see 76 Send Your Work to Reviewers**).

TIP

While previewing, it's smart to switch among the different display resolutions to make sure that your page will still look good to visitors using differing display resolutions (800×600 and 1024×768 are the most common). You can switch resolutions by right-clicking the Windows desktop, choosing **Properties**, and then clicking the **Settings** tab in the dialog box that appears.

NOTE

You can repeat steps 2 and 3 as many times as you want—making changes, previewing, and then making more changes—until your page looks perfect.

Publish | **Save for Later** | **Cancel** | **Link**

Normal | Default Font | 12 | **B** *I*

The Beanstalk Audio Primer

Table of Contents

1. About Home Theater
   o Surround Sound Types
   o How Many Speakers?
   o Speaker Position
2. About Audio Receivers
3. About Turntables
4. About Speakers

① **Open the Page in Edit Mode**

File	
New Page...	Ctrl+N
Edit Page	Ctrl+Shift+E
Publish	Ctrl+Shift+P
Publish as New Page...	
Save	Ctrl+S
Save for Later	Ctrl+Shift+L
Cancel Draft	
Preview in Browser	F12
E-mail Review	
Export...	
Page Setup...	
Print...	Ctrl+P
Print Preview...	
Roll Back to Previous Version...	
Delete Page...	
Work Offline	
Drafts	▶
Recently Published Pages	▶
Exit	Ctrl+Q

② **Choose File, Preview in Browser**

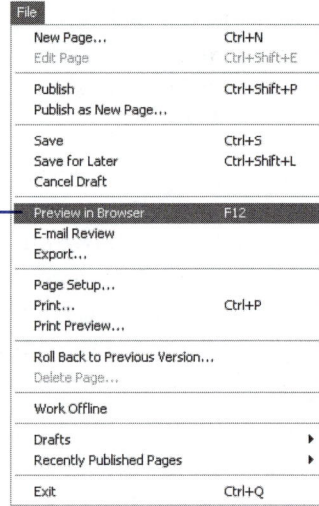

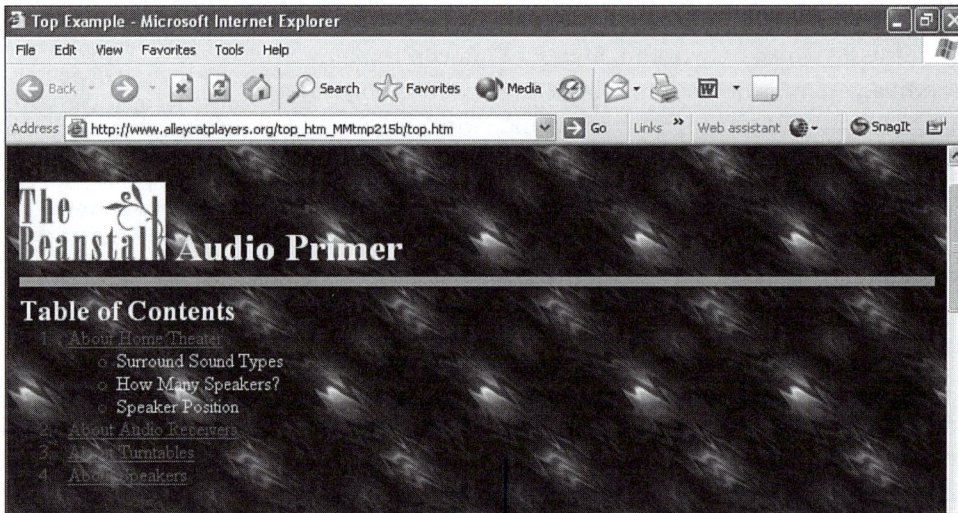

Top Example - Microsoft Internet Explorer

File   Edit   View   Favorites   Tools   Help

Back | Search | Favorites | Media

Address http://www.alleycatplayers.org/top_htm_MMtmp215b/top.htm   Go   Links   Web assistant   SnagIt

The Beanstalk Audio Primer

Table of Contents

1. About Home Theater
   o Surround Sound Types
   o How Many Speakers?
   o Speaker Position
2. About Audio Receivers
3. About Turntables
4. About Speakers

③ **Evaluate the Page**

76 Send Your Work to Reviewers

Sending your work to reviewers ("email review") is a variation on the Preview in Browser idea. As in the preview, Contribute publishes the page to a temporary online directory for review. However, when you use email review, you also generate an email message addressed to anyone who needs to check or approve your work containing a link that takes those reviewers directly to the online preview.

The reviewers can check your work and then send you comments or corrections by reply email. Note that the reviewers cannot edit, annotate, or do anything else to the page—it's secure. They can only review it, test it, and tell you what they think.

1 Open the Page in Edit Mode

Start while viewing the page in Edit mode, when you feel the draft is about done. To send out a page you're not currently editing, open the page and switch to Edit mode before step 2.

2 Click the Send for Review Button

From the menu bar, choose **File, E-mail Review**. Contribute opens a new email message (in the default email program on your computer) containing a link that will lead reviewers to an online copy of your draft.

3 Choose the Email Option

In the Send for Review dialog box, select the **Send e-mail with link to a preview of the draft** option.

4 Enter the Email Addresses of Reviewers

In the **To:** line of the email message, enter the email address of every reviewer you want to evaluate the draft.

Before sending, you can add a personal message to the body of the email message—notes of things in your draft to pay particular attention to, a request to respond by a certain date, and so on.

Before You Begin

✔ 74 About Publishing
✔ 75 Preview Your Work

TIP

From the time you send out an email review until such time as you publish that page (or cancel the draft), Contribute displays a message underneath the toolbar in Edit mode whenever you open that page reminding you of when you sent out the review and offering a link to the last draft sent out. The reminder helps you avoid making too many more changes before getting feedback on what you've already done.

NOTE

Contribute posts a copy of your draft online in a temporary folder for reviewing purposes (it won't displace any official copy of the page currently online). When you either publish this page or cancel the draft later, Contribute automatically deletes the temporary copy.

1 Open the Page in Edit Mode

2 Click the Send for Review Button

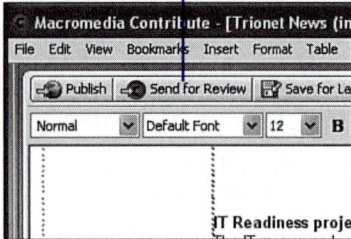

3 Choose the Email Option

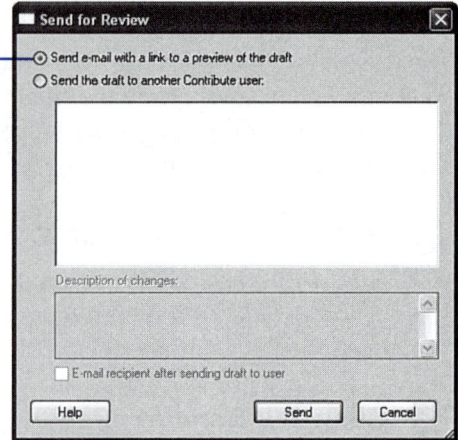

5 Send the Message

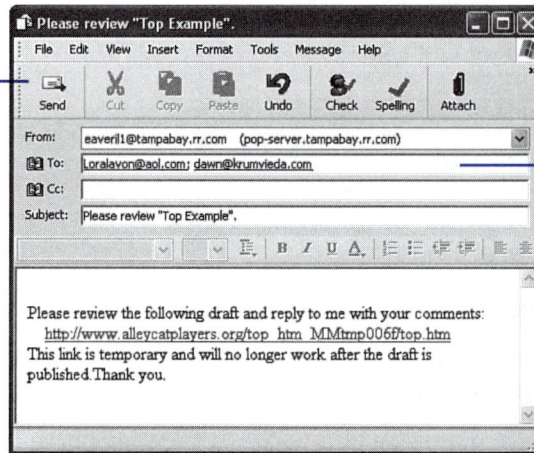

4 Enter the Email Addresses of Reviewers

5 Send the Message

Press the **Send** button to send the email message as you would any other message composed in your email program.

77 Add Keywords and Descriptions to Pages

Web search engines and directories such as Yahoo! and Excite sometimes use the keywords encoded in your page to categorize your pages when their automated web searches come across your site and catalog it. Some search engines display your actual description text in the hit list when a search finds your page.

To put it another way: If your page is about tires, and you want anyone searching for "tires" in a search engine to find your page in the hit list, you boost your chances by adding "tires" as a keyword for your page. If you want to phrase a description that will concisely attract those tire buyers to choose your page from that hit list, it's good to have added a description.

1 Open the Page in Edit Mode

Start while viewing the page in Edit mode.

2 Choose Format, Keywords, and Description

From the menu bar, choose **Format, Keywords and Description**. The **Page Keywords and Description** dialog box appears.

3 Add (or Edit) Keywords

In the **Keywords** pane, type or edit the keywords for this page, leaving a single space (with no commas or other punctuation) between each keyword.

4 Add (or Edit) the Description

In the **Description** pane, type a brief, well worded description of the page or site.

5 Click OK

Click **OK** and the keywords and description are saved with the page file. When you publish this page, the keywords and description become available online.

Before You Begin

✔ **74** About Publishing

KEY TERMS

Keywords and the *description* are optional bits of information included as text in the HTML files of your web pages. This information is invisible to people who view your page online, but it helps online search engines catalog and describe your page, and it also helps them know when to include your page in the hit list from a search.

NOTE

It may take days or weeks before search engines get around to cataloging your page after you add keywords and a description. Be patient, and don't expect immediate results—they'll find you eventually. On some sites—including Yahoo! and Excite—you can add your site manually; look for a link similar to Add My URL.

1 Open the Page in Edit Mode

2 Choose Format, Keywords, and Description

3 Add (or Edit) Keywords

4 Add (or Edit) the Description

5 Click OK

---

78 Publish Edited Pages

Before You Begin

✔ **74** About Publishing

✔ **75** Preview Your Work

✔ **76** Send Your Work to Reviewers

Most of the time when you publish, you'll be publishing an edited version of a page that's already online—the quickest and easiest kind of publishing.

Things get a little more complicated when you've linked from that page other pages that haven't been published yet—but when that occurs, Contribute leads you through what you need to do, all the while making sure that all the necessary files get uploaded and that the links in your pages work the way they're supposed to.

2 **Click Publish**

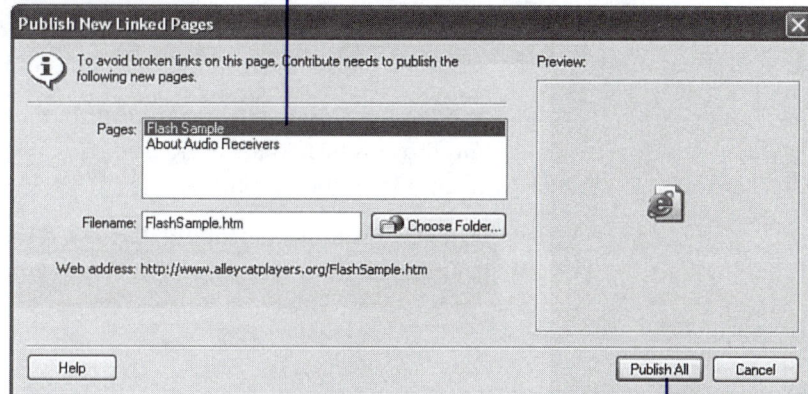

1 **Open the Page in Edit Mode**

3 **Check for Unpublished New Pages**

4 **Click Publish All**

1 ## Open the Page in Edit Mode

Start while viewing the finished page in Edit mode, after you have made any final changes and incorporated feedback from reviewers.

2 Click Publish

Click the **Publish** button on the Edit toolbar. If the page does not contain links to any new unpublished pages, after a few moments, Contribute will display a message that it's busy publishing. (Skip ahead to step 4 to see what happens next.) If the page *does* contain links to new unpublished pages, the **Publish New Linked Pages** dialog box appears, and you need to move on to step 3.

3 Check for Unpublished New Pages

The list of **Pages** in the **Publish New Linked Pages** dialog box shows all new pages linked to from the one you're publishing.

One by one, select each page and read its filename in the box labeled **Filename**. If necessary, change the filename in the box. (You can optionally click the **Choose Folder** button and choose the folder in which the file will be saved online.)

4 Click Publish All

Click the **Publish All** button to publish the page you started with in step 1, plus new unpublished pages it links to (if any).

While publishing your page, Contribute displays a message reporting that it's busy publishing and displays the progress of the publishing in a line graph.

After publishing, Contribute displays a message congratulating you on publishing successfully. When you click **OK** to clear the message, you'll see the finished online versionof the page in Browse mode.

NOTE

If you change the filename and/or folder of an unpublished new page in step 3, Contribute will automatically update the link URLs in your page so that they still point to those pages as you intended.

---

79 **Publish New Pages**

Before You Begin

✔ **74** About Publishing

✔ **75** Preview Your Work

✔ **76** Send Your Work to Reviewers

✔ **78** Publish Edited Pages

The easiest (and best) way to publish a new page is to add a link to that page in an existing page and then to publish the existing page. During publishing, Contribute will publish the new page as well (**see** **78** **Publish Edited Pages**).

However, there might be some circumstances under which you want to publish a new page solo, without linking to it first. For example, another contributor might be responsible for creating the link to that page, whereas you're charged only with creating the new page. Or, you might want to put something online that's only for folks to whom you have sent a link, not for the general public.

If you've created a new page and don't want to publish it by first publishing an existing page that links to it, here are the steps.

1 **Open the New Page in Edit Mode**

Start while viewing the finished new page in Edit mode, after you have made any final changes and have incorporated feedback from reviewers.

2 **Click Publish**

Click the **Publish** button on the Edit toolbar. The **Publish New Page** dialog box appears.

3 **Check the Filename**

Read the page's filename in the box labeled **Filename** and change it if necessary. You can optionally click the **Choose Folder** button and choose the folder in which the file will be saved online.

4 **Click Publish**

Click the **Publish** button on the **Publish New Page** dialog box. If the page does not contain links to any other new unpublished pages, after a few moments Contribute will display a message that the page is being published.

While publishing your page, Contribute displays a message reporting that it's busy publishing and displays the progress of the publishing in a line graph.

5 **Click OK**

After publishing, Contribute displays a message congratulating you on publishing successfully. When you click **OK** to clear the message, you'll see the finished online version of the page in Browse mode.

TIP

If you do create a new page to which someone else is responsible for creating the link, make sure you tell (or email) that contributor the filename and URL of the new page.

NOTE

If the page *does* contain links to other new unpublished pages, the **Publish New Linked Pages** dialog box appears; see step 3 in `78` **Publish Edited Pages**.

2 Click Publish

Publish | Save for Later | Cancel | Link | Image | Table | PayPal

Normal | Default Font | 12 | **B** *I*

February 2005

SUNDAY	MONDAY	TUESDAY	WEDNESDAY	THURSDAY	FRIDAY	SATURDAY
		1	2	3	4	5
6	7	8	9	10	11	12
13	14	15	16	17	18	19
20	21	22	23	24	25	26
27	28					

1 Open the New Page in Edit Mode

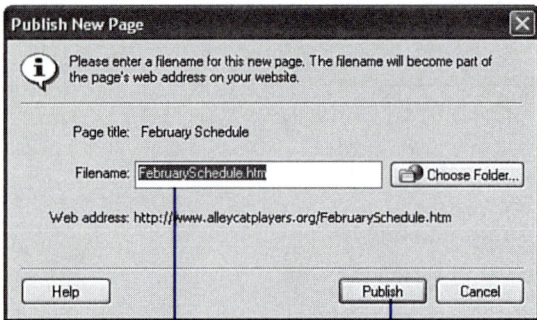

Publish New Page

Please enter a filename for this new page. The filename will become part of the page's web address on your website.

Page title: February Schedule

Filename: FebruarySchedule.htm   Choose Folder...

Web address: http://www.alleycatplayers.org/FebruarySchedule.htm

Help   Publish   Cancel

3 Check the Filename

4 Click Publish

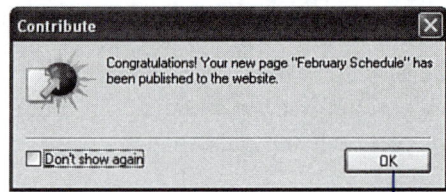

Contribute

Congratulations! Your new page "February Schedule" has been published to the website.

☐ Don't show again   OK

5 Click OK

80 Restore Published Pages to Their Previous Versions

Even with all the careful steps of previewing your work and sending it to reviewers, it's possible (likely, even) that an error will find its way online. When this happens, you can simply edit the page to fix the error, but sometimes it can be difficult to retrace your steps that carefully.

As a failsafe, Contribute includes a "rollback" feature that lets you easily replace the current online version of a file with an older version of the same file. You don't have to use the most immediate preceding version; depending upon how the administrator has set things up, there might be as many as 99 previously published versions from which you may choose.

1 Browse to the Page to Roll Back

The rollback feature doesn't work in Edit mode. Use the Contribute browser to open the current online version of the page that you'd like to roll back.

2 Choose File, Actions, Roll Back to Previous Version

From the menu bar, choose **File, Roll Back to Previous Version**. The **Roll Back Page** dialog box appears.

3 Choose the Version to Which to Roll Back

The dialog box lists available previous versions of the page, the contributor who published them, and the date each was published. (The most recent previous version is at the top of the list.) Use this information to select the version to use and click on it.

4 Click Roll Back

Click the **Roll Back** button on the dialog box. Contribute replaces the online version of the page with the earlier version you selected.

Before You Begin

✔ **74** About Publishing

TIP

After you roll back a page, the version you just replaced will thereafter appear as a choice in the **Roll Back Page** dialog box, so later on you can "roll back your rollback" and return to that version, if necessary.

1 Browse to the Page to Roll Back

2 Choose File, Actions, Roll Back to Previous Version

3 Choose the Version to Which to Roll Back

4 Click Roll Back

PART IV

Administering Websites

12

Basic Site Administration Tasks

IN THIS CHAPTER:

"Contribute site administration" is a mouthful, but it sounds more complicated than it is. It's nothing like server maintenance, network administration, or other jobs the name may call to mind. Really, it's a simple matter of getting users connected to the sites they'll edit and choosing what they may edit within those pages.

The first parts of site administration—setting up connections, preferences, and the administrator—are covered in this chapter. After those tasks are taken care of, you'll find the final steps of administration in Chapter 13, "Managing Roles and Sharing Connections."

81 About Site Administration

Before You Begin

✔ **1** About Connections

See Also

➔ **99** Send Connections to Contributors

🔍 KEY TERMS

Connection—The bundle of settings that enables a user to access and edit a site (or an administrator to administer a site). Connections are quickly and easily created with the Connection Wizard (or Connection Assistant on a Mac).

Connection key—A file that enables a connection for a user. After creating connections, administrators typically distribute these keys to users in email messages.

Although Contribute does let you violate it at times, there is a natural order in which initial site administration tasks should be performed:

1. Create a *connection* to each website users will edit (see **82** **Create or Edit Connections with the Wizard**).

2. Set *preferences* on each user's computer, governing such things as which optional, external programs may be used from within Contribute for such tasks as image editing (see **85** **About Preferences**).

3. Create *roles*—logical groupings of users who will share the same permissions (see **90** **Create a New Role**).

4. Edit *role settings*—the settings that determine what types of editing activities users in a group may perform. For example, a group of users may all be denied (or granted) the ability to delete pages from the site.

5. Send *connection keys* to users (see **99** **Send Connections to Contributors**).

In and among these key tasks, you might also need to confirm and/or change the administrator email address, choose whether to enable

Contribute's rollback feature, and make provisions for alternate index file names and URL mapping—though all of these activities may be optional or even unnecessary on your system, depending upon how your server has been configured and how other Contribute settings have been set up.

82 Create or Edit Connections with the Wizard

If you are the administrator or if your administrator has provided you with the network information to create a connection yourself, you can do so easily by firing up Contribute's Connection Wizard. If you should be the administrator but haven't been so assigned within Contribute, the Wizard also lets you assign yourself as such while setting up the connection.

When any aspect of a connection needs changing, the Connection Wizard provides an easy way to move through all the current connection settings, so you can change what you need to change.

Before you fire up the Wizard, make sure you have all the information you need for creating a connection. You'll need to know the following:

- Each user's name and email address—A username and email address are used to identify each user. One way in which Contribute uses this identification is to prevent multiple users from editing the same web page at the same time.

- The web address (URL) of the website or the network path to the website (for web pages on local intranets)—The network path is the location of the website within your company's intranet.

- FTP or SFTP connection information—If you connect to the website using FTP or Secure FTP, you must know the address of the FTP server and also the username and password for connecting to the FTP server.

With this information in hand, creating a connection with the Wizard is a simple matter of filling in the blanks.

Before You Begin

✔ **81** About Site Administration

NOTE

On a Mac, the Connection Wizard is called the "Connection Assistant."

NOTE

It might seem logical to send out connection keys to users as soon as you've created them, but first you need to set up permission groups (see Chapter 13, "Managing Roles and Sharing Connections").

TIP

You might want to go over this list with the webmaster, network administrator, or other person responsible for your company's web server before setting up connections to make sure you have the necessary technical info—such as the FTP address—on hand before you start.

My Connections

② **Click Create**

| Create... | Import... | Edit... | Remove | Rename | Disable | Administer... |

Website Name	Address	Role	Administrator
Tutorial Website	file:///D|/Documents%20and%20Settings/Snell/Local%20...	Administrator	tutorial_user@t...
Alley Cat Players	http://www.alleycatplayers.org/	Administrator	eaveril1@tampa...

☐ Don't connect to websites at startup (improves Contribute startup time)

| Help | | Close |

Edit **View** **Bookmarks** **Insert** **Format**

Undo	Ctrl+Z
Redo	Ctrl+Y
Cut	Ctrl+X
Copy	Ctrl+C
Paste	Ctrl+V
Paste Text Only	Ctrl+Shift+V
Clear	
Select All	Ctrl+A
Find...	Ctrl+F
Preferences...	
My Connections...	
Administer Websites	▶

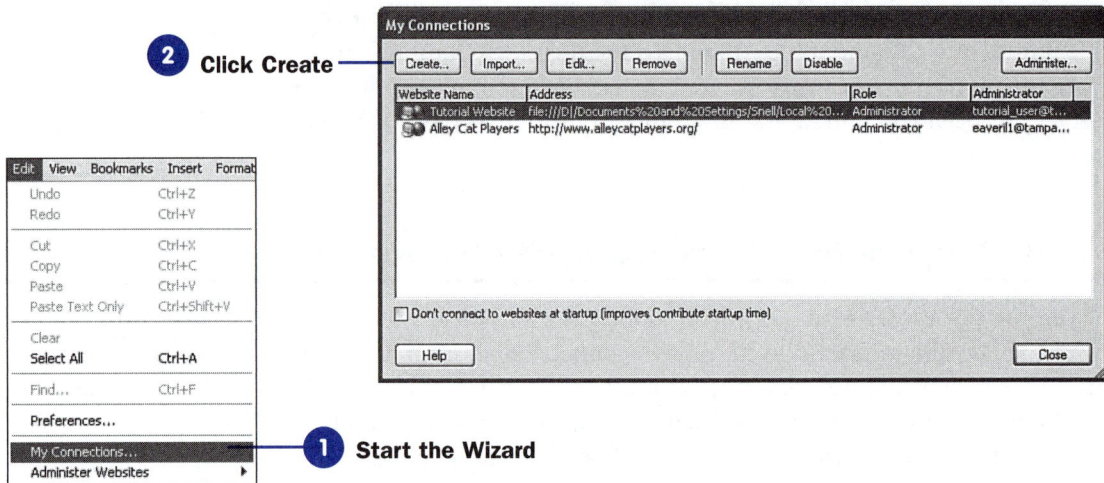

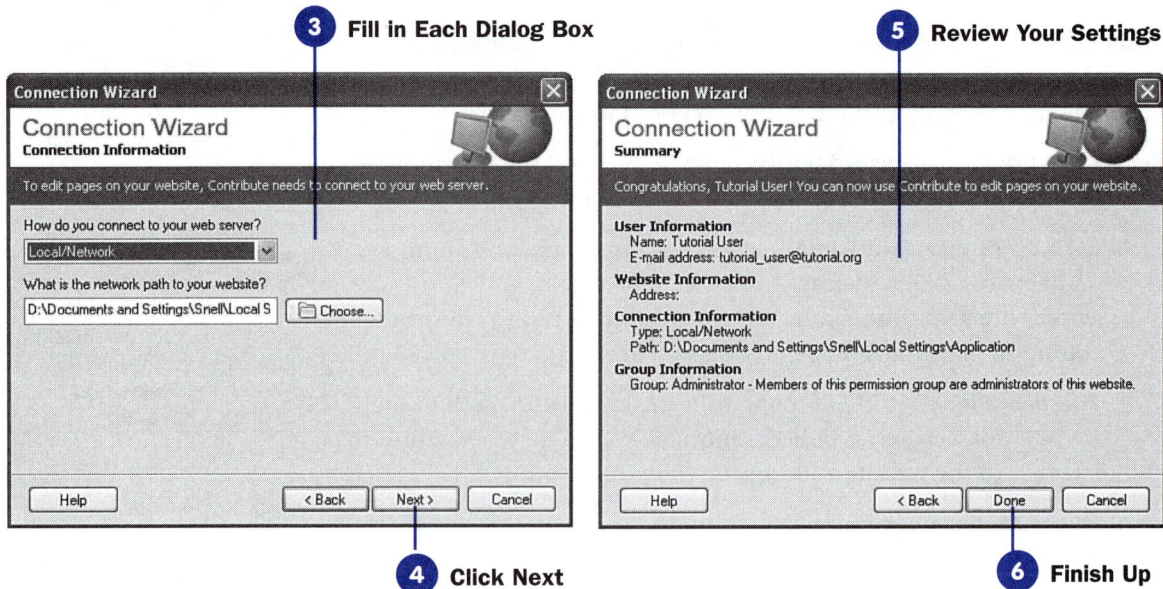

① **Start the Wizard**

③ **Fill in Each Dialog Box**

Connection Wizard

Connection Wizard
Connection Information

To edit pages on your website, Contribute needs to connect to your web server.

How do you connect to your web server?

`Local/Network`

What is the network path to your website?

`D:\Documents and Settings\Snell\Local S` 📁 Choose...

| Help | | < Back | Next > | Cancel |

④ **Click Next**

⑤ **Review Your Settings**

Connection Wizard

Connection Wizard
Summary

Congratulations, Tutorial User! You can now use Contribute to edit pages on your website.

User Information
Name: Tutorial User
E-mail address: tutorial_user@tutorial.org

Website Information
Address:

Connection Information
Type: Local/Network
Path: D:\Documents and Settings\Snell\Local Settings\Application

Group Information
Group: Administrator - Members of this permission group are administrators of this website.

| Help | | < Back | Done | Cancel |

⑥ **Finish Up**

---

① **Start the Wizard**

From Contribute's menu bar, choose **Edit, My Connections** (in Windows) or **Contribute, My Connections** (on a Mac) to start the Wizard. The **My Connections** dialog box opens.

---

2 **Click Create**

Click **Create**. The Wizard opens to guide you through setting up a new connection.

3 **Fill in Each Dialog Box**

As in any wizard, the Connection Wizard displays a series of dialog boxes, each one requesting specific information required to set up a connection. Respond to each dialog as fully and accurately as you can.

4 **Click Next**

After completing each dialog box, click **Next** (in Windows) or **Continue** (on a Mac).

5 **Review Your Settings**

When you arrive at the **Summary** dialog box, review the settings you've entered or changed.

6 **Finish Up**

If the settings reported on the Summary screen are correct, click **Done** (in Windows) or **Finish** (on a Mac) to complete the connection. The Wizard closes, and the main page of the website appears in the Contribute browser.

TIP

At any time while working through the wizard, you can click the **Back** button to move backward through the dialog boxes and make changes. You might do this if you suddenly realize you have made a mistake, or if you just want to recheck your input before you arrive at the Summary dialog box.

---

83 **Become Administrator of a Website**

When a website does not already have an administrator (usually defined when the connection is set up; see **82** **Create or Edit Connections with the Wizard**), you can declare yourself the administrator simply by setting up a password as described in this task.

Once you become the administrator, you control all access to the folders in the website, you can assign roles and other settings (as described in Chapter 13, "Managing Roles and Sharing Connections"), and you can send connection keys to other Contribute users.

Before You Begin

✔ **81** About Site Administration

✔ **82** Create or Edit Connections with the Wizard

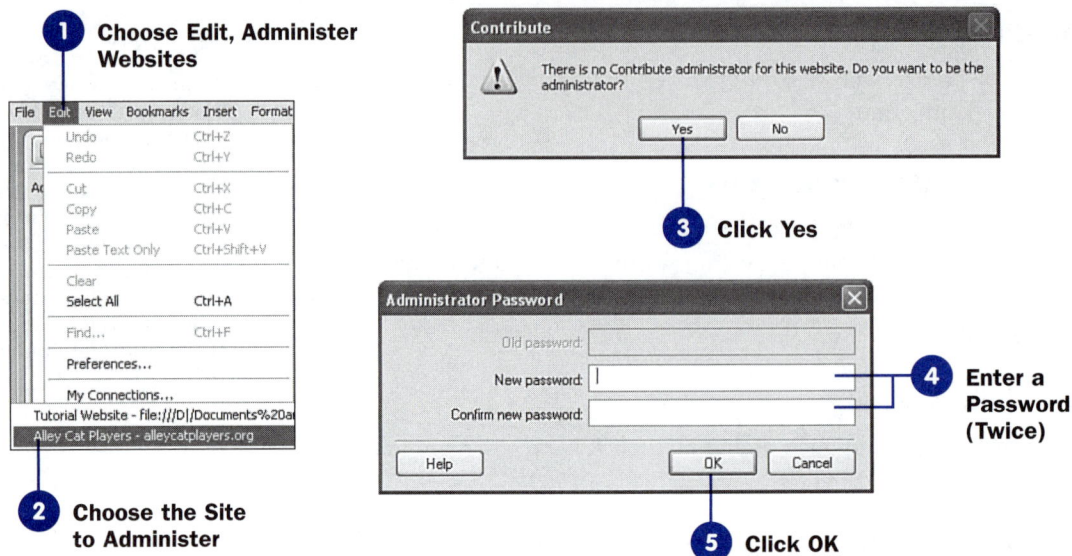

Choose Edit, Administer Websites

Contribute

⚠ There is no Contribute administrator for this website. Do you want to be the administrator?

[Yes] [No]

3 Click Yes

File   Edit   View   Bookmarks   Insert   Format
Undo   Ctrl+Z
Redo   Ctrl+Y

Cut   Ctrl+X
Copy   Ctrl+C
Paste   Ctrl+V
Paste Text Only   Ctrl+Shift+V

Clear
Select All   Ctrl+A

Find...   Ctrl+F

Preferences...

My Connections...
Tutorial Website - file:///D|/Documents%20a
Alley Cat Players - alleycatplayers.org

Administrator Password

Old password:

New password: |

Confirm new password:

[Help]   [OK]   [Cancel]

4 Enter a Password (Twice)

2 Choose the Site to Administer

5 Click OK

✎ **NOTE**

If you don't see the site you want to administer in step 2, you don't yet have a connection to it. To become administrator of a site to which you don't yet have a connection, run the Connection Wizard and declare yourself the administrator while doing so (**see 82 Create or Edit Connections with the Wizard**).

💡 **TIP**

Changing the password makes you the administrator, but you still need to change the administrator email address to your own (see **84 Change the Administrator Email, Password, and Enabling Rollback**).

1 Choose Edit, Administer Websites

Choose **Edit, Administer Websites**. As soon as you point to **Administer Websites**, that menu item is displaced by a list of sites to which you have a connection.

2 Choose the Site to Administer

Click on the Web site address to administer. If the site has no administrator, a prompt appears asking whether you want to be the administrator.

3 Click Yes

Choose **Yes**. The **Administrator Password** dialog box opens.

4 Enter a Password (Twice)

Type a password in **New password** and then type it again in **Confirm new password**. Then click **OK**. The **Administer Website** dialog box opens.

5 Click OK

In the **Administer Website** dialog box, you can configure or edit roles, as described in Chapter 13. However, if all you wanted to do was declare yourself the administrator, you're done. Click **OK** to close the **Administer Website** dialog box.

84 Change the Administrator Email, Password, and Enabling Rollback

After you have changed the administrator or become a new administrator, only the administrator password is changed—you still need to change the administrator email address so that Contributor queries regarding this site will come to you (and so that the reply address on connections you send out will be yours).

While changing the administrator email address, you'll have the opportunity to change the password and to configure one of the most important sitewide settings—whether to permit users to perform rollbacks.

1 Choose Edit, Administer Websites

Choose **Edit, Administer Websites**. As soon as you point to **Administer Websites**, that menu item is displaced by a list of sites to which you have a connection.

2 Choose the Site to Administer

Click on the website address to administer. Contribute prompts for your administrator password.

3 Click Administration

On the **Administer Website** dialog box, click the **Administration** link. The **Administration** dialog box appears.

4 Change the Administrator Email Address

Under **Contact e-mail address**, type your email address.

5 Click Rollbacks

In the left column, click the **Rollbacks** link.

Before You Begin

✔ 81 About Site Administration

✔ 82 Create or Edit Connections with the Wizard

✔ 83 Become Administrator of a Website

NOTE

If you don't see the site you want to administer in step 2, you don't yet have a connection to it. You must first create a connection to a site and also be named the administrator before you can administer it. (See 82 **Create or Edit Connections with the Wizard** and 83 **Become Administrator of a Website**.)

1 Choose Edit, Administer Websites

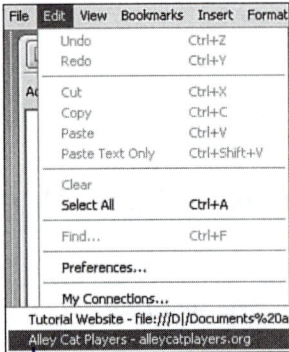

File	Edit	View	Bookmarks	Insert	Format

Undo Ctrl+Z
Redo Ctrl+Y

Cut Ctrl+X
Copy Ctrl+C
Paste Ctrl+V
Paste Text Only Ctrl+Shift+V

Clear
Select All Ctrl+A

Find... Ctrl+F

Preferences...

My Connections...

Tutorial Website - file:///D|/Documents%20a
Alley Cat Players - alleycatplayers.org

2 Choose the Site to Administer

3 Click Administration

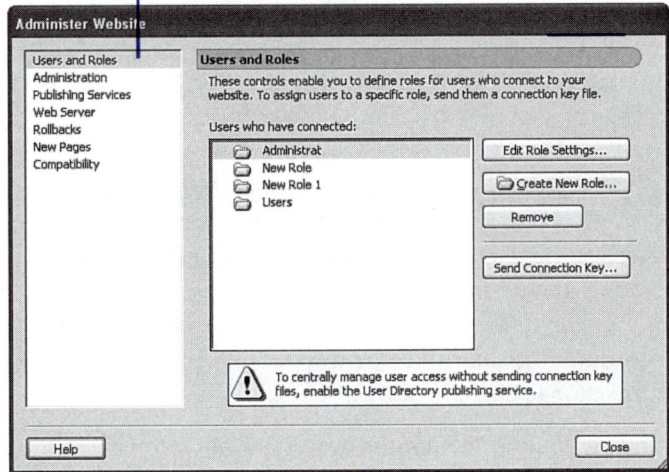

Administer Website

Users and Roles
Administration
Publishing Services
Web Server
Rollbacks
New Pages
Compatibility

Users and Roles

These controls enable you to define roles for users who connect to your website. To assign users to a specific role, send them a connection key file.

Users who have connected:

Administrat
New Role
New Role 1
Users

Edit Role Settings...
Create New Role...
Remove
Send Connection Key...

⚠ To centrally manage user access without sending connection key files, enable the User Directory publishing service.

Help   Close

4 Change the Administrator Email Address

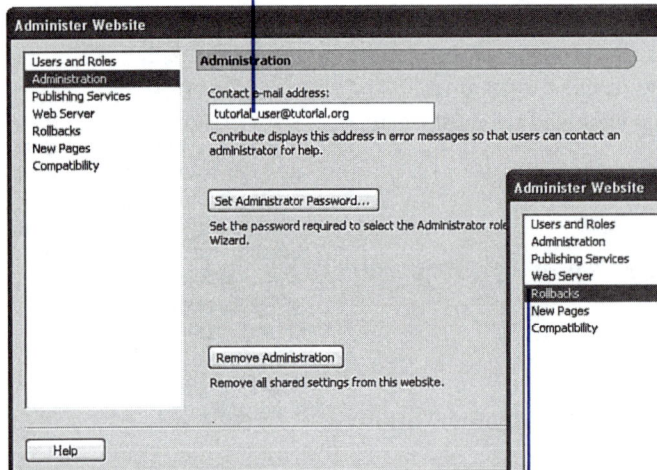

Administer Website

Users and Roles
Administration
Publishing Services
Web Server
Rollbacks
New Pages
Compatibility

Administration

Contact e-mail address:

tutorial_user@tutorial.org

Contribute displays this address in error messages so that users can contact an administrator for help.

Set Administrator Password...

Set the password required to select the Administrator role Wizard.

Remove Administration

Remove all shared settings from this website.

Help

6 Enable or Disable Rollbacks

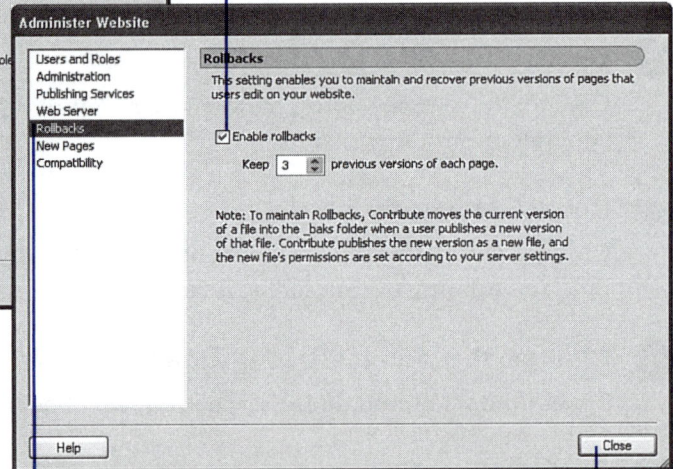

Administer Website

Users and Roles
Administration
Publishing Services
Web Server
Rollbacks
New Pages
Compatibility

Rollbacks

This setting enables you to maintain and recover previous versions of pages that users edit on your website.

☑ Enable rollbacks

Keep 3 ⬍ previous versions of each page.

Note: To maintain Rollbacks, Contribute moves the current version of a file into the _baks folder when a user publishes a new version of that file. Contribute publishes the new version as a new file, and the new file's permissions are set according to your server settings.

Help   Close

5 Click Rollbacks

7 Click Close

6 **Enable or Disable Rollbacks**

Use the check box provided to enable or disable rollbacks for this site.

7 **Click Close**

When done changing settings, click **Close**.

TIP

If in step 6 you choose to enable rollbacks (by checking the box), use the **Keep** list to choose the number of previous versions of the site to keep available to users (up to 99).

85 **About Preferences**

Unlike roles, which are set up by the administrator for whole groups of users at a time, *preferences* are settings managed separately on each user's computer. Preferences may be changed by the administrator or the user. The settings are divided onto five different tabs in the **Preferences** dialog box:

- Use the **General** tab to choose general options, such as what dictionary to use for spell-checking.

- Use the **File Editors** tab to choose external programs to be used for editing certain file types managed within Contribute. For example, you can select an editing program for JPEG pictures; when you choose **Edit Image** from the pop-up menu for an image, that's the program that opens.

- Use the **Firewall** tab to configure your company firewall settings into Contribute to avoid communication problems.

- Use the **Invisible Elements** tab to choose whether to display section anchors as little flags when you're editing a page containing anchors.

- Use the **Security** tab to set up a Contribute startup password.

86 Set Preferences

Before You Begin

✔ **81** About Site Administration

✔ **85** About Preferences

TIP

When faster table editing has been enabled in a user's preferences, the user must click outside the table or switch to another draft or the browser each time the user wants the table redrawn.

You can set (or change) the preferences for a user at any time. The following steps lead you through each option on each tab. Of course, you can open the **Preferences** dialog box, change only what you want, and jump right back out again to get on with other tasks.

1 Open the Preferences Dialog Box

From Contribute's menu bar, choose **Edit**, **Preferences** (in Windows) or **Contribute**, **Preferences** (on a Mac).

2 Choose Editing

From the category list, choose **Editing** to set editing options.

3 Choose Whether to Use Faster Table Editing

Enabling faster table editing prevents Contribute from redrawing the table each time the user changes it, which can speed up editing of large tables.

4 Choose Whether to Enable Screen Reader Support

Enabling this option disables offscreen page rendering so that a screen reader can be used.

5 Choose a Dictionary

From the list of spelling dictionaries, choose the one you want the Contribute spell-checker to use.

6 Choose File Editors

Choose **File Editors** from the category list on the left to begin the process described in steps 8–11 by which you can choose external editors for various file types.

Edit View Bookmarks Insert Format

Undo	Ctrl+Z
Redo	Ctrl+Y
Cut	Ctrl+X
Copy	Ctrl+C
Paste	Ctrl+V
Paste Text Only	Ctrl+Shift+V
Clear	
Select All	Ctrl+A
Find...	Ctrl+F
Preferences...	
My Connections...	
Administer Websites	▶

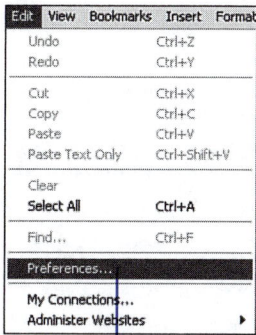

1 Open the Preferences Dialog Box

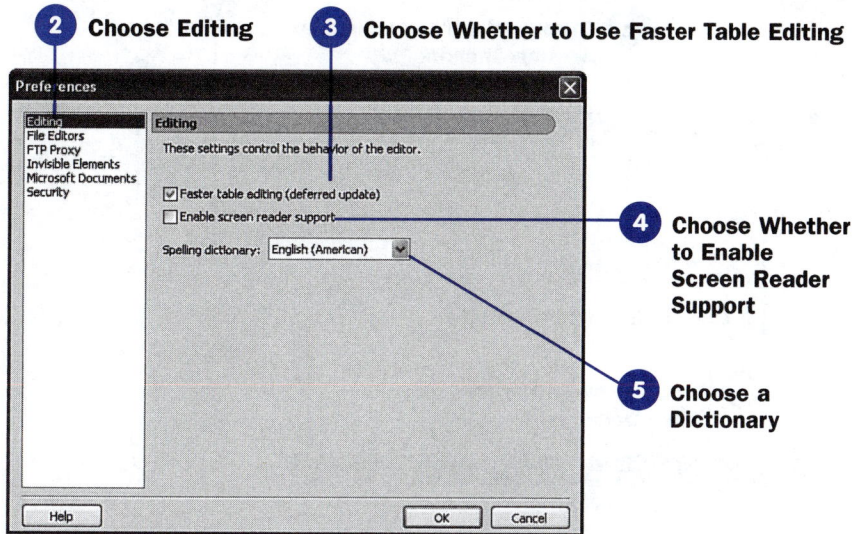

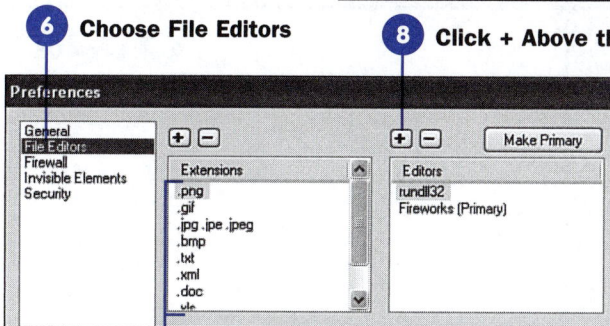

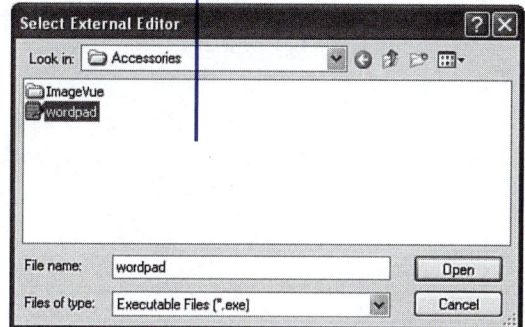

2 Choose Editing

3 Choose Whether to Use Faster Table Editing

Preferences

Editing
File Editors
FTP Proxy
Invisible Elements
Microsoft Documents
Security

Editing

These settings control the behavior of the editor.

☑ Faster table editing (deferred update)

☐ Enable screen reader support

Spelling dictionary: English (American)

Help   OK   Cancel

4 Choose Whether to Enable Screen Reader Support

5 Choose a Dictionary

6 Choose File Editors

Preferences

General
File Editors
Firewall
Invisible Elements
Security

Extensions
.png
.gif
.jpg .jpe .jpeg
.bmp
.txt
.xml
.doc
.xls

Editors
rundll32
Fireworks (Primary)

➕ ➖   Make Primary

7 Select a File Type

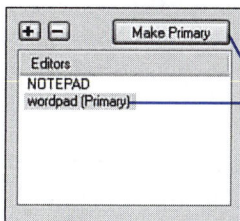

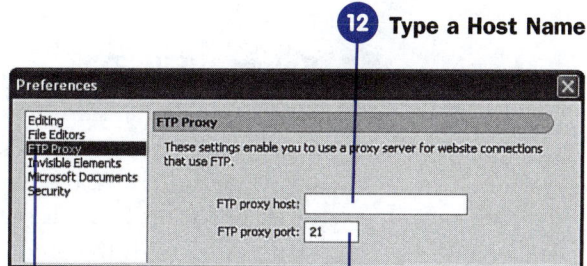

8 Click + Above the Right Pane

9 Navigate to the Program

Select External Editor

Look in: Accessories

📁 ImageVue
📄 wordpad

File name: wordpad   Open

Files of type: Executable Files (*.exe)   Cancel

➕ ➖   Make Primary

Editors
NOTEPAD
wordpad (Primary)

10 Choose the Program

11 Choose FTP Proxy

Preferences

Editing
File Editors
FTP Proxy
Invisible Elements
Microsoft Documents
Security

FTP Proxy

These settings enable you to use a proxy server for website connections that use FTP.

FTP proxy host:

FTP proxy port: 21

12 Type a Host Name

13 Type a Port Number

CHAPTER 12: Basic Site Administration Tasks

15 Choose Whether to Display
Section Anchors

17 Choose Security

18 Choose Whether to Require
a Contribute Password

Preferences

General
File Editors
Firewall
Invisible Elements
Security

☑ Show section anchors when editing a page

14 Choose Invisible Elements

16 Choose How to Handle Inserted
Office Documents

Preferences

General
File Editors
Firewall
Invisible Elements
Security

☐ Require Contribute startup password

Password:

Confirm password:

Enter a startup password to prevent unauthorized users from modifying
your website using Contribute on this machine. This setting also encrypts
connection information on this machine for added security. Please
choose Help for more information.

Preferences

Editing
File Editors
FTP Proxy
Invisible Elements
Microsoft Documents
Security

Microsoft Documents

This setting controls the way Contribute handles Microsoft Office
documents.

When inserting a Microsoft Office document into Contribute:

○ Insert the contents of the document into the current draft
○ Insert the document as FlashPaper into the current draft
○ Create a link to the document
◉ Ask whenever I insert a Microsoft Office document into Contribute

Help   OK   Cancel

Help   OK   Cancel

19 Click OK

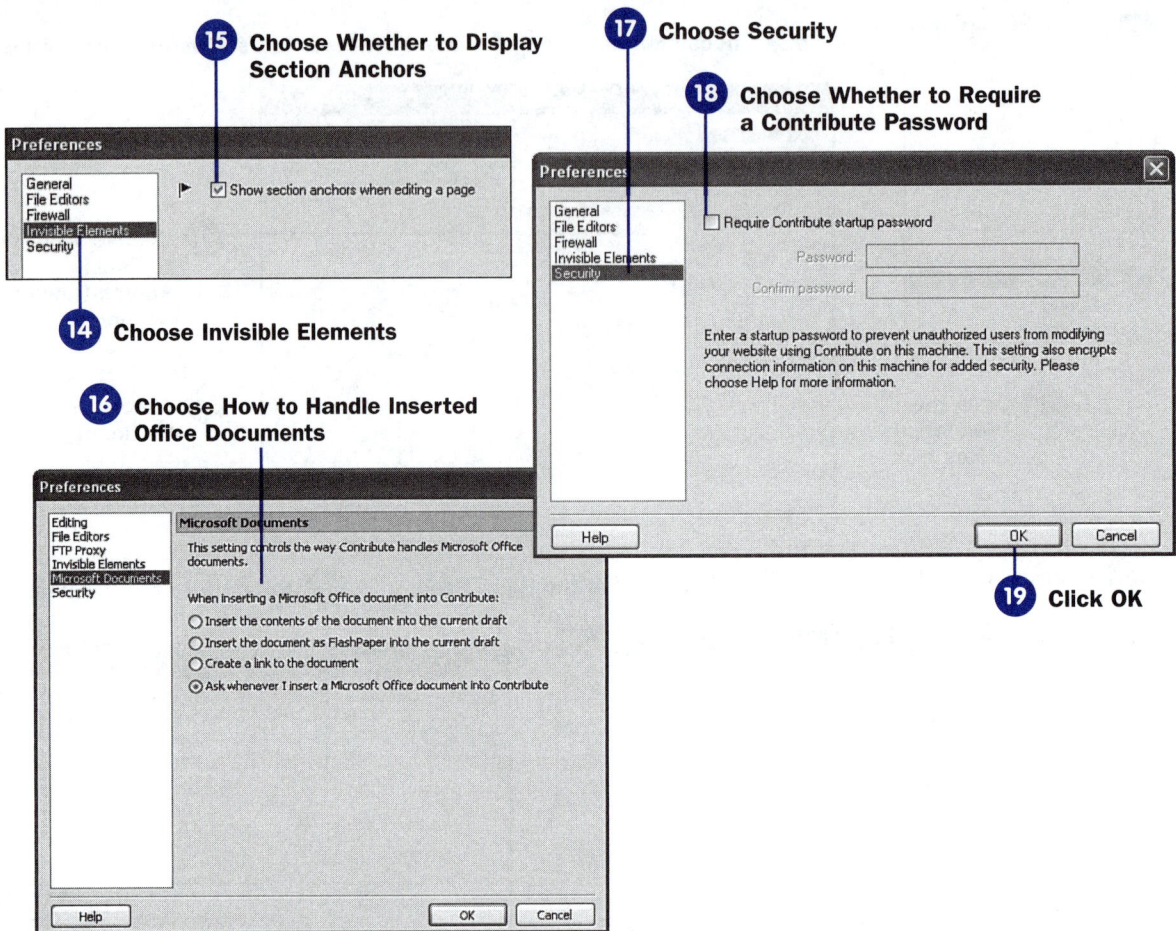

7 Select a File Type

In the list of Extensions near the center of the dialog box, click the
file type for which you want to choose an editor. Editing programs
associated with that file type appear in the right pane. If the program you want to use is selected, move on to another file type or
skip to step 12. If the program is not listed, perform steps 9–11 to
add it.

8 **Click + Above the Right Pane**

Above the right pane, click the plus sign (+) to open the **Select External Editor** dialog box.

9 **Navigate to the Program**

Use the **Select External Editor** dialog box to navigate to the application you want to add, select it, and click the **Open** button. The program now appears in the right pane.

10 **Choose the Program**

In the right pane, select the program you want Contribute to open for editing the file type selected in the list of Extensions and then click the **Make Primary** button.

11 **Choose FTP Proxy**

Select **FTP Proxy** from the category list on the left to enter the proxy hostname and port.

12 **Type a Host Name**

In the FTP proxy **host** box, type the name of the proxy host.

13 **Type a Port Number**

In the **FTP proxy port** box, type the network port number for FTP access.

14 **Choose Invisible Elements**

Select **Invisible Elements** from the category list on the left to choose whether to display section anchors as little flags when you're editing a page containing anchors.

15 **Choose Whether to Display Section Anchors**

Select or deselect the **Show section anchors when editing a page** box.

16 **Choose How to Handle Inserted Office Documents**

Choose **Microsoft Documents** from the category list, and select an option to choose what should happen by default when the user places a Microsoft Office document on a Contribute site.

TIP

Leaving section anchors visible when in Edit mode is usually a good idea; otherwise, users might be unaware when a page is already set up with anchors for them to link to and might take the time and trouble to add new anchors (see **57** Link to a Particular Spot Within a Page).

NOTE

If you check the check box in step **18** to require a password, you must also type a password for the site in the **Password** box and then type the same password again in the **Confirm password** box.

17 Choose Security

Select **Security** from the category list on the left to choose whether to require a password for starting Contribute.

18 Choose Whether to Require a Contribute Password

To add an extra layer of security, you can require the user to type a password in order to open Contribute. If you choose this option, Contribute will prompt for the password at startup.

19 Click OK

When done setting preferences, click **OK** to close the Preferences dialog box.

87 Set Index Page Filenames

Before You Begin

✔ **81** About Site Administration

TIP

You might need to consult with your company's web server administrator to learn which index page filenames your server uses and in what order.

NOTE

When a server can't find the index file among its list of alternate index filenames, it displays the "404" message (cannot find page).

The *index page* for a website is the default web page a visitor sees upon entering a site when a particular page file is not specified in the URL the visitor enters.

For example, on many websites, if the user supplies only the site address (such as **http://www.alleycatplayers.org**) without specifying a page on that site, a page such as **index.html** is the one that automatically appears. Other common index file names are **index.htm**, **default.htm**, **welcome.htm**, and **default.html**. The particular index file name to use is configured in the server.

Most web servers are also set up with *alternate* index page filenames, which select from a list of options the page to display when no page is indicated in the URL. They do this by trying, one at a time and in a particular order, each filename in the list of alternates. The server might first try **index.html**; if no such file is found on the site, the server might next try **index.htm**, **default.html**, and so on. After the server finds one of the files in the list, it stops looking and displays that page.

Contribute is preconfigured with a list of popular index page filenames, and if your site's index file is on that list, there's nothing more you need to do. However, if your index page filenames aren't on the list, you will need to add them, and you'll need to set the order in which Contribute tries the available names.

1 Choose Edit, Administer Websites

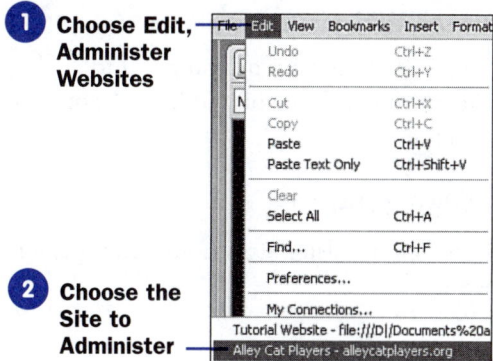

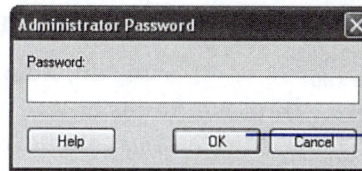

3 Enter Your Password and Click OK

2 Choose the Site to Administer

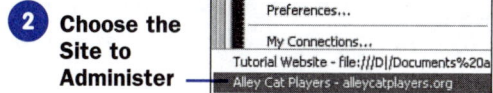

4 Click Web Server

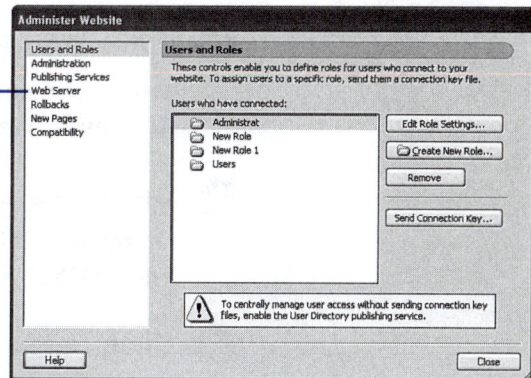

6 Type the Filename

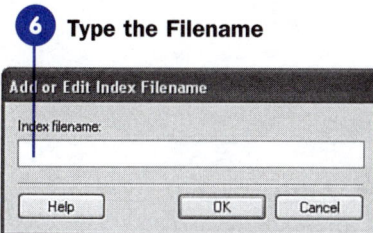

5 Click Index Files, Then Click Add

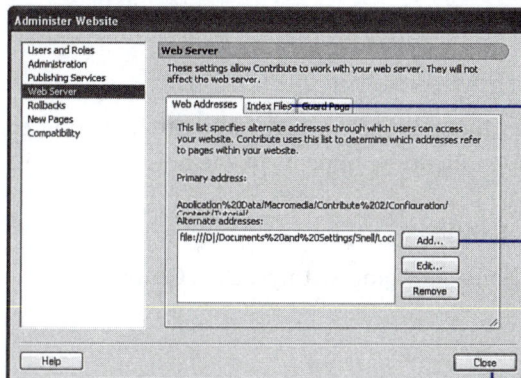

7 Click Close

NOTE

If you don't see the site you want to administer in step 2, you don't yet have a connection to it. You must first create a connection to a site and also be named the administrator before you can administer it (**see** **82** **Create or Edit Connections with the Wizard** and **83** **Become Administrator of a Website**).

1 Choose Edit, Administer Websites

Choose **Edit, Administer Websites**. As soon as you point to **Administer Websites**, that menu item is displaced by a list of sites to which you have a connection.

2 Choose the Site to Administer

Click on the website address to administer. Contribute prompts for your administrator password.

3 Enter Your Password and Click OK

Type your administrator password and then click **OK** to open the **Administer Website** dialog box.

4 Click Web Server

On the **Administer Website** dialog box, click the **Web Server** link. The **Web Server** dialog box appears.

5 Click Index Files, Then Click Add

Click the **Index Files** tab and then click the **Add** button to display the **Add or Edit Index Filename** dialog box.

6 Type the Filename

Enter an index filename in the box provided and click **OK**. The new index filename appears at the bottom of the list.

7 Click Close

When done changing settings, click **Close**.

88 Choose Alternate Web Addresses

In principle, each web address (URL) online points to one and only one domain, which is associated with one and only one IP address, which is shared by no other domain.

However, in practice, web servers use a variety of tricks to host multiple domains. A server can be configured to map multiple web addresses to different IP addresses or to access multiple web addresses from a single IP address. To do this, servers often apply a technique called *URL mapping*, which is accomplished in several different ways:

- Multiple DNS aliasing—Two or more domain name server (DNS) aliases point to an IP address. When connecting to a server that uses multiple DNS aliases, Contribute treats each of the aliases as a different website.

- Virtual servers—Two or more DNS aliases point to the same server, but appear to visitors as different websites. Servers set up with virtual servers can serve up different pages depending on the visitor's address. This gives them the capability, for example, to deliver "localized" content to users accessing the site from different geographical locations.

- Port numbers—These divide a domain name into multiple websites, often to deliver different software functions based on the visitor accessing the site.

If your server uses alternate URLs, you must set up the alternate URLs in the sitewide permissions in Contribute. Otherwise, when users connect to a Contribute website, they may use a different address than the one specified in Contribute, which can cause some pages to behave unreliably. Here's how to add your website's alternate URLs to the sitewide settings.

1 Choose Edit, Administer Websites

Choose **Edit, Administer Websites**. As soon as you point to Administer Websites, that menu item is displaced by a list of sites to which you have a connection.

Before You Begin

✔ **81** About Site Administration

✔ **87** Set Index Page Filenames

🔦 **TIP**

You might need to consult with your company's web server administrator to determine whether your server uses alternate URLs and to learn which URLs to use.

1 **Choose Edit, Administer Websites**

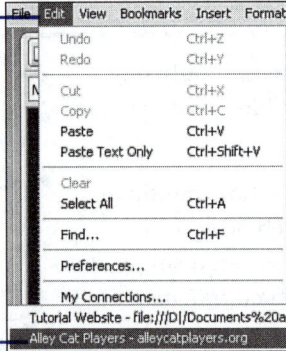

File	Edit	View	Bookmarks	Insert	Format
	Undo		Ctrl+Z		
	Redo		Ctrl+Y		
	Cut		Ctrl+X		
	Copy		Ctrl+C		
	Paste		Ctrl+V		
	Paste Text Only		Ctrl+Shift+V		
	Clear				
	Select All		Ctrl+A		
	Find...		Ctrl+F		
	Preferences...				
	My Connections...				

Tutorial Website - file:///D|/Documents%20a(

Alley Cat Players - alleycatplayers.org

2 **Choose the Site to Administer**

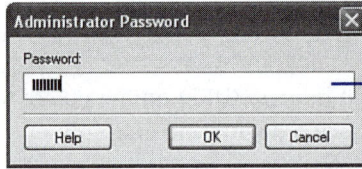

Administrator Password

Password:

‖‖‖‖‖‖

Help   OK   Cancel

3 **Enter Your Password and Click OK**

Add or Edit Alternate Address

Alternate website address (URL):

http://www.alleycats.org/

Help   OK   Cancel

6 **Type the Alternate URL**

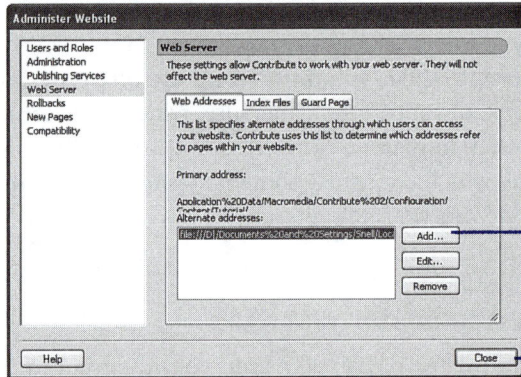

Administer Website

Users and Roles
Administration
Publishing Services
Web Server
Rollbacks
New Pages
Compatibility

Users and Roles

These controls enable you to define roles for users who connect to your website. To assign users to a specific role, send them a connection key file.

Users who have connected:

- Administrat
- New Role
- New Role 1
- Users

Edit Role Settings...
Create New Role...
Remove
Send Connection Key...

⚠ To centrally manage user access without sending connection key files, enable the User Directory publishing service.

Help   Close

4 **Click Web Server**

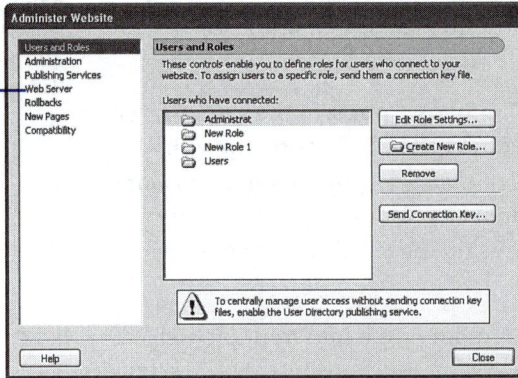

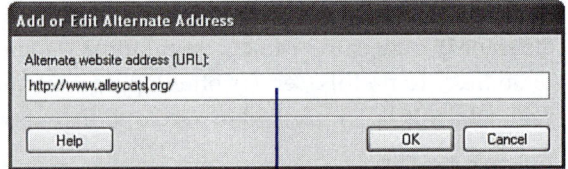

Administer Website

Users and Roles
Administration
Publishing Services
Web Server
Rollbacks
New Pages
Compatibility

Web Server

These settings allow Contribute to work with your web server. They will not affect the web server.

Web Addresses | Index Files | Guard Page

This list specifies alternate addresses through which users can access your website. Contribute uses this list to determine which addresses refer to pages within your website.

Primary address:

Application%20Data/Macromedia/Contribute%202/Configuration/
Content/Tutorial

Alternate addresses:

file://D|/Documents%20and%20Settings/Shal/Loc

Add...
Edit...
Remove

5 **Click Add**

Help   Close

7 **Click Close**

2 Choose the Site to Administer

Click on the Web site address to administer. Contribute prompts for your administrator password.

3 Enter Your Password and Click OK

Type your administrator password and then click **OK** to open the **Administer Website** dialog box.

4 Click Web Server

On the **Administer Website** dialog box, click the **Web Server** link. The **Web Server** dialog box appears.

5 Click Web Addresses, Then Click Add

Click the **Web Addresses** tab and click the **Add** button.

6 Type the Alternate URL

Enter an alternate URL in the box provided and click **OK**. The new URL appears in the list.

7 Click OK

Click **OK** to close the **Add or Edit Alternate Address** dialog box, then click **Close**.

13

Managing Roles and Sharing Connections

IN THIS CHAPTER:

Contribute is all about control—giving contributors enough control to add the content they're responsible for, but also restricting those users from making changes they don't need to make, preventing mistaken edits and other changes to the site that the Webmaster would then need to clean up.

That control is governed by the *roles* (selected bundles of users with common needs or responsibilities) and *role settings*.

In this chapter, you (as administrator) take control: You define roles and settings. Having done that, you take the final step in deploying Contribute—sending connection keys to users.

89 About Roles

Roles are simple enough: They're just selected lists of users who will edit Contribute websites. You can divide up your users into groups any way you like—and you can include a given user in more than one group. The thing to remember is that role settings always apply to a whole group. You can't give one user in a group the power to edit a particular thing and restrict another user in the same group from doing so. Of course, all members in a role edit the same site or the same folders within that site.

Before creating roles and settings, you'll want to spend some time looking at the available options and deciding which users you want in which role. You might wind up simply creating a different role for each company department, or you might put less experienced computer users in a role to which you assign very restrictive settings and more experienced users in another role with settings that enable greater control.

PART IV: Administering Websites

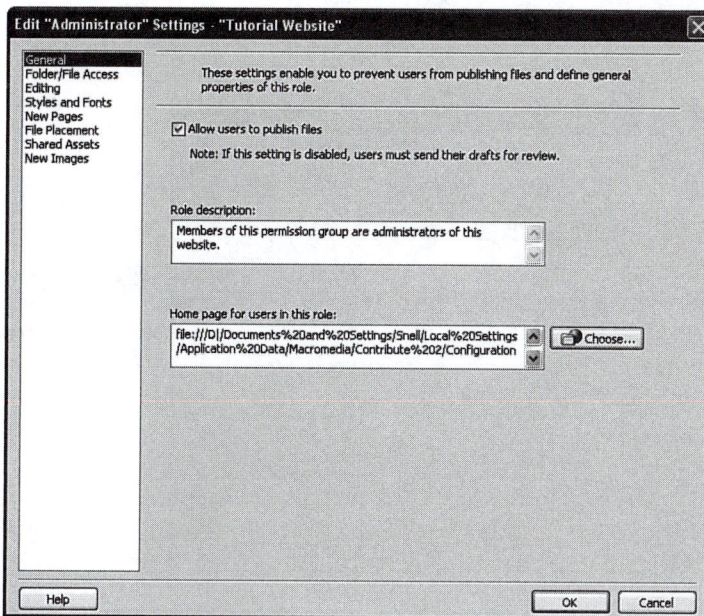

Editing role settings.

After you've created your roles, you can define the settings for each role. Settings are defined on a dialog with a list of categories along the left, each of which opens a different list of settings on the right.

90 Create a New Role

Before you can define the settings for a role, you must create that role. When you create a new connection, two roles are set up automatically to get you started: **Administrators** and **Users**. It's taken for granted that you'll probably want to grant Contribute administrators greater editing power than other users. For example, you might want to enable administrators of a site to delete pages, but deny that power to users.

If you have only a small group of users editing a particular site, the Users role might be all you need. However, if you have a larger number of users, you'll need to set up a separate role for each set of settings you intend to define.

Before You Begin

✔ **89** About Roles

1 Choose Edit, Administer Websites

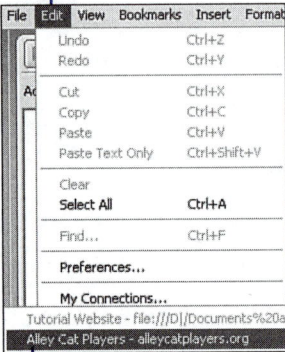

File | Edit | View | Bookmarks | Insert | Format

Undo	Ctrl+Z
Redo	Ctrl+Y
Cut	Ctrl+X
Copy	Ctrl+C
Paste	Ctrl+V
Paste Text Only	Ctrl+Shift+V
Clear	
Select All	Ctrl+A
Find...	Ctrl+F
Preferences...	
My Connections...	

Tutorial Website - file:///D|/Documents%20a
Alley Cat Players - alleycatplayers.org

2 Choose the Site to Administer

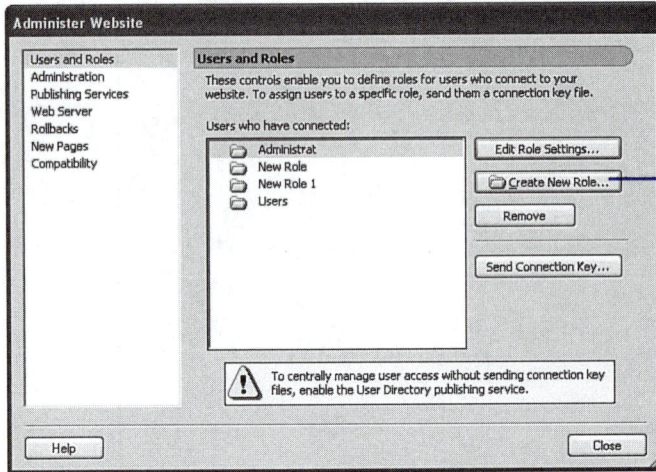

Administer Website

Users and Roles
Administration
Publishing Services
Web Server
Rollbacks
New Pages
Compatibility

Users and Roles
These controls enable you to define roles for users who connect to your website. To assign users to a specific role, send them a connection key file.

Users who have connected:

- Administrat
- New Role
- New Role 1
- Users

Edit Role Settings...
Create New Role...
Remove

Send Connection Key...

3 Click Create New Role

⚠ To centrally manage user access without sending connection key files, enable the User Directory publishing service.

Help   Close

4 Choose a Role to Copy From

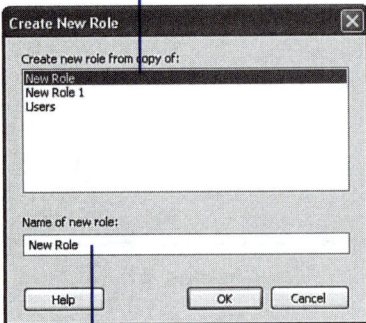

Create New Role

Create new role from copy of:
New Role
New Role 1
Users

Name of new role:
New Role

Help   OK   Cancel

5 Name the Group

Administer Website - Alley Cat Players - alleycatplayers.org

Sitewide settings
These settings apply to all Contribute users editing pages on your website.

Sitewide Settings...

Permission groups
Permission groups limit what Contribute users can do on your website. To restrict a user to a specific group, send a connection key to the user.

Administrator
Users
Marketing
Development
Sales

Edit Group...
New...
Duplicate...
Delete

6 Create More Groups

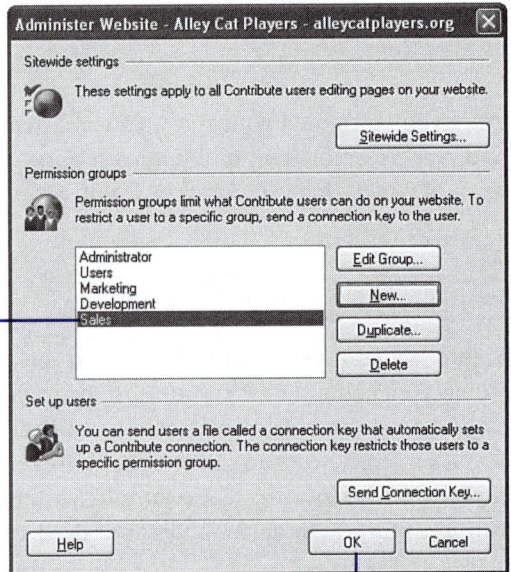

Set up users
You can send users a file called a connection key that automatically sets up a Contribute connection. The connection key restricts those users to a specific permission group.

Send Connection Key...

Help   OK   Cancel

7 Click Close

1 ## Choose Edit, Administer Websites

Choose **Edit, Administer Websites**. As soon as you point to **Administer Websites**, that menu item is displaced by a list of sites to which you have a connection.

2 ## Choose the Site to Administer

Click on the website address to administer. Contribute prompts you for your administrator password. Type your administrator password and then click **OK** to open the **Administer Website** dialog box.

3 ## Click Create New Role

In the **Administer Website** dialog box, click the **Create New Role** button. The Create New Role dialog box appears.

4 ## Choose a Role to Copy From

From the list of roles, choose the role whose settings most closely match the role you are creating.

5 ## Name the Group

Type a name for this group in the **Name of new role** box and then click **OK**.

6 ## Create More Groups

Repeat steps 3 and 4 for each group you want to add.

7 ## Click Close

To close the **Administer Website** dialog box, click **Close**.

---

91 ## Set General Role Settings

The "general" role settings let you type a description for the role to help identify it and choose a different home page on the site for this group than the regular home page for the site. For example, if this role will edit only a particular page on the site, you can set that page up as their "home" page so that Contribute takes them right to it when they connect.

NOTE

If you don't see the site you want to administer in step 2, you don't yet have a connection to it. You must first create a connection to a site and also be named the administrator before you can administer it (see **82** Create or Edit Connections with the Wizard and **83** Become Administrator of a Website).

Before You Begin

✔ **89** About Role

✔ **90** Create a New Role

1 Choose Edit, Administer Websites

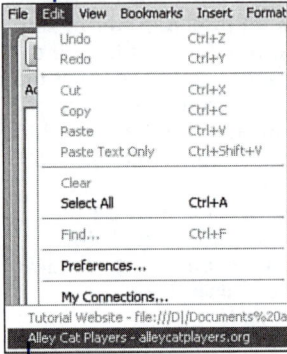

3 Choose a Role

4 Click Edit Role Settings

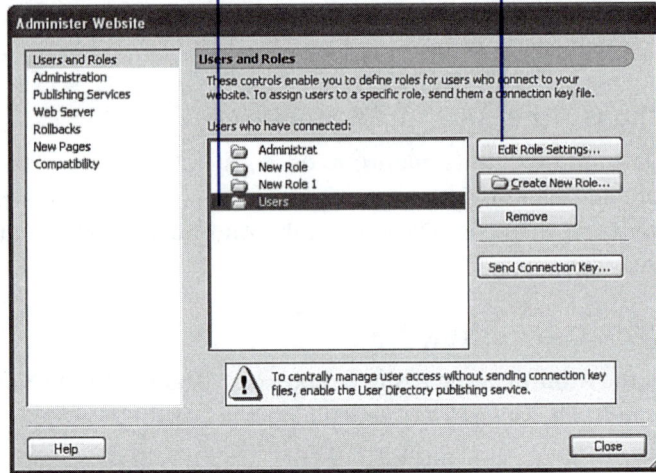

2 Choose the Site to Administer

5 Click General

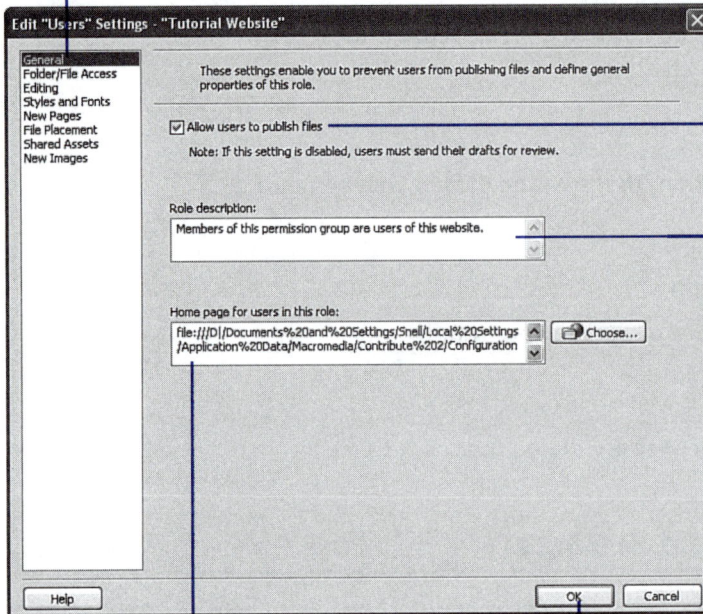

6 Choose Whether Users in the Role May Publish

7 Describe the Role

8 Choose a Role Home Page

9 Choose Again or Click OK

1 ## Choose Edit, Administer Websites

Choose **Edit, Administer Websites**. As soon as you point to Administer Websites, that menu item is displaced by a list of sites to which you have a connection.

2 ## Choose the Site to Administer

Click on the website address to administer. Contribute prompts you for your administrator password. Type your administrator password and then click **OK** to open the **Administer Website** dialog box.

3 ## Choose a Role

In the list of roles, choose the one for which you want to edit settings.

4 ## Click Edit Role Settings

Click the **Edit Role Settings** button to open the settings for the role you selected in step 3.

5 ## Click General

In the list of categories on the left of the dialog box, click **General** (if it is not already selected).

6 ## Choose Whether Users in the Role May Publish

Check the check box to enable users in this role to publish their work.

7 ## Describe the Role

Type a description of this role and the website the role edits in the upper text box.

8 ## Choose a Role Home Page

The **Home page** text box shows the current home page for the website. If you (or the website's author) have set up role-specific home pages, you can change the home page for this role by clicking the **Choose** button and then selecting the new home page from a list of files on the site.

9 **Choose Again or Click OK**

Choose another category in the left panel to edit other settings (as described throughout this chapter), or click **OK** to close the **Edit Role Settings** dialog box and then click **Close** to close the **Administer Website** dialog box.

92 **Set Folder and File Access Role Settings**

Before You Begin

✔ **89** About Roles

✔ **90** Create a New Role

The file/folder access permissions could be the most important you'll define. You use these permissions to determine whether users can edit any page on a site to which they have a connection, or only pages in certain folders. You also choose here whether users in the group can delete pages from the site.

TIP

If you intend to limit a role's editing to pages in certain folders, you'll first need to work with the website's webmaster or author to isolate those pages within one or more folders on the server.

1 **Choose Edit, Administer Websites**

Choose **Edit, Administer Websites**. As soon as you point to **Administer Websites**, that menu item is displaced by a list of sites to which you have a connection.

2 **Choose the Site to Administer**

Click on the website address to administer. Contribute prompts you for your administrator password. Type your administrator password and then click **OK** to open the **Administer Website** dialog box.

3 **Choose a Role**

In the list of roles, choose the one for which you want to edit settings.

4 **Click Edit Role Settings**

Click the **Edit Role Settings** button to open the settings for the role you selected in step 3.

5 **Click Folder/File Access**

In the list of categories to the left of the dialog box, click **Folder/File Access**.

1 Choose Edit, Administer Websites

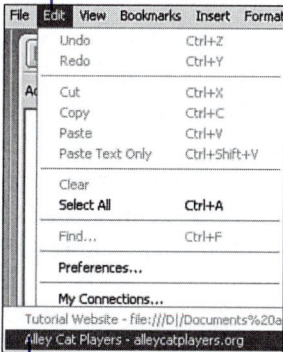

2 Choose the Site to Administer

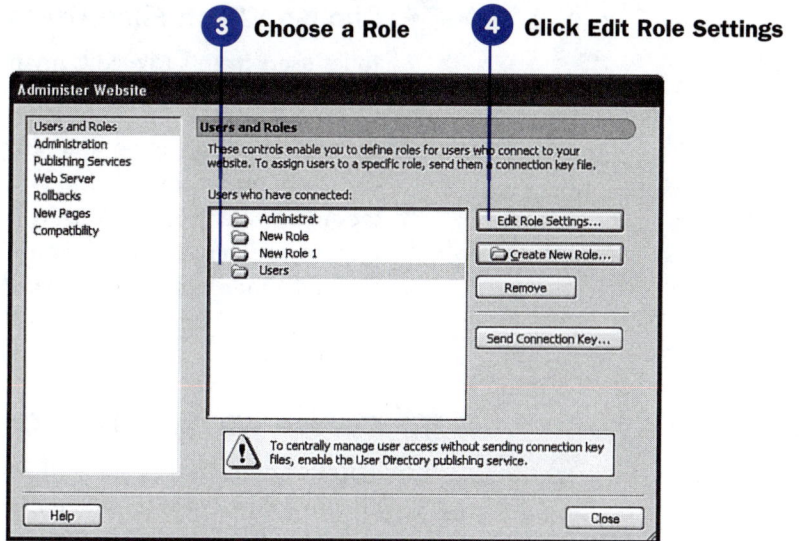

3 Choose a Role

4 Click Edit Role Settings

5 Click Folder/ File Access

6 Choose Which Files Users May Edit

7 Choose Whether Users Can Delete Pages

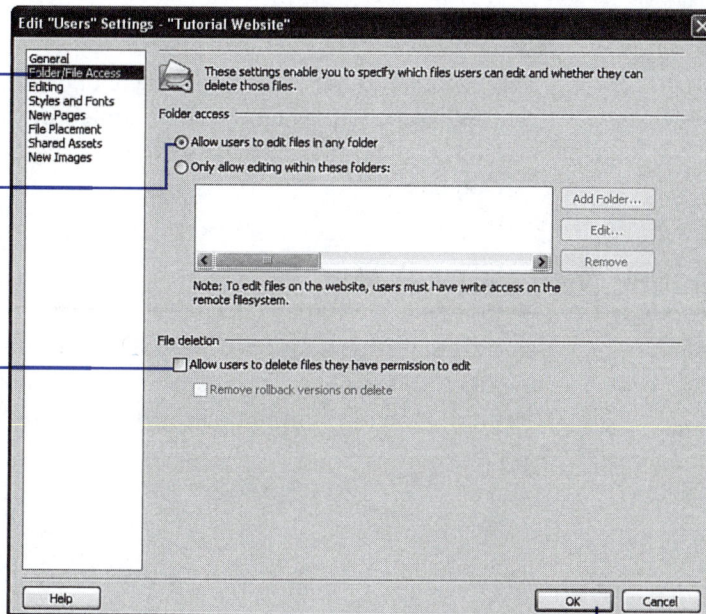

8 Choose Again or Click OK

6 Choose Which Files Users May Edit

To let users in this role edit any file in any folder on the site, click **Allow users to edit files in any folder.**

To restrict this role to editing only files contained in particular folders, click **Only allow editing within these folders** and then click the **Add Folder** button. A list of all folders in the site appears. Choose a folder you want this role to be permitted to edit and then click the **Open** button. Click the **Add Folder** button again to add more folders; when you are finished, all the folders this group may edit appear in the Folder access list.

7 Choose Whether Users Can Delete Pages

To allow users in this role to delete pages from the folders they edit, choose **Allow users to delete files they have permission to edit.** If you do not choose this option, users in this role won't be able to delete pages.

8 Choose Again or Click OK

Choose another category in the left panel to edit other role settings (as described throughout this chapter) or click **OK** to close the dialog box and then click **Close** to close the **Administer Website** dialog box.

---

93 Set Editing Role Settings

Before You Begin

✔ **89** About Roles

✔ **90** Create a New Role

Sometimes, restricting users from editing certain folders and from deleting pages isn't enough. You might want even tighter control over what users can do, and assuming that level of control begins with the editing settings.

1 Choose Edit, Administer Websites

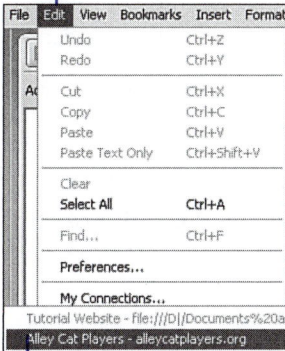

4 Click Edit Role Settings

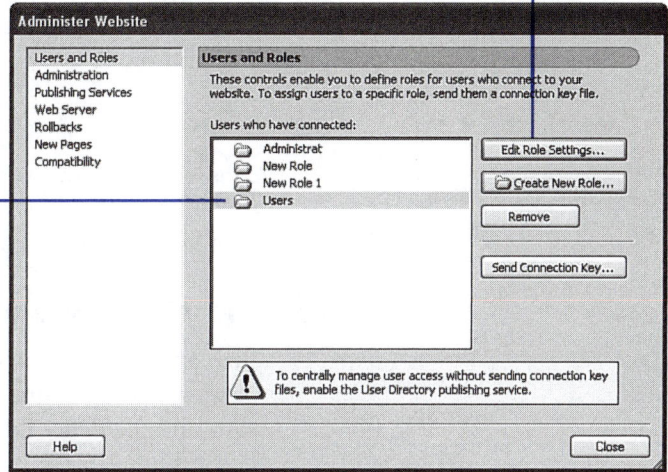

3 Choose a Role

2 Choose the Site to Administer

6 Choose Options for General Editing Restrictions

5 Click Editing

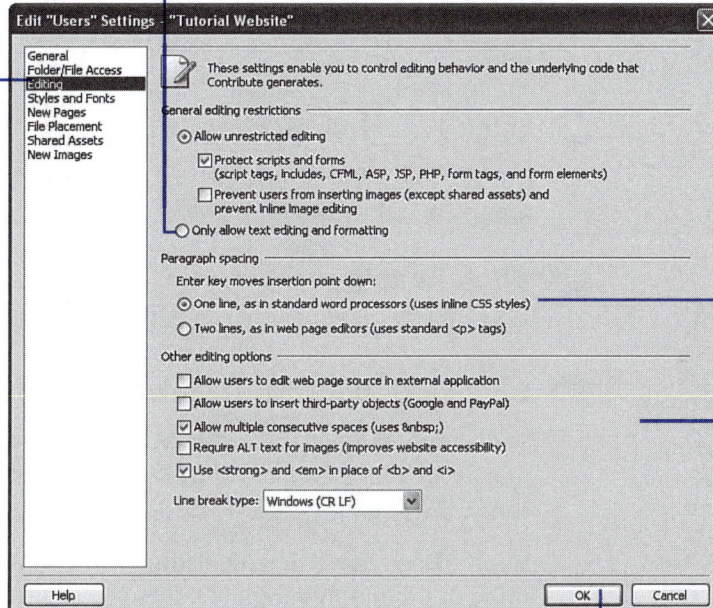

7 Choose Options for Paragraph Spacing

8 Choose Among Options for Other Editing Tasks

9 Choose Again or Click OK

Here you can prevent users from inadvertently changing important script coding embedded in page files, decide whether pressing the **Enter** key when editing text simply breaks the line (as in a word processor) or inserts a blank line and starts a new paragraph (as in a web-authoring program), and more.

1 Choose Edit, Administer Websites

Choose **Edit, Administer Websites**. As soon as you point to **Administer Websites**, that menu item is displaced by a list of sites to which you have a connection.

2 Choose the Site to Administer

Click on the website address to administer. Contribute prompts you for your administrator password. Type your administrator password and then click **OK** to open the **Administer Website** dialog box.

3 Choose a Role

In the list of roles, choose the one for which you want to edit settings.

4 Click Edit Role Settings

Click the **Edit Role Settings** button to open the settings for the group you selected in step 3.

5 Click Editing

In the list of categories on the left of the dialog box, click **Editing**.

TIP

By default, the **Protect scripts and forms** option is selected, and for most roles, it's probably wise to leave it selected. Contribute provides users with no tools for editing this code, and few users will possess the skill to edit it properly, anyway.

6 Choose Options for General Editing Restrictions

Select from the options in the **General Edition Restrictions** section of the dialog box to control the general types of changes users can make to pages.

Select **Allow unrestricted editing** to permit users to change anything at all in non-template pages.

Select **Protect scripts and forms** to prevent users from deleting (intentionally or not) embedded script and form code such as script tags, server-side includes, ColdFusion tags, ASP tags, JSP tags, PHP tags, and form tags.

Select **Prevent users from inserting images…** to block users from inserting or editing inline images.

Select **Only allow text editing and formatting** to restrict users to making only text and text formatting changes to pages, preventing them from adding, deleting, or changing tables, images, links, or plug-ins.

7 **Choose Options for Paragraph Spacing**

The standard method of separating paragraphs in web pages is the HTML **<p>** tag, which inserts a single blank line between paragraphs. However, in pages using CSS styles, it's also possible to break paragraphs in a more word-processor-like way, where one press of the **Enter** key ends a paragraph, two presses insert a blank line, three presses insert two blank lines, and so on. The **Paragraph spacing** section of the **Edit Role Settings** dialog box lets you choose which method Contribute users apply when they hit the **Enter** key:

One line, as in standard word processors applies CSS tags to let users end paragraphs and insert blank lines, just as they would with a word processor.

Two lines, as in Web page editors makes Contribute behave more like a standard web-authoring program, applying a **<p>** tag to end a paragraph and insert one (and only one) blank line each time the user presses **Enter**.

8 **Choose Among Options for Other Editing Tasks**

The **Other editing options** section offers a few final, random choices:

Select **Allow users to edit web page source in external application** to enable users to change the HTML source code of a Contribute page in another editing program.

Select **Allow users to insert third-party objects (Google and Paypal)** to enable users to embed Google (to provide site visitors with web searching) or PayPal (to provide online payments) objects in their sites.

> **TIP**
>
> Allowing Contribute to apply CSS styles, as you would if you selected the **One line, as in standard word processors** option, gives users more control over the formatting and layout of pages. Unlike straight HTML, however, CSS is not universally recognized among browsers, although all recent versions of Internet Explorer and Netscape do support CSS.

> **TIP**
>
> The "other" editing options are mostly about choosing between the strictest application of standard web page coding or a more flexible, but perhaps less universally recognized, alternative. The default settings for these are pretty good choices; as a rule, unless you have a really good reason to change them, it's best to leave these options alone.

> **KEY TERM**
>
> **Accessibility**—A general term for accommodations made in software and web pages to enable those with various disabilities to make use of them. Common accessibility measures include coding descriptive "alternate" text describing a site's images, which can be read by the text-to-speech software used by those with visual impairments.

Select **Allow multiple consecutive spaces (uses)** to enable users to insert multiple consecutive spaces between words, like this. When this option is not selected, pages edited in Contribute will show only a single space between words, no matter how many times the user presses the spacebar.

Select **Require ALT text for images** to instruct Contribute to prompt users any time they neglect to use a feature that would make the page more accessible to people with disabilities.

Select **Use <strong> and <em> in place of <b> and <i>** to have Contribute encode the *<strong>* (for bold) and *<em>* (emphasis, for italics) tags instead of the more common *<b>* and *<i>* tags when the user formats text as bold or italic. Choosing this option makes the HTML code generated by Contribute more in line with current HTML practices.

Open the **Line break type** list to choose the character combination coding Contribute uses to indicate the ends of lines in a paragraph. Windows is the default (and probably best) choice. If the site is to be deployed on a Mac- or Unix-based server, you might want to change the line break type to match the system type used. Check with the site's webmaster to determine the type of server and line break setting to use.

9 Choose Again or Click OK

Choose another category in the left panel to edit other categories (as described throughout this chapter) or click **OK** to close the dialog box and then click **Close** to close the **Administer Website** dialog box.

---

94 **Set Style and Font Role Settings**

Before You Begin

✔ **89** About Roles

✔ **90** Create a New Role

Carefully selected text fonts and paragraph styles are a big part of giving a page design identity—an identity you could want to protect and preserve, even with multiple editors doing their thing to the content.

The style and font settings let you control how users in a group can apply styles and fonts, so you can ensure that changes to the words don't inadvertently cause changes in the page's personality.

1 Choose Edit, Administer Websites

Choose **Edit**, **Administer Websites**. As soon as you point to **Administer Websites**, that menu item is displaced by a list of sites to which you have a connection.

2 Choose the Site to Administer

Click on the website address to administer. Contribute prompts you for your administrator password. Type your administrator password and then click **OK** to open the **Administer Website** dialog box.

3 Choose a Role

In the list of roles, choose the one for which you want to edit permissions.

4 Click Edit Role Settings

Click the **Edit Role Settings** button to open the settings for the role you selected in step 3.

5 Click Styles and Fonts

In the list of categories on the left of the dialog box, click **Styles and Fonts**.

6 Choose Style Options

Select **Allow users to apply styles** to allow users to apply paragraph styles to text. When this option is not selected, users can't apply paragraph styles, and the style list does not even appear on the Edit toolbar. If you enable the **Allow users to apply styles** option, you have two more choices to make about which kinds of styles to include in the Style list on the Edit toolbar:

Choose **Include HTML heading styles in the Style menu** to enable the user to apply the standard HTML style tags: Paragraph, Heading 1, Heading 2, and so on.

Choose **Include CSS styles in the Style menu** to enable the user to apply any CSS styles included in the page's stylesheet by the website's author.

TIP

For more about paragraph styles, see **17** About **Text Formatting** and **18** **Change the Style of Text.**

TIP

Letting Contribute apply CSS styles, as you would if you selected the **Include CSS styles in the Style menu** or the **Inline CSS styles** options in the Styles and Fonts part of the dialog box, gives users more control over the formatting and layout of pages. Unlike straight HTML, however, CSS is not universally recognized among browsers, although all recent versions of Internet Explorer and Netscape do support CSS.

1 Choose Edit, Administer Websites

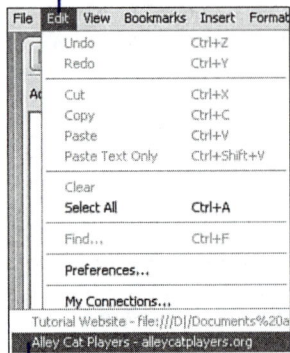

4 Click Edit Role Settings

File Edit View Bookmarks Insert Format

Undo	Ctrl+Z
Redo	Ctrl+Y
Cut	Ctrl+X
Copy	Ctrl+C
Paste	Ctrl+V
Paste Text Only	Ctrl+Shift+V
Clear	
Select All	Ctrl+A
Find...	Ctrl+F
Preferences...	
My Connections...	

Tutorial Website - file:///D|/Documents%20a
Alley Cat Players - alleycatplayers.org

2 Choose the Site to Administer

Administer Website

Users and Roles
Administration
Publishing Services
Web Server
Rollbacks
New Pages
Compatibility

Users and Roles

These controls enable you to define roles for users who connect to your website. To assign users to a specific role, send them a connection key file.

Users who have connected:

📁 Administrat
📁 New Role
📁 New Role 1
📁 Users

Edit Role Settings...
Create New Role...
Remove
Send Connection Key...

⚠ To centrally manage user access without sending connection key files, enable the User Directory publishing service.

Help   Close

3 Choose a Role

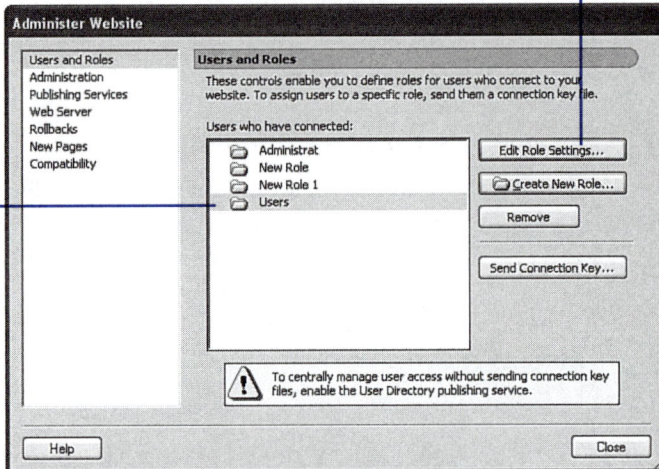

Edit "Users" Settings - "Tutorial Website"

General
Folder/File Access
Editing
Styles and Fonts
New Pages
File Placement
Shared Assets
New Images

A These settings control the types of style and font formatting that users can apply.

Style support: Document-level CSS (<span class="styleName">)

☑ Allow users to apply styles (displays the Style menu)
   ☑ Include HTML heading styles (<h1>, ...) in the Style menu
   ☑ Include CSS styles in the Style menu
      ⦿ Show all CSS styles
      ○ Show only CSS styles included in CSS filter file:

      📁 Choose...

☑ Allow users to apply fonts and sizes (displays the Font and Size menus)
   Apply sizes using: Pixels
☑ Allow users to apply bold, italic, underline, strikethrough, and fixed width styles
☑ Allow users to apply font color and background color

Help   OK   Cancel

5 Click Styles and Fonts

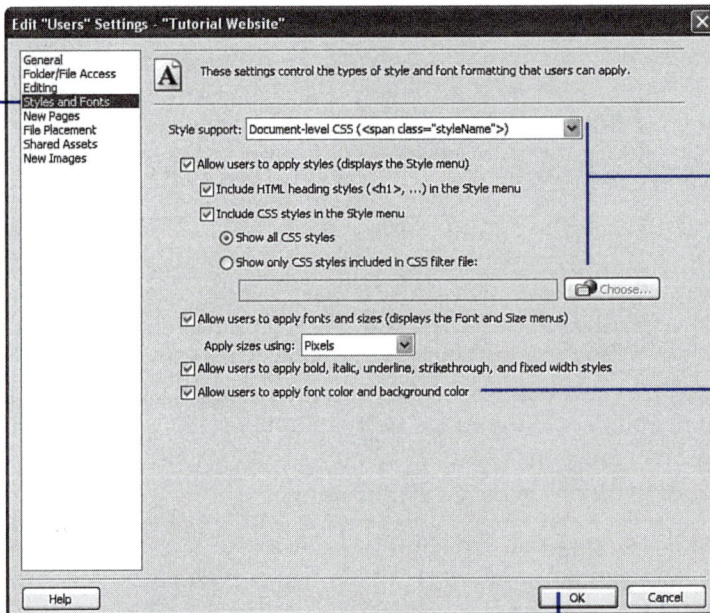

6 Choose Style Options

7 Choose Font Options

8 Choose Again or Click OK

7 Choose Font Options

Select **Allow users to apply fonts and sizes** to enable the Font and Size lists in the Edit toolbar. When this option is not selected, users can edit text, but cannot change its font or size. If you enable the **Allow users to apply fonts and sizes** option, you have a few more choices to make about which kinds of styles to include in the Style list on the Edit toolbar:

Select **HTML tags** to enable Contribute to apply fonts using HTML font tags. This is the most standard and widely used method for defining fonts in web pages.

Select **Inline CSS styles** to enable Contribute to apply fonts using inline CSS font tags. This method is less widely used than HTML tags, but it enables more varied font choices and works just fine for nearly all up-to-date browsers. If you enable this option, you may also select an option from the **Apply sizes using** list to determine which unit of measurement to display for font size in the Edit toolbar: **Points**, **Pixels**, or **Ems**.

8 Choose Again or Click OK

Choose another category in the left panel to edit other categories (as described throughout this chapter) or click **OK** to close the dialog box and then click **Close** to close the **Administer Website** dialog box.

TIP

None of the choices for **Apply sizes using** really enables exact control of text size. A *point* is 1/72nd of an inch, so 18-point type would be 1/4" high, although the actual size depends on the resolution and monitor size. A *pixel* is one dot on the screen. Pixel measurements are handy because they keep the size of text relative to other text sizes the same, regardless of the display resolution. *Ems* are tricky; they are a relative measurement that differs from font to font. Ems can be good when accessibility is important, however, because em-sized text is easily enlarged by programs used by those with visual impairments.

95 Choose Settings for New Web Pages

The new pages settings let you control which types of new pages users in a role can add to the site. You can, for example, restrict users to adding pages only based on particular templates or only to pages based on copies of other pages on the site. Like the style and font permissions, these options help you ensure that new pages added to the site match the rest of the site in style and format.

1 Choose Edit, Administer Websites

Choose **Edit, Administer Websites**. As soon as you point to **Administer Websites**, that menu item is displaced by a list of sites to which you have a connection.

Before You Begin

✔ **89** About Roles
✔ **90** Create a New Role

2 Choose the Site to Administer

Click on the website address to administer. Contribute prompts you for your administrator password. Type your administrator password and then click **OK** to open the **Administer Website** dialog box.

3 Choose a Role

In the list of **roles**, choose the one for which you want to edit settings.

4 Click Edit Role Setting

Click the **Edit Role Settings** button to open the settings for the role you selected in step 3.

5 Click New Pages

In the list of categories on the left of the dialog box, click **New Pages**.

6 Choose How Users Can Create New Pages

Select one, two, or all of the choices for how users will be permitted to add new pages to the site:

Create a blank page enables users to add new, blank pages.

Use built-in sample pages enables users to add new pages based on the samples included with Contribute.

Create a new page by copying any page on the website enables users to add new pages by making copies of existing pages on the site and then editing them.

Create a new page by copying a page from this list enables users to add new pages based on non-Dreamweaver templates created especially for your company or this site, usually by the website's author. If you select this option, use the **Add** button to open a dialog box for navigating to and selecting the template files. These templates will be displayed in the list of templates the user sees after choosing to add a new page based on a template (**see** **60** **Use a Template to Make a New Page**).

1 Choose Edit, Administer Websites

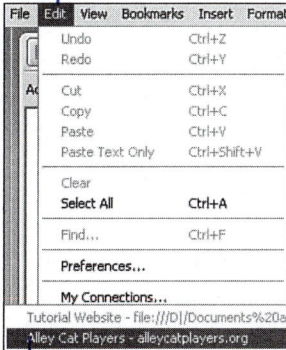

4 Click Edit Role Settings

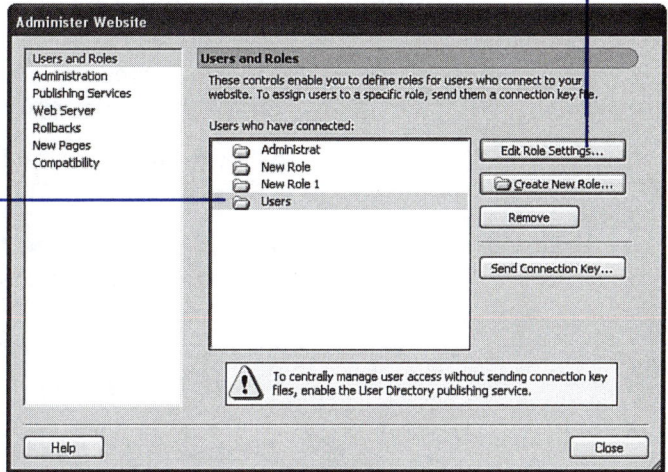

3 Choose a Role

2 Choose the Site to Administer

5 Click New Pages

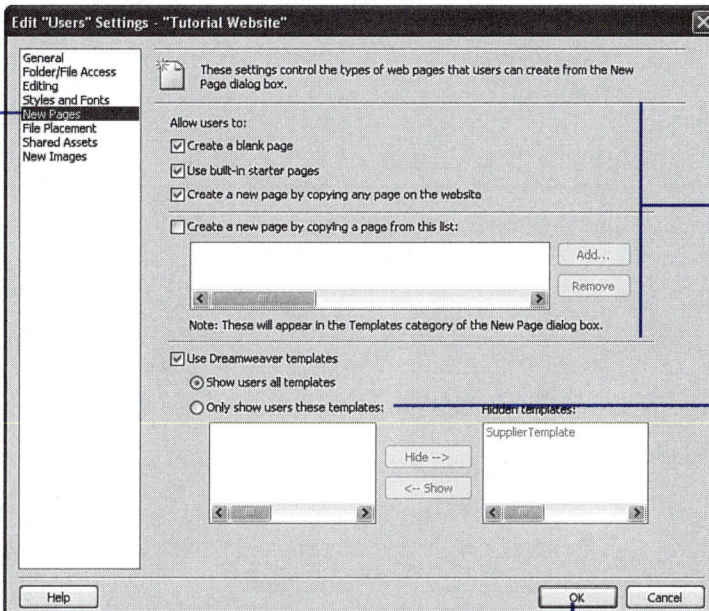

6 Choose How Users Can Create New Pages

7 Choose Whether to Use Dreamweaver Templates

8 Choose Again or Click OK

7 Choose Whether to Use Dreamweaver Templates

The **Use Dreamweaver templates** option lets users add new pages based on templates created in Dreamweaver, especially for your company or this site, usually by the Web site's author. If you choose this option, you also have a few other choices to make:

Select **Show users all templates** to allow users to see and use all Dreamweaver templates set up for this site.

Select **Only show users these templates** to allow users to see and use only certain templates. After choosing this option, select the templates shown in the list one at a time, clicking **Hide** (to hide the page from users in this group) or **Show** (to enable users to see and use the selected template).

8 Choose Again or Click OK

Choose another category in the left panel to edit other permission categories (as described throughout this chapter) or click **OK** to close the dialog box and then click **Close** to close the **Administer Website** dialog box.

96 Set File Placement Role Settings

Before You Begin

✔ **89** About Roles

✔ **90** Create a New Role

The File Placement role settings settings enable you to control where and how images and other linked files in websites edited by this role are stored. You can choose different placement rules for images, Microsoft Office and PDF files, and all others, and you can create new categories of external files. The File Placement settings also enable you to limit the size of linked files used by this role.

1 Choose Edit, Administer Websites

Choose **Edit, Administer Websites**. As soon as you point to **Administer Websites**, that menu item is displaced by a list of sites to which you have a connection.

2 Choose the Site to Administer

Click on the website address to administer.

1 Choose Edit, Administer Websites

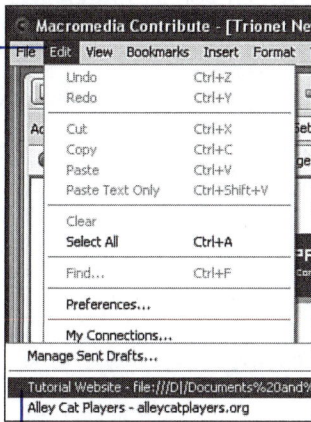

3 Choose a Role

4 Click Edit Role Settings

2 Choose the Site to Administer

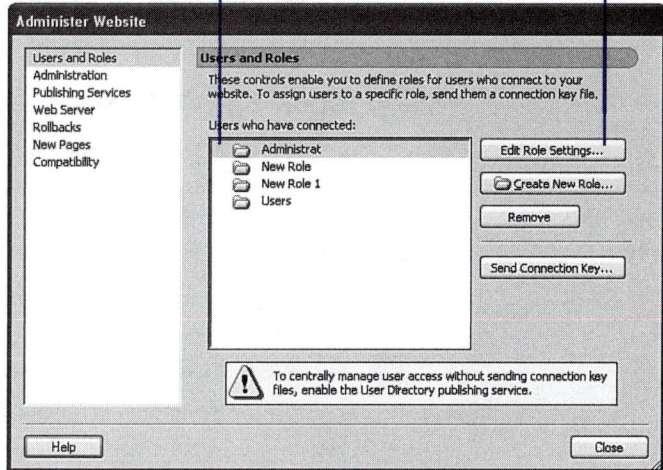

5 Click File Placement

6 Choose Your File Placement Rules

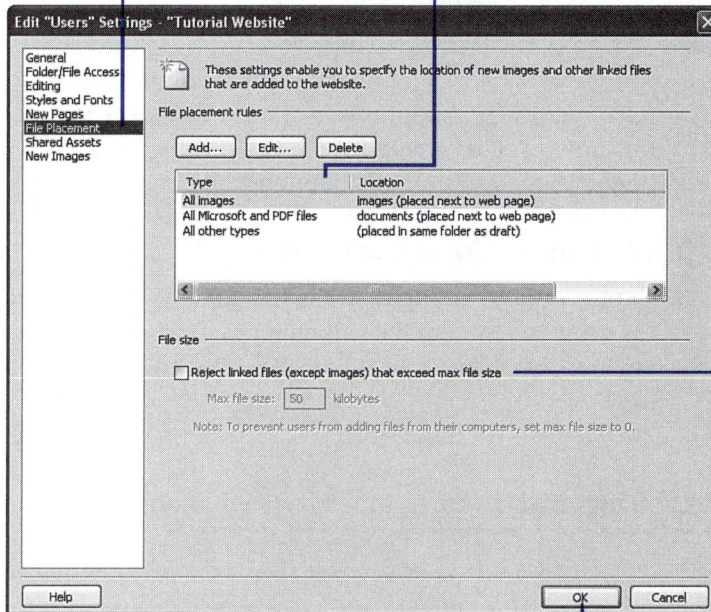

7 Choose a Maximum Linked File Size

8 Choose Again or Click OK

③ Choose a Role

In the list of roles, choose the one for which you want to edit settings.

④ Click Edit Role Settings

Click the **Edit Role Settings** button to open the settings for the role you selected in step 3.

⑤ Click File Placement

From the list of categories on the left, choose **File Placement**.

⑥ Choose Your File Placement Rules

Use the options provided to create or edit file placement rules. To review or edit any of the three default rule sets (**all images, Microsoft and PDF, all others**), choose a rule set and click the **Edit** button. To create a new rule set for placement of another file type, click **Add**.

⑦ Choose a Maximum Linked File Size

Use the check box to impose a maximum allowable linked file size, and enter the maximum file size in the **Max file size box**. Users in this role will not be permitted to insert linked files (other than images) larger than the maximum.

⑧ Choose Again or Click OK

Choose another category in the left panel to edit other settings (as described throughout this chapter), or click **OK** to close the dialog box and then click **Close** to close the Administer Websites dialog box.

TIP

The maximum linked file size you define in Step 8 applies to all linked files except images. To control the size of image files, see **98** **Choose Settings for New Images**.

---

97 **Set Shared Assets Role Settings**

Before You Begin

✔ **89** About Roles

✔ **90** Create a New Role

The Shared Assets role settings enable you to create and manage a list of shared assets, such as images or other linked files stored on the server and inserted in multiple pages, by multiple users—for example, a logo image to go atop every page.

---

1 Choose Edit, Administer Websites

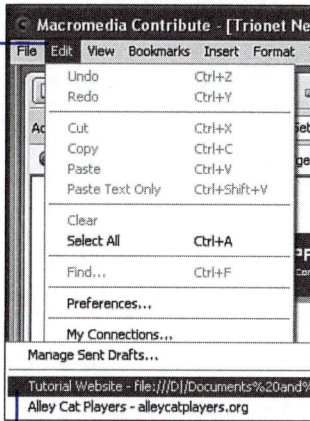

3 Choose a Role

4 Click Edit Role Settings

2 Choose the Site to Administer

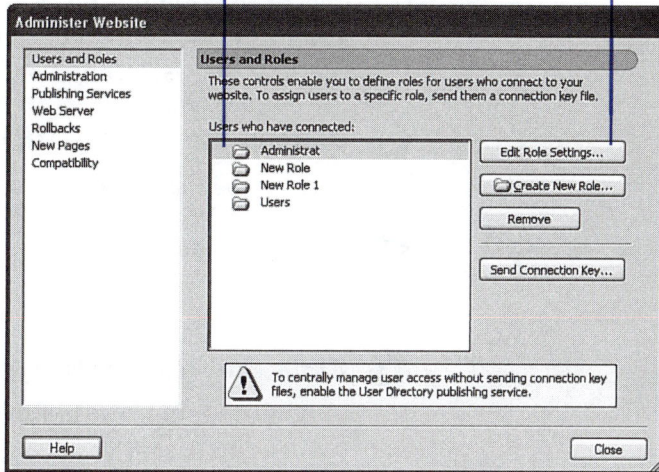

5 Click Shared Assets

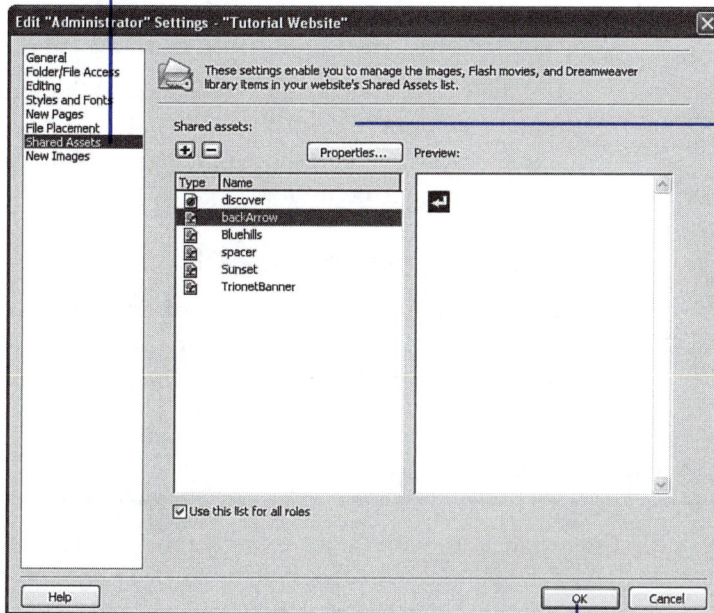

6 Create and Manage Your Shared Assets List

7 Choose Again or Click OK

1 Choose Edit, Administer Websites

Choose **Edit, Administer Websites**. As soon as you point to **Administer Websites**, that menu item is displaced by a list of sites to which you have a connection.

2 Choose the Site to Administer

Click on the website address to administer.

3 Choose a Role

In the list of roles, choose the one for which you want to edit settings.

4 Click Edit Role Settings

Click the **Edit Role Settings** button to open the settings for the role you selected in step 3.

5 Click Shared Assets

From the list of categories on the left, choose **Shared Assets**.

6 Create and Manage Your Shared Assets List

Use the options provided to create or edit the shared assets list. To add a new asset to the list, click the plus (**+**) button. To change the name or ALT text of a shared image, select the image in the list and click the **Properties** button.

TIP

Check the **use this list for all roles** check box to enforce this list across all roles. If you leave the box unchecked, these shared assets settings will apply only to the role you selected in step 3.

7 Choose Again or Click OK

Choose another category in the left panel to edit other settings (as described throughout this chapter), or click **OK** to close the dialog box and then click **Close** to close the Administer Websites dialog box.

---

98 Choose Settings for New Images

Before You Begin

✔ **89** About Roles

✔ **90** Create a New Role

The new images settings govern only one aspect of new images: size. You have the option to allow users to add new images of any size. However, users unschooled in the effects of oversized image files (slow page response, clogged server disks, and so on) could unknowingly insert unnecessarily large image files in pages. These settings enable you to limit file size to keep the site responsive.

PART IV: Administering Websites

1 Choose Edit, Administer Websites

Choose **Edit, Administer Websites**. As soon as you point to **Administer Websites**, that menu item is displaced by a list of sites to which you have a connection.

2 Choose the Site to Administer

Click on the website address to administer. Contribute prompts you for your administrator password. Type your administrator password and then click **OK** to open the **Administer Website** dialog box.

3 Choose a Role

In the list of roles, choose the one for which you want to edit settings.

4 Click Edit Role Settings

Click the **Edit Role Settings** button to open the settings for the role you selected in step 3.

5 Click New Images

In the list of categories on the left, click **New Images**.

6 Enable Contribute Image Processing

Check the **Enable Contribute image processing when inserting images** check box to enable the other new image settings. If you clear this check box, Contribute will not automatically limit image sizes for this role.

7 Choose the Maximum Area

Select **Automatically reduce image dimensions if they exceed these limits** and complete the fields below it to limit the maximum size (screen area) of an inserted image and define the maximum JPEG quality allowed. When a user in this role inserts a larger image and/or one with a higher JPEG quality setting, the image will be automatically reset within the limits.

1 Choose Edit, Administer Websites

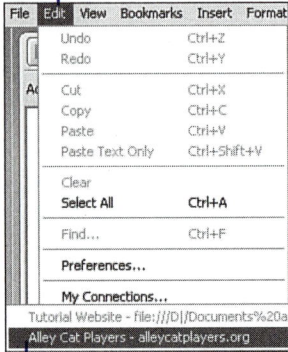

4 Click Edit Role Settings

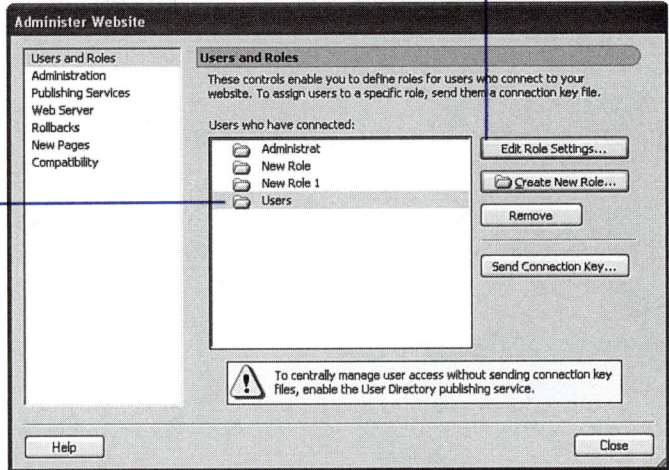

File	Edit	View	Bookmarks	Insert	Format

Undo	Ctrl+Z
Redo	Ctrl+Y
Cut	Ctrl+X
Copy	Ctrl+C
Paste	Ctrl+V
Paste Text Only	Ctrl+Shift+V
Clear	
Select All	Ctrl+A
Find...	Ctrl+F
Preferences...	
My Connections...	
Tutorial Website - file:///D|/Documents%20a	
Alley Cat Players - alleycatplayers.org	

Administer Website

Users and Roles
Administration
Publishing Services
Web Server
Rollbacks
New Pages
Compatibility

Users and Roles

These controls enable you to define roles for users who connect to your website. To assign users to a specific role, send them a connection key file.

Users who have connected:

- Administrat
- New Role
- New Role 1
- Users

Edit Role Settings...

Create New Role...

Remove

Send Connection Key...

⚠ To centrally manage user access without sending connection key files, enable the User Directory publishing service.

Help   Close

3 Choose a Role

2 Choose the Site to Administer

5 Click New Images

Edit "Users" Settings - "Tutorial Website"

General
Folder/File Access
Editing
Styles and Fonts
New Pages
File Placement
Shared Assets
New Images

These settings control the way images are inserted into pages. They do not affect images inserted from shared assets.

☑ Enable Contribute image processing when inserting images

⊙ Automatically reduce image dimensions if they exceed these limits:

Max width: 700 pixels

Max height: 700 pixels

JPEG quality: 70 percent

○ Reject images that exceed max file size

Max file size: 64 kilobytes

Note: To prevent users from inserting and editing images, select Editing on the left, then enable the option to only allow text editing and formatting.

Help   OK   Cancel

6 Enable Contribute Image Processing

7 Choose the Maximum Area

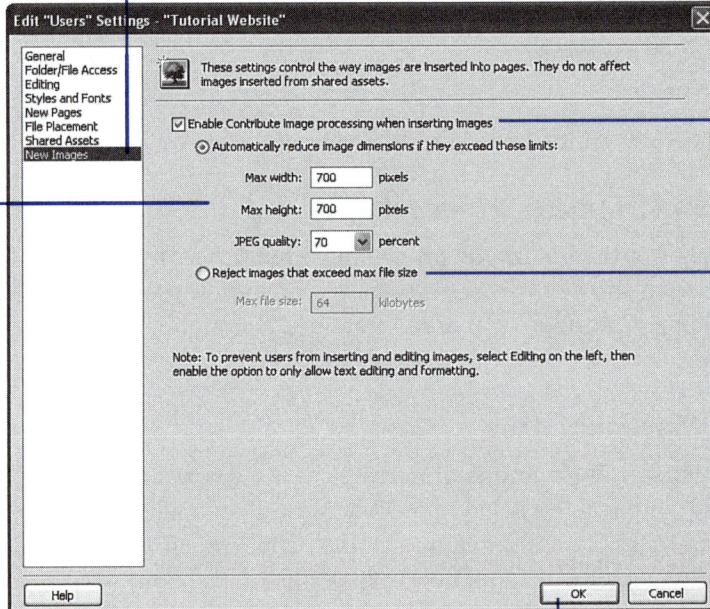

8 Choose the Maximum File Size

9 Choose Again or Click OK

8 Choose the Maximum File Size

Select **Reject images that exceed max file size**, and enter a maximum file size in the field below it, to prevent users in this role from inserting image files larger than the maximum you define.

9 Choose Again or Click OK

Choose another category in the left panel to edit (as described throughout this chapter) or click **OK** to close the dialog box and then click **Close** to close the **Administer Website** dialog box.

99 Send Connections to Contributors

After you've created your roles and defined their settings, it's time to send out connection keys to users so that they can connect to the site and edit (within the limits of their role) the content for which they're responsible.

Sending connection keys is a snap—Contribute opens up a Wizard (or Assistant on a Mac) that leads you through each step.

1 Choose Edit, Administer Websites

Choose **Edit, Administer Websites**. As soon as you point to **Administer Websites**, that menu item is displaced by a list of sites to which you have a connection.

2 Choose the Site to Administer

Click on the website address to administer. Contribute prompts you for your administrator password. Type your administrator password and then click **OK** to open the **Administer Website** dialog box.

3 Choose a Role

On the **Administer Websites** dialog box, select the roles to which you want to send connection keys.

Before You Begin

✔ **89** About Roles

✔ **90** Create a New Role

✔ **91** Set General Role Settings

✔ **92** Set Folder and File Access Role Settings

✔ **93** Set Editing Role Settings

✔ **94** Set Style and Font Settings

✔ **95** Choose Settings for New Web Pages

✔ **98** Choose Settings for New Images

1 Choose Edit, Administer Websites

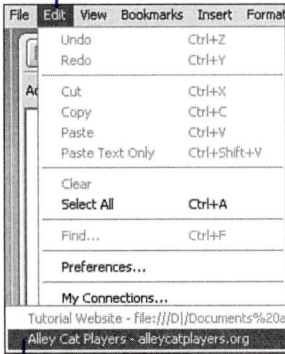

4 Click Send Connection Key

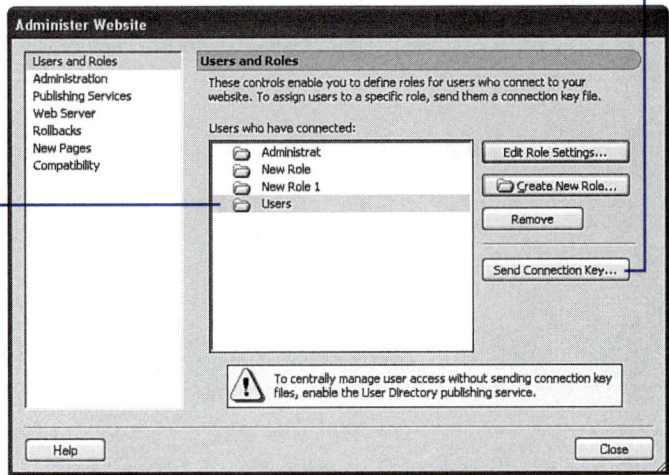

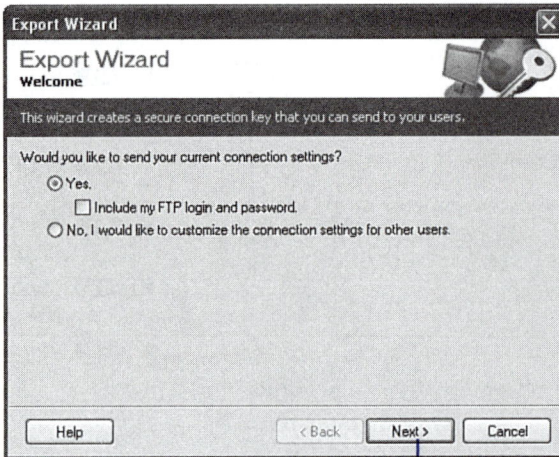

3 Choose a Role

2 Choose the Site to Administer

5 Flip Through the Pages

4 **Click Send Connection Key**

Click the **Send Connection Key** button to open the Export Connection Wizard (in Windows) or the Export Connection Assistant (on Mac).

5 **Flip Through the Pages**

Choose from the options presented on each page of the Wizard or Assistant, clicking **Next** (in Windows) or **Continue** (on Mac) to move forward from screen to screen.

Index

A

drag and drop, 67

Dreamweaver, locating editable regions, 21

E

E-mail Address button, 110

E-mail Review command (File menu), 169

email

    changing administrator, 187-189

    reviews, 169-171

Edit menu commands

    Administer Websites, 186

    Find, 48

    My Connections, 19, 25, 184

    Paste, 40

    Paste Text Only, 40

    Preferences, 14, 190

    Redo, 15

    Undo, 15

Edit mode, 10-12

Edit Page button, 10-11, 156, 160

Edit Role Settings dialog box

    Allow users to apply fonts and sizes option, 217

    Allow users to apply styles option, 215

    Create a blank page option, 218

    Create a new page by copying a page from this list option, 218

    Create a new page by copying any page on the website option, 218

    HTML tags option, 217

    Include CSS styles in the Style menu option, 215

    Include HTML paragraph and heading styles in the Style menu option, 215

    Inline CSS styles option, 217

New Images option, 225

Non-template editing section, 212

Only show users these templates option, 220

Options for Other Miscellaneous Editing Tasks section, 213

Options for Paragraph spacing section, 213

Other editing options section, 213

Protect scripts and forms section, 212

Show users all templates option, 220

Styles and Fonts option, 215

Use built-in sample pages option, 218

Use Dreamweaver templates option, 220

Edit toolbar, 12, 72

editable regions, 21

editing

    connections, locating editable regions, 21

    content, 4-5, 153-156

    images

        in links, 112

        in tables, 92-93

    text, 34-38

        links, 112

        selecting to edit, 35

        tables, 91

    web pages, publishing, 172-174

<em> tag, 214

ems, 217

Enable button, 29

enabling

    connections, 27-29

    rollback, 187-189

Enter key, 34, 84

Excel (Microsoft), inserting documents into websites, 141-146

Export Connection Assistant (Mac), 229

Export Connection Wizard, 229

How can we make this index more useful? Email us at indexes@samspublishing.com

237

J - K

L

M

N

O

S

How can we make this index more useful? Email us at indexes@samspublishing.com

241

T

How can we make this index more useful? Email us at indexes@samspublishing.com

243

in a Snap

Jump In Anywhere!

Organized into a series of **short**, **clearly written**, **well-illustrated** lessons, all *In a Snap* books in the Sams Teach Yourself series let you **zero right in** on that one particular task you need to accomplish right now—and then they let you get back to work.

Learning how to do new things with your computer shouldn't be tedious or time-consuming. It should be quick, easy, and maybe even a little bit fun.

Digital Photography with Adobe Photoshop Album in a Snap

Jennifer Fulton and Scott M. Fulton III
0-672-32568-3
$24.99 US/$35.99 CAN

Mac OS X Panther in a Snap

Brian Tiemann
ISBN: 0-672-32612-4
$24.99 US • $35.99 CAN

eBay in a Snap

Preston Gralla
ISBN: 0-672-32646-9
$19.99 US • $28.99 CAN

Macromedia Contribute 3 in a Snap

Ned Averill-Snell
ISBN: 0-672-32516-0
$24.99 US • $35.99 CAN

iLife '04 in a Snap

Jinjer Simon
ISBN: 0-672-32577-2
$24.99 US • $35.99 CAN

Key Terms

Don't let unfamiliar terms discourage you from learning all you can about Macromedia Contribute. If you don't completely understand what one of these words means, flip to the indicated page, read the full definition there, and find techniques related to that term.